# Scotland
# and the music hall,
## 1850–1914

MANCHESTER
UNIVERSITY PRESS

STUDIES IN
POPULAR
CULTURE

General editor:  Professor Jeffrey Richards

# Scotland
# and the music hall,
# 1850–1914

**PAUL MALONEY**

Manchester University Press

Manchester and New York

distributed exclusively in the USA by Palgrave

The right of Paul Maloney to be identified as the author of this work
has been asserted by him in accordance with the Copyright, Designs
and Patents Act 1988.

Published by Manchester University Press
Oxford Road, Manchester M13 9NR, UK
and Room 400, 175 Fifth Avenue, New York, NY 10010, USA
www.manchesteruniversitypress.co.uk

Distributed exclusively in the USA by
Palgrave, 175 Fifth Avenue, New York,
NY 10010, USA

Distributed exclusively in Canada by
UBC Press, University of British Columbia, 2029 West Mall,
Vancouver, BC, Canada V6T 1Z2

British Library Cataloguing-in-Publication Data
A catalogue record for this book is available from the British Library

Library of Congress Cataloging-in-Publication Data applied for

ISBN    0 7190 6146 6    hardback
        0 7190 6147 4    paperback

First published 2003

11  10  09  08  07  06  05  04  03        10  9  8  7  6  5  4  3  2  1

Typeset in Adobe Garamond and Gill Sans by
D R Bungay Associates, Burghfield, Berks

Printed in Great Britain by
Bookcraft (Bath) Ltd, Midsomer Norton

# STUDIES IN POPULAR CULTURE

There has in recent years been an explosion of interest in culture and cultural studies. The impetus has come from two directions and out of two different traditions. On the one hand, cultural history has grown out of social history to become a distinct and identifiable school of historical investigation. On the other hand, cultural studies has grown out of English literature and has concerned itself to a large extent with contemporary issues. Nevertheless, there is a shared project, its aim, to elucidate the meanings and values implicit and explicit in the art, literature, learning, institutions and everyday behaviour within a given society. Both the cultural historian and the cultural studies scholar seek to explore the ways in which a culture is imagined, represented and received, how it interacts with social processes, how it contributes to individual and collective identities and world views, to stability and change, to social, political and economic activities and programmes. This series aims to provide an arena for the cross-fertilisation of the discipline, so that the work of the cultural historian can take advantage of the most useful and illuminating of the theoretical developments and the cultural studies scholars can extend the purely historical underpinnings of their investigations. The ultimate objective of the series is to provide a range of books which will explain in a readable and accessible way where we are now socially and culturally and how we got to where we are. This should enable people to be better informed, promote an interdisciplinary approach to cultural issues and encourage deeper thought about the issues, attitudes and institutions of popular culture.

*Jeffrey Richards*

´For
Lorna

# Contents

# Contents

# List of illustrations

# List of tables

# General editor's foreword

Music hall was the principal popular medium of entertainment in nineteenth-century Britain. Hitherto, much of the scholarly work on the subject has concentrated on London. This book is unique and groundbreaking in that it is the first systematic scholarly account of the music hall in Scotland. Not only is this valuable in itself, but throughout the book Maloney engages productively and instructively with the other leading scholars on the subject (Dagmar Kift, Dave Russell, Peter Bailey, Gareth Stedman Jones and Laurence Senelick among them), continually drawing comparisons and contrasts between the development of the music hall and its evolution in England.

Maloney demonstrates conclusively that although there was a fruitful and mutually enriching interchange between Scotland and England, Scottish music hall had a distinctively different economic and social profile. In particular, it encountered strong and sustained disapproval from the Presbyterian Church, played an important role in the evolution of Scottish popular theatre, and influenced the entertainments staged by temperance organisations and the municipal authorities.

Regularly citing illuminating evidence from vivid contemporary sources, Maloney charts the development of Scottish music hall, carefully examining every facet of the industry. He traces the origins, training, remuneration and career profiles of the performers, examines the nature of the entertainment, and analyses the social composition of the audience. He assesses the popular perception of the music hall and its role in the construction of class, national and imperial identities. Richly illustrated, thoroughly documented, engagingly written, subtly argued and always accessible, this is a major contribution to our understanding of the nature and function of music hall in the British Isles.

*Jeffrey Richards*

# Acknowledgements

I have a great many people to thank for their help with this book and the Strathclyde University postgraduate thesis on which it is based.

Firstly my supervisor, Callum G. Brown, for being a model of constructive criticism and encouragement, and to whom I am hugely indebted; Andrew Jackson of Glasgow City Archive for extracting the Glasgow City Valuation roll material; Elizabeth Watson of the Scottish Theatre Archive; the staff of the Glasgow Room of the Mitchell Library, Glasgow; Andrew Pollock of the People's Palace, Glasgow, and his volunteer colleague William Gallacher for invaluable advice; Richard Mangan of the Raymond Mander & Joe Mitchenson Theatre Collection; Jim Pratt of Aberdeen City Library for his help with research on the North-east; and the staffs of the West Search Room, National Archives of Scotland, Edinburgh; Glasgow University Archives; Strathclyde University Archives; Dundee Central Library, Local Studies Dept.; Dundee City Archives; Edinburgh Central Library; and Edinburgh City Archives.

Other individuals and organisations who helped with a range of enquiries include Dr Christopher C. Lee and David A. Roberts of Paisley Museum & Art Galleries; Mrs Benvie, Curator, Montrose Museum & Art Gallery; Dorothy Thompson of the Museum of the Cumbraes, Millport; Largs & District Historical Society; and Dr Alasdair Durie, of the Department of Social and Economic History, Glasgow University; Brian Lochrin for his assistance with photographic reproductions; Robert Bain and Archie Foley of the Scottish Music Hall Society; Brian Kirk and Mrs Elizabeth Kirk of Fyfe and Fyfe Ltd; Graham Cruickshank; David Cheshire; Adam McNaughtan and Ted Bottle.

I would also like to thank Jeffrey Richards and Alison Whittle of Manchester University Press for their understanding and support.

As part of original purpose of this research was to learn more about the lives of working music-hall performers, my initial doubts concerned where I would find details of these largely unreported careers, from a period that is rapidly moving beyond living memory. I would therefore like to express my gratitude to all those who responded to my appeals in the *Sunday Post* and the *Scots Magazine*, and particularly the following people for supplying information about their relatives who worked on the Scottish variety stage before the First World War: Mr and Mrs Robert Bain; Mary Barrow; Mrs Janet W. Baxter; Mrs May Burns; Mr Michael C. Davis; Mrs Greta Eves; Mrs J. Hart; Mr and Mrs T. I. Graham; Mr Jim Smith; and Mrs Rita Wallace. Much of the value of this book comes from the material they contributed.

An earlier version of Chapter 7, 'Patriotism, Empire and the Glasgow Music Hall', appeared in the journal *Scotlands*. I would also like to thank the following for their assistance with the section on Scottish performers overseas: Clay Djubal of the School of English, Media Studies & Art History, University of Queensland, for his generosity in supplying material from his own researches on the Clay circuit; Frank Van Straten; Dave Moran; Catherine O'Donoghue of the Performing Arts Museum, Victorian Arts Centre, Melbourne; Judith Murphy of the John Oxley Library of the State Library of Queensland; and Christopher Smith of Queensland Performing Arts Museum.

Notwithstanding the assistance of the above, any errors or omissions in this book are entirely my own.

On a personal note, I would like to thank my parents, David and Edwina Maloney, for passing on their interest in and love of the theatre and its history; my sons Jonathan and Robbie for their understanding on all the occasions when this project consumed my energies; and above all, my wife Lorna, for all her support and encouragement during this project.

Finally, the completion of the book brings full circle a family connection with the subject: as a small girl in September 1940 my mother-in-law Rosemary Murray (née Young), on the occasion of his opening the West Kilbride Red Cross Fancy Fair, presented a walking stick to the veteran Sir Harry Lauder.

# 1

# Introduction

Music hall was the most successful popular theatre form of the nineteenth century. From its beginnings in the back rooms of pubs in the 1830s and 1840s, it quickly became the first theatre genre to be marketed as commercial mass entertainment. At the height of its popularity in the years leading up to the First World War, the music-hall industry in Britain entertained 25 million people a year and employed 80,000. The scale of this rise was nearly as rapid as the decline that followed, as cinema quickly overtook it in popularity in the interwar years. By the 1950s and the arrival of television, music hall was effectively dead as a mass entertainment. Within its hundred-year reign, music hall was hugely influential to British culture. Its songs were the popular currency of the era, played on barrel organs, sung by buskers in the street, by workers in the workplace, on works outings and holidays, and sold as sheet music to be played and sung at home around the piano. Its humour and styles penetrated the Victorian and Edwardian mind, shaping ways of thinking about pleasure and entertainment, as well as providing much of the vocabulary for everyday life.

Music hall's cultural significance extended far beyond its value as entertainment. Like modern tabloids, its 'take' on contemporary politics was felt to embody mainstream popular sentiment. Its performers mimicked royalty and politicians, offering satire and affectionate parody of the leaders of the British Empire, and lampooning middle-class patrician values. It was the source of social and constitutional commentary to millions of British people, providing the vital medium for the expression of national as well as local identities. Yet it would be wrong to view the music hall solely as a piece of plebeian popular culture. Commercialisation of the form led inevitably to pressure to attract middle-class audiences. To the historian, music hall is fascinating because of the tension created between its social agenda – its songs about and for working people in largely urban industrial contexts – and the rapid widening of its audience to include the middle classes. It became part of the great British social experiment.

Music hall's performing material similarly offered a shorthand to the social attitudes and class prejudices of its predominantly working-class audience. The prototypical genres it evolved, in a performing milieu in which artists had only a couple of minutes to impress and win over a potentially hostile audience, are still as recognisable as those of Dickens and Mayhew in our social map of the period: the cockney 'Coster' comedian; the blacked-up 'nigger' minstrel; the 'Hebrew' comedian, and the 'Scotch comic'. The last persona, largely defined in the public mind by Harry Lauder, has an uncomfortable cultural resonance in Scotland, derived from its associations with the sentimentalised Kailyard school of literature and drama: the twentieth-century Scottish poet Hugh MacDiarmid wrote that he had 'never met a single intelligent Scot who would be seen at a Lauder performance'.

In fact, to modern sensibilities, the derogatory impact of the Scotch comic's parody of the drunken, kilt-clad Scot probably fell well short of the repellent aspects of some of the other ethnic characterisations mentioned. The reality of the Victorian music hall was much more the world of Bernard Manning than that of 'The Good Old Days', a comparison which might seem crass, but perhaps better encapsulates the uneasiness of the relationship with wider society than first seems the case. A cheerful diatribe of racial and social incorrectness, subtly differentiated to reflect regional and social predilections and circumstances, music hall represented nothing so much as the cusp of respectability – in attitude, demeanour and perception – and the never-far-off threat of vulgarity; the taint of the fairground enshrined in permanent urban context, with all its gas-lit horrors of drunken lawlessness, riot and violence. In Scotland, where music hall's development was closely linked to older fairground entertainments, it wasn't surprising that middle-class fear of civil disorder associated with fairs remained high: in Dundee in 1864 a drunken battle between Irishmen and local youths at the town's Stobb's Fair needed extensive police action to bring it under control; at the same year's Lady Mary Fair, an act in which a man skinned live rats with his teeth before biting their heads off was discontinued at the request of the police, the *Advertiser* castigating the depravity of those who watched 'so inhuman a spectacle'. In 1889 a riot at Aberdeen's Bon-Accord music hall provoked press alarm that 'Young Aberdeen … bids fair to rival a Glasgow-Irish audience or the denizens of Whitechapel'.[1]

The bulk of research on music hall to date has primarily concerned England, and particularly London, understandably given the city's dominance

Jack (Jock) Mills (The Wise Man)

of the national music-hall industry. However, the development of music hall in Scotland was different in a number of important respects, largely relating to the structure of Scottish society and its industrial and economic development. Taken collectively, these provide a markedly different model of a music-hall culture.

As a result, Glasgow is in many aspects more representative of the wider industrial experience of Britain than London. There are three main factors for this, each of which forms an important part of the architecture of this book.

In the first place, music hall in Scotland emerged in a religious climate more representative of the industrial towns and villages of Northern England, South Wales and Ulster. It was one marked by longstanding Presbyterian disapproval, which dated back to the Reformation, of music, theatre and entertainment generally. While attitudes had moderated in the eighteenth century, allowing for the establishment of patent theatres in Edinburgh and Glasgow, the first half of the nineteenth saw a renewal of clerical attacks on all forms of commercial entertainment. Even social reformers providing alternatives to pub-based amusements found themselves in the firing line. The introduction of teetotal Saturday Evening Concerts in Glasgow in the 1850s was denounced on the grounds that such events, by trying to lure the public away from boozy alternatives to more wholesome entertainments, nevertheless encouraged the dissemination of the entertainment culture, and made young people even less likely to attend church. Moreover, whatever its motives, the entertainment itself failed to meet the only criterion by which it could be considered valid – that of glorifying God and drawing participants nearer to His works.[2] Such stridency reflected the pressure that traditional church doctrines came under from the increase in leisure in the early nineteenth century. The period was in any case one of profound turmoil for organised religion in Scotland. The Free Church leader Thomas Chalmers held urbanisation responsible for the decline in church attendance and the wider breakdown of society, particularly in cities, which he saw resulting in 'the palpable increase, from year to year, of a profligate, profane, and heathen population'.[3] Most serious among the social ills identified was alcohol, the consumption of which reached its high point in Scotland between 1830 and 1850. In the 1840s Glasgow had 3,400 pubs, one for every 150 inhabitants, while Dundee had one for every 24 families.[4]

The religious response to the crisis was evangelicalism, which evolved from the 1780s as a radical religious reform movement determined to reclaim the urban working classes from their dissolute, godless torpor. From the foundation of the Sunday school movement in the 1780s, evangelicalism inspired a stream of volunteer organisations that actively befriended working people in their homes and at leisure. Their chosen method, the promotion of constructive or rational leisure pursuits, involved a wide range of improving activities intended to encourage self-discipline and sociability while (as importantly), diverting working people away from the temptations of the public house. While most of these activities – day excursions and picnics, and outdoor and sporting pursuits such as bowls, rambling, cycling, cricket and football – were unexceptionable, and usually had an overtly religious or educational dimension, others involving music and the performing arts soon brought conflict with established Presbyterian practice.

The promotion of choral music, which saw the establishment of the Glasgow Choral Union in 1862, inevitably led to questioning of the narrow role of music in church services, usually restricted to unaccompanied singing by congregations that often remained seated. In 1854 the Aberdeen journalist William Carnie, himself founder of a Harmonic Choir, argued for the lifting of the ban on organ and other instruments, on the grounds that music's elevating influence should not be constricted. But it took the Scottish visits of the American revivalists Dwight Moody and Ira Sankey between 1873 and 1875, and the enormous popular success of hymns sung to harmonium accompaniment that followed, for the eventual accession to demands for instrumental music in services.

These shifts by evangelicalism to reclaim popular music for religion and restraint heightened condemnation of 'unrespectable' forms of entertainment. Dancing came under attack for licentiousness. The gentrified version of 'traditional' country dancing evolved in the late eighteenth century – which drew inspiration from the music of the great fiddler Niel Gow, painted by Raeburn and commemorated by Burns, and the polite interpolations of the dancing master Francis Peacock – came in for censure in the 1830s. Aberdeen temperance soirées, which included rousing recitations and singing, nevertheless balked at the over-stimulation of dancing. In 1884 the Rev. Alexander Bannatyne of the Union Free Church in Aberdeen warned against the pernicious influence of the Waltz and other partner dances in which 'the flings and springs and the artistic circles, and the close-bosomed wheeling and whirling' were too obvious an incitement to promiscuity.[5]

If social dancing and sacred music remained contentious, Presbyterian abhorrence of theatre was deeply entrenched. As a result, Scottish theatre managers fought a constant battle to validate even mainstream theatre genres of the politer sort in the face of profound religious scepticism. North-east impresario William McFarland used his promotional newssheet *The Comet* to emphasise the moral character of the plays visiting his Dundee and Aberdeen theatres, reminding 'those clergy who identify themselves with wholesale condemnation of the theatre' that in *Uncle Tom's Cabin*, the protagonist's line '"No, massa, my body is yours, but my soul belongs to One who's bought it and paid for it, and is able to keep it" [was] as strictly Evangelical a sentiment as was ever heard in any church or chapel'.[6] If legitimate theatre had a problem justifying itself before this constituency (and many genres of popular theatre were definitely beyond the pale), then music hall, with its drink-sodden public-house associations, faced an almost impossible task.

The 'Unco' guid' – the religiously righteous – remained a highly influential force in Scottish society up until the 1950s. Their intractable opposition to almost any form of secular entertainment, coupled with their close connections to municipal government, working-class political movements, unions and volunteer organisations, disposed a formidable body of opinion against entertainments such as music hall. In practice, however, the very extremity of the position militated against adherence to it. People would find their amusement somewhere, and, as Hamish Fraser has suggested, the absence of a sanctioned middle course sometimes made for a more violent reaction in response.[7] The exuberance – almost desperation – of the wilder strands of Scottish popular culture in the late nineteenth and early twentieth centuries, whether in excessive drinking, betting, dancing or on the football terraces, was a reflection of the Presbyterian conundrum: damned if you did, damned if you didn't. But the sober, dour tone of much public life in Scotland in the nineteenth century was a legacy of the Kirk.

A second factor linking Glasgow with the wider northern experience was the willingness of Scottish evangelical and temperance organisations, and through them municipal authorities, faced from the 1840s with the increasing demand for popular amusements, to grasp the nettle and actively engage in promoting musical entertainments themselves. This was particularly the case in Glasgow, where the scale of this operation constituted a subsidised sector that operated alongside the commercial music hall market. Given the dynamism and interventionist social agenda of Scottish evangelical and temperance organisations, and their determination to permeate every area of working-class life, it was perhaps inevitable that they would become directly involved in providing moral amusements. The argument was one of social pragmatism, the reformers warning the Kirk that

It is all very well to inveigh against public-houses, theatres, and music halls, but where is the toiler, be he working man, clerk or shopkeeper, to go for required recreation? Those who have been foremost in condemning the entertainments of the present day have done little to insist in providing recreation for the people.[8]

The temperance movement, the most influential offshoot of evangelicalism, arrived in Scotland in 1829, to be followed by teetotalism in the form of the Total Abstainers' Union, The Good Templars (1869), the Rechabites, and a range of other organisations, including the Band of Hope, which taught teetotal values to children. Dagmar Kift has pointed out that many English non-conformist and temperance groups viewed entertainments such as music hall as an unwelcome distraction from rational uses of recreation. Where such organisations did concern themselves with the area of commercial entertainments, as in a report on drunkenness in Sheffield in 1853, they called for the introduction of cheap moral amusements but made little effort to provide them.[9] In contrast, several Scottish temperance organisations responded to public demand for affordable entertainments by promoting popular concerts themselves. The Aberdeen Total Abstainers Union mounted a series of Popular Saturday Evening concerts from 1841, while the Glasgow Abstainers' Union Saturday Night Concerts in the City Hall began in 1854 and ran uninterrupted for sixty years. From 1872 the Glasgow Good Templars' Harmonic Society gave concerts in three city-centre halls – in Bridgeton, Wellington Street and the Gorbals. The performers moved between venues by cab and, as with the Abstainers', included both 'serious' artists, performing classical and sacred repertoire, and music-hall stars, who gave a mildly detoxified version of their acts, including Scotch comic songs and patter. Moreover Glasgow City Council began its own series of Corporation Penny Concerts in the late 1890s, annual attendance for which had reached 80,000 by the 1900 season.

This harnessing of the power of popular entertainment for proselytising purposes was highly significant, particularly in Glasgow. By the 1860s such concerts constituted a prestigious rival circuit to that of commercial music halls, one which played an important role in the careers of visiting and resident performers, who were often themselves the products of temperance influences: as a boy the young Lauder's first performance was at a Band of Hope concert, while the Scotch comic W. F. Frame was a lifelong Good Templar. Moreover, voluntary organisations were now entertainment managers. By booking acts and mixing with performers, officers of temperance, evangelical and socialist organisations, and through them municipal politics, were brought into contact with music hall managers and performers. For all their boozy taint, music-hall 'pro's were sharing concert platforms with amateur choral singers from Glasgow cathedral. The eliding of these worlds, temperance and commercial music hall, went a long way towards filling the vacuum left by Calvinist and Presbyterian incomprehension of the pleasure ethic.

A third aspect in which Glasgow is more representative of the wider industrial experience concerns the particular resonance of music hall in Scottish society, and its place in the Scottish theatre tradition. Although legitimate playhouses were well established in the main Scottish cities by the early nineteenth century, they were a comparatively late development. In Dundee, the Theatre Royal that opened at Yeaman Shore in 1801 was the city's first permanent theatre, before which it had relied upon visits by touring troupes, while 'The profession was held in stern reprobation, as elsewhere throughout Scotland'.[10] One of the effects of the historic suppression of professional theatre had been to focus the balance of theatrical activity on the wooden and canvas booth theatres, known as gaffs or geggies, which appeared at traditional fairs and on semi-permanent pitches in town and city centres. These fit-up theatres, which offered everything from melodramas to cut-down versions of Shakespeare, constituted a vigorous popular theatre tradition, featuring energetic and often grisly stage fights, interspersed with music and singing, and plenty of interaction with the audience. The rise in the early nineteenth century of the National Drama, a home-produced canon of plays depicting characters and events from Scottish history and literature, centring on the works of Walter Scott, briefly succeeded in combining the popular and middle-class audience for the playhouses. But with the arrival of rail travel in the 1840s, which brought with it an influx of southern touring companies, and the subsequent demise of the stock companies of actors at the larger Scottish theatres, many leading practitioners of the National Drama, and something of its spirit, retreated to the fairground circuit. In this context, the music hall that evolved in Scotland had a special place in the nation's theatrical life: highly influenced by the fairground tradition, it was not, as in England, necessarily seen as a cruder appendage to an aesthetically rich legitimate theatre, but rather as something much closer to the mainstream, and to the Scots vernacular stage which constituted many people's experience of theatre-going. This image of music hall and its successor, pantomime, in the wake of the National Drama's decline, as enshrining a popular Scottish people's theatre, has been articulated by several commentators, including Barbara Bell, who has written that 'As part of the popular "theatre", music hall educated the next generation of Scottish performers, playwrights and audience'.[11] In this context the Scottish music hall can be seen to have been directly in the line of a mainstream Scottish popular theatre tradition that continued through the socialist plays of Joe Corrie and the Fife Miners' Players, who performed their one-act plays to working-class audiences in music halls and variety theatres, to the radical popular theatre of companies such as Wildcat and John McGrath's 7:84 Theatre Company in the 1970s and 1980s, who claimed its legacy as their own.

Glasgow was the hub of Scottish theatre activity. As one of the largest centres of music hall outside London, Glasgow possessed a plethora of halls and variety theatres, and a resident as well as migrant population of actors and performers. But it also had a distinctive music hall culture that it projected into the wider world of music hall. In part this derived from its place at the centre of a national, as opposed to regional, musical and cultural tradition: from their earliest days Glasgow halls offered a combination of locally based Scottish performers and imported English acts, an environment where leading 'British' stars could score important professional triumphs, but in a milieu where Scottish music and humour was predominant, and where special ire was reserved for 'that most pathetic of Glasgow sounds, an English music-hall song given with a local accent'.[12] Glasgow was known for producing and testing stars, for nurturing styles of performance and humour, and for developing new ways of organising and managing this new mass entertainment. The three contextual factors discussed already – music hall's development within a Presbyterian society, the promotion of rival entertainments by municipal and temperance bodies, and music hall's position within the broader mainstream of Scottish theatre – are vital to the understanding of this development, and are all themes of this book. In developing them, and in seeking to compare the Scottish experience with that of London, the book will focus on Glasgow as its main model and point of comparison. The reasons for this are that in most respects Glasgow proved the most important centre of activity. While not as economically dominant in Scotland as London was in England, it nevertheless dwarfed in almost all aspects of its economic and social development the other three principal Scottish cities – Edinburgh, Dundee and Aberdeen. A centre of heavy manufacturing and Second City of the Empire, Glasgow owed its rapid expansion to industrialisation, making it a more representative example of the industrial revolution than London; it was from its earliest development the centre of a sizeable music-hall industry, with some seven halls in the late 1850s, at a time before Edinburgh possessed even a single such venue; and the dynamism of its municipal gospel and religious and reforming organisations made it, in the words of Callum Brown, 'arguably the most innovative centre for religious voluntary organisations in the English-speaking world'.[13] Above all, Glasgow offers a model of a dynamic, confident metropolitan centre, buoyed by economic and financial muscle, yet operating on a quite different social and cultural model to that of English cities.

So while we will explore developments in Scotland generally, focussing on the four Scottish centres, not least for older entertainment traditions that fed into music hall's development, the main focus will remain on Glasgow. At the two extremes of popular culture – the religious puritanism of evangelical teetotalism, and the alcohol-lubricated world of music-hall entertainment – Glasgow excelled. Nowhere can the music hall as a genre be contextualised better than in that city of religion, industry and empire.

Although a considerable literature has built up on the subject of the Victorian and Edwardian music hall, almost everything produced to date has concerned developments either in London or in towns and cities in northern England. While a number of recent books and collections have concerned the Scottish music hall, notably Frank Bruce's *Scottish Showbusiness*, an excellent popular survey of Scottish music hall and variety (Edinburgh, National Museums of Scotland, 2000), there remains no full-length academic work on the subject, which, apart from a handful of scholarly articles and unpublished theses, has been almost entirely neglected.[14] As a corollary, the most significant recent publication in the field, Dagmar Kift's *The Victorian Music Hall: Culture, Class and Conflict* (Cambridge, Cambridge University Press, 1996) sets out to redress this imbalance by contrasting London with work on regional centres, including Glasgow, in an attempt to adduce broader national trends on a range of topics that includes licensing and audiences.

Allowing for the wide range of subjects and methodologies adopted, most English research has centred on two main themes, which frequently overlap; firstly, the role of music hall in class identity, and the degree to which the social composition of the audience changed in the course of its commercial expansion; and, secondly, the question of whether music hall's apparent Conservative political bias from the 1890s contributed to the growth of popular nationalism or Jingoism.

Dealing first with the issue of social identity, music hall's origins as a working-class entertainment, developed in the backrooms of pubs, are not disputed (although recent researchers, notably Jim Davis and Michael Booth, have questioned whether it deserves to be seen in isolation, arguing that the working-class audience for popular theatre forms such as melodrama, was far greater than has hitherto been acknowledged[15]). Where opinions sharply diverge, however, is over whether music hall continued to reflect working-class political and social values during its subsequent commercial development.

From the 1870s onwards, music hall managements began a concerted attempt to improve the public image of the entertainment, with a view to broadening its potential audience to include the middle classes. Further marketing innovations introduced by the music-hall syndicates, notably the Moss group, from the 1890s continued the process. If recent studies of the social composition of English audiences suggest that they largely failed in this, and that music hall remained a generally working- or lower-middle-class experience throughout the period under investigation, this is not to say that the social tone and political agenda of music hall had not undergone a profound transformation.

The auditoriums of the new Palaces of Varieties, as music halls were known from the 1880s, were sub-divided into socially segregated areas that allowed the different social groups in the audience to enter and leave by separate exits, precluding inter-class contact. Similarly, great care had been taken to remove vulgar or offensive elements from performing material, to upgrade the theatre furnishings, and to guarantee the propriety of all aspects of the proceedings. If the middle classes did not necessarily arrive for the performance, their spiritual presence was nevertheless very much felt. Given this, the debate about music hall's social profile has shifted ground; the audience may have been largely working class, but the environment in the auditorium now deferred to middle-class sensibilities and notions of respectability.

Where, in this context, did music hall's dynamic lie? Not surprisingly, several leading writers have identified developments between the 1870s and 1900s as amounting to a process of embourgeoisement that subverted the working-class ethos of earlier music hall. The most outspoken, Laurence Senelick, has gone so far as to characterise music hall of the 1880s as a fundamentally middle-class institution, which functioned as an agent of social control by espousing middle-class values to working-class audiences. He further contends that, far from being the voice of the common people, views and attitudes expressed in music-hall performing material were often not those generally held by the working people of the audience, but represented rather the overt propagandising of select establishment interest groups and élites. In asserting this, Senelick quotes the liberal theorist J. A. Hobson's view that as a means of influencing a popular audience the music halls were 'a more potent educator than the church, the school, the political meeting, or even than the press'.[16]

Gareth Stedman Jones, whose key work preceded Senelick's and was in many ways the groundbreaking contribution in the field, also based his research on London. Stedman Jones similarly attests to music hall's

Conservative political bias in the 1890s, but unlike Senelick views this not as an imposition by outside forces, but rather as a genuine reflection of working-class political attitudes. His thesis is that the period between 1870 and 1900 saw the development of a new working-class leisure culture, politically conservative and inward-looking in character, that reflected widespread disenchantment with mainstream politics following the failure of the trade unions to achieve their political objectives. Stedman Jones' critique places music hall at the centre of this 'culture of consolation' that grew up around 'the pub, the racetrack and the music hall'.[17]

Although Stedman Jones' model will receive regular consideration, several important differences between conditions in London and Glasgow are immediately evident. Firstly, the depressed economic circumstances he describes, where changing work practices led to men in skilled trades losing ground to un-skilled or semi-skilled workers, an increase in home working and a decline in work-centred culture, were all exacerbated by the fact that, for various reasons, London did not develop large-scale factory production until after the period in question. Stedman Jones accepts that the same demoralisation and alienation of the workforce would probably not have occurred in the more homogeneous industrial communities of the north, where trade unions played a central role in the culture.[18] This was indeed the case in Glasgow, where over the same period industrial organisation was moving toward expansion and large-scale workshop and factory production. Whatever the divisive pressures exerted on Glasgow workers as a result of internal competition within the labour force, there was at least the collective identity and consciousness that went with the work-centred culture of heavy industries. In fact the period from the early 1890s that Stedman Jones identifies as the crucial phase in London working-class political apathy coincided with the birth and growth of Independent Labour Party (ILP) influence in Glasgow.[19]

A second contributory factor cited by Stedman Jones was the failure of middle-class evangelical and temperance reformers, who 'by the Edwardian period, it had become inescapably clear ... had failed to recreate a working class in its own image'.[20] This seems far from clear in the context of Glasgow, with its dominant Presbyterian culture, where if anything by the 1890s the centre ground was perceived as having already been conceded to the reformers. Stedman Jones similarly asserts that by the turn of the century the London working classes had rejected middle-class values and social mores, in favour of a pragmatic accommodation of their own that recognised the value of conspicuous propriety. He suggests that

'Respectability' did not mean church attendance, teetotalism or the possession of a post office savings account. It meant the possession of a presentable Sunday suit, and the ability to be seen wearing it.[21]

Peter Bailey has developed this idea, contending that the urban working-class adoption of middle-class social mores was selective by intention, and amounted to role playing for social and professional advantage. Bailey proposes that 'respectability was practised in a more limited and situational sense than that of a lived ideal or permanent code of values' and 'was assumed as a role (or cluster of roles) as much as it was espoused as an ideology'.[22]

This certainly has a resonance for Scottish Presbyterian society, but is surely less than the whole picture. The fact that, as Stedman Jones concedes, it was all many working-class families could do to maintain the outward semblance of respectability, in terms of dress and conduct, should not be taken as a blanket rejection of the wider system of values propagated by reformers. In Glasgow's case, there is evidence that the influence of reformers was far more widely disseminated and profoundly felt than was the case in London, not least because, as has been mentioned, reforming groups and the Municipality itself became involved in the promotion of music-hall entertainment through temperance and Saturday-afternoon concerts as a way of luring working audiences away from the corrupting influence of the commercial halls. That a sizeable part of the city's entertainment audience was under this sort of moral supervision must have had a strong residual influence. Elspeth King writes of the effect of the Municipal Gospel:

> The important factor was that all of these different social elements were providing a wide range of leisure and cultural opportunities which were not only open to all, but which were offered with the kind of zeal and enthusiasm of which only people who want to reform, save or re-structure their society are capable. What may have been a counter-cultural manifestation in the 1850s, as in the case of the Abstainers' Union concerts, was the dominant culture by 1900.[23]

Stedman Jones' quotation of Marie Lloyd's statement that 'Why, if I was to try and sing highly moral songs they would fire ginger ale bottles and beer mats at me'[24] contrasts with reports of Glasgow audiences rejecting visiting artists whose performances they found lewd. The Glasgow author J. J. Bell wrote of visiting the Scotia in dubious Stockwell Street as a youth in the 1880s ('none too savoury. Constables in pairs walked up and down'), and seeing the London star Bessie Bellwood get hissed off the stage by the working-class Glasgow audience for throwing her skirts up as she danced in what was felt to be a shameless manner.[25]

A later researcher, Penny Summerfield, encapsulated a central weakness in Stedman Jones' theory – that 'it assumes that the culture of consolation was created largely by the working class alone' and '[it] neglects the social relations which were contextual to the developing music hall and which it also helped to create'.[26] In contrast, Summerfield maintains that music hall was almost completely a product of its marketing as a proto-modern capitalist leisure enterprise, and that its final form emerged as a product of the tension between its promoters and licensing authorities concerned to control the social behaviour of citizens. Her statement that 'The evolution of music hall was a process of deliberate selection, later made to look natural and inevitable' is a view that has come to be shared by other writers, including Peter Bailey.

Of these critics Stedman Jones, Senelick and Bailey have sought to place music hall within a wider social construct of working-class life. In contrast, the main preoccupation of Scottish researchers has been the issue of Scottish cultural identity and self-image, particularly with regard to the music-hall stereotype generated by Lauder and other Scotch comics. In her survey of popular leisure in Glasgow, Elspeth King decries the failure of Scottish music hall to produce a genuine expression of Scottish culture.

> The escapist stereotype developed in urban Glasgow by Frame, the boot and soor milk boy and apprentice engineer, was the 'Bonnie Hieland Laddie', resplendent in kilt and toorie, accompanied by pipes and dispensing incomprehensible pawky patter and sprigs of heather indiscriminately. This gross caricature was further developed and refined by a visit to the USA, where he took Carnegie Hall by storm in 1898, and was subsequently copied by Lauder and others.[27]

This view of the Scotch comic as a travesty that has wrought immense damage to Scottish self-perception and esteem has recently been challenged. In a 1996 essay on the comedian W. F. Frame, the authors Alasdair Cameron and Adrienne Scullion suggest that the blanket excoriation of music-hall Scottishness deserves re-evaluation, on the grounds that

> the totemic images of the Scotch comic – the cocksure Highland laddie, the interfering husband-seeking spinster and the gossiping village-worthies or (their urban equivalents) the window-hangers – were approved and even celebrated as symbols of a nationality which, under normal circumstances, audiences were never allowed to express.[28]

Cameron and Scullion contend that the Highland dress and extravagant Tartanry were merely the product of music hall's performing conventions, in which acts lasted little more than five minutes and had to grab the audience's attention in the first two. Viewed in this light, they argue, the artificiality of the stage construct was far less important than its attempt to provide a positive cultural definition that was recognisable to disparate elements in the audience. In this respect the essay is an elaboration of an earlier one in which Cameron argued that the natural constituency for these acts went beyond their sentimental appeal to displaced highlanders, to embrace urban Scots suffering from a form of cultural disenfranchisement.

> Tartan, St Andrew's flags and some kind of national imagery, however simplistic, was a means of creating a national identity. This was particularly important in a theatre which appealed to the working class who were not receiving the direct benefits of Empire and who were uninterested in the sophistry of the apologists for Union. Such audiences were not British but Scottish, and the images they saw on stage made sense when associated with performers who spoke like them and with whom they could identify.[29]

But if the audience was Scottish, where did its cultural identity reside, given the divide between Highlands and Lowlands? And how did these 'performers who spoke like them' speak? The dangers of easy assumptions regarding shared or 'common' language as a benchmark of national identity are pointed out by Bill Findlay in his chapter on the comic actor James Houston.[30] Whilst emphasising that demand for Scots material increased dramatically in the nineteenth century, when 'Scots speech was the daily norm for Lowland Scots in Victorian Scotland', Findlay also suggests that the comic persona of the 'pawky' stage Scot dressed in Highland garb but speaking Scots 'had a long pedigree in Scottish entertainment' that stretched back through characters in Scott and the National Drama. In other words the 'grotesque' hybrid comfortably predated music hall.

Given that the Scottish writers discussed have largely centred on notions of Scottish identity, a number of other important perspectives can be applied to the nature of music hall in Scotland.

The first is the need for a detailed study of music hall in Glasgow, the centre of the Scottish industry, and in particular its class identities. Although this has been largely passed over in the rush to engage with issues of national identity, a clear understanding of Glasgow music hall's class affiliations is in any case essential to a balanced appreciation of the appeal of nationalist sentiments. English music-hall performers, most of whom were working class, topped most bills in Glasgow from the 1870s onwards and enjoyed considerable popularity with the public. Given the cultural and linguistic divisions in the native Scottish audience already discussed, Alasdair Cameron's statement that the Glasgow public preferred performers 'with whom they could identify' could just as well have been referring to social class as to shared nationality.

In any case the social dynamic of music hall's appeal, which may have been complex, needs clarifying in the specific context of Glasgow. Although other writers have suggested that music halls in some English cities may have drawn their audiences from specific social groups, I would support Penny Summerfield's view that most halls were probably socially heterogeneous, aiming to attract all social classes by offering admission at a wide range of prices.[31] In the case of Glasgow, where there were never more than four or five halls in the city centre for any sustained period before the 1900s, it seems unlikely that managers could have afforded to overlook any potential section of the community, even if the *de facto* audience was largely drawn from one social grouping.

That there were clearly different sorts of music hall is evident from ticket pricing, conditions of performance and first-hand descriptions. If the new Glasgow Empire in the late 1900s was hardly *Sunday Night at the London Palladium*, then the Panopticon in Trongate in the same period (then featuring four shows a day, starting with a morning performance for night workers fresh from the graveyard shift) must have been approaching the sort of rough New York burlesque house depicted in *The Night They Raided Minsky's*. The question to be investigated is whether there was a pattern to this difference, a hierarchy as such, which would presuppose the existence of a 'better' class of audience. An initial suspicion is that the main factor may prove to have been location, and that the larger city-centre halls attracted what middle-class custom there was (in itself debatable), while smaller outlying halls, which offered generally inferior acts, played to largely local audiences.[32]

As things are, the lack hitherto of detailed information on Glasgow leads to generalisations. Assertions such as Scullion and Cameron's that the arrival of the Moss–Stoll circuit in the 1890s 'marks the demise of a locally organised popular entertainment theatre', whilst accurate in terms of identifying a historical trend, are misleading in their implications. In fact what might be termed 'low' or unre-constructed popular music hall did not die out in the late 1890s but survived in less splendid venues adjacent to the city centre, such as the Panopticon in Trongate and the Queen's at Glasgow Cross, and elsewhere mutated into the new format of cine-variety. In addition, a satellite circuit of smaller predomi-nantly working-class halls in surrounding towns such Paisley, Govan, Greenock, Falkirk and Hamilton (where the wooden Hippodrome was forced to close down for a week during the prolonged coal strike of 1912) continued much as before.[33]

This book will therefore argue that the survival of a viable working-class music hall, which existed parallel to the large city-centre variety theatres in the period up to and after the First World War, was a distinctive feature of Glasgow music hall. Moreover that, as part of its diverse nature, this important strand of music-hall activity did remain locally organised and responsive to local demand. Substantiating this claim will involve an examination of the cultural roots of music hall in local Glasgow communities, touching on the popularity of amateur nights, the use of the buildings themselves for political meetings and soup kitchens, the role of music-hall songs as common currency, and an exami-nation of the social and political (as opposed to national) content of music-hall material.

But as the argument is reliant on also establishing the continued existence of a 'live' working-class performing tradition, a second area to be investigated will be the Scottish music-hall profession itself. This survey of Scottish performers will be divided into three separate chapters: the first will examine Scottish artists' social origins, career patterns and lifestyle, together with the various professional rites of passage by which performers gained access to work on the lucrative national circuits and in London; the second chapter will investigate the music-hall community in Glasgow, and attempt to assess its size and composition, and social mobility; the third chapter will examine the professional culture that devel-oped amongst music-hall performers from the 1870s onwards, the level of social acceptance or respectability that music hall enjoyed with the wider public, and whether perceptions altered with the establishment of variety as a mass entertain-ment in the years leading up to the First World War.[34]

As I have suggested, an investigation of Glasgow's localised performing cul-ture will be a particular feature of this section. Between the 1850s and 1914 music-hall performers in Glasgow gained experience through an informal feeder system that consisted of a combination of local concerts held in small public halls, Free and Easies, temperance and Harmonic Society competitions, charitable benefits and 'bursts'.[35] When some of these institutions began to wane in the early 1900s, cine-variety and the regular amateur nights held in many of the larger halls continued to provide opportunities for members of the audience to perform. This system, which represented much more of a con-tinuum than the image of relentless change that is sometimes depicted, con-tinued to provide the direct link between the audience/community and performer that some critics maintain died with the disappearance of the music-hall chairman in the 1880s. It moreover continued to produce performers trained in precisely the skills of 'patter' that were claimed to be in decline, who went on to become leading stars of mainstream variety. In addition, the sense of performers being 'of' the community was further reinforced in the case of

Glasgow by the existence of numbers of part-time or semi-professional performers, whose occasional appearances on the lower reaches of bills kept alive
the participatory principle of earlier music-hall forms.

A third set of themes to be explored will concern the relationship of Scottish
identity to manifestations of Imperialism in music-hall performance. These will
be examined on various levels. One objective will be to look for evidence of a possible link between support for the cause of Empire, and the economic reality of
Scottish industry's reliance on export markets for continued industrial growth. If
it remains to be seen whether music hall in Glasgow in the 1890s was as politically
Conservative (or at least as consistently so) as it was in London, there is certainly
considerable evidence of widespread promotion of Imperialism generally
between the 1870s and 1914. Penny Summerfield suggests that the character of
'Jingoism' was largely dependent on the specific audience being addressed. If this
was the case, the question remains whether, given the economic importance of
colonial markets for manufactured goods, Scottish music-hall audiences' enthusiasm for notions of Empire, in all their various manifestations, should be viewed
in a rather different light to the cynicism and xenophobia that Stedman Jones and
Senelick believe characterised English audiences. This is not to claim that
Scottish audiences need necessarily have made a conscious link between colonial
expansion and the security of jobs in heavy industries at home. Causal effect in
this case could be more abstruse. To London workers involved in light industries
and small shop production, the broader sweep of overseas and colonial policies
no doubt seemed remote; in the case of Glasgow, workers engaged in the manu-
facture of railway locomotives and shallow-draught river steamers built for
export to such overseas markets as India, China and South Africa were provided
with a direct correlation between the source of their employment and the importance of securing spheres of influence overseas. It will be seen whether references
to these economic issues surface in performance material.

Another aspect of Imperialism to be examined will be how Glasgow music
hall's espousal of the cause of Queen and Empire through patriotic anthems was
reconciled with the simultaneous popularity of what could be termed Scottish
national songs – generally heroic ballads celebrating incidents and individuals
from Scottish history. Although such songs were usually positive and forward-
looking, proud rather than brooding over past injustices, and generally avoided
identifying the English by name, their general tenor was Jacobite, and left little
doubt as to the identity of the old enemy behind past wrongs unrighted. The
*Scotia Music-Hall Songbook* provides a typical mix of both genres, with rousing
Imperialist paeans such as 'Hurrah for the Life of a Sailor!' and 'Cheer Boys

Cheer' (for Mother England!) printed alongside similarly inspirational nation-alist hymns such as 'Draw the Sword, Scotland!', 'Hurrah for the Bonnets of Blue' and 'Where Hath Scotland Found Her Fame'. The fact that songs of the latter type were warmly received by audiences who clearly responded to their appeal to a distinct Scottish patriotism, but who then went on to participate avidly in other songs that required them to fight for Old England's Glory, seems incongruous enough to bear investigating further. The underlying question is exactly what the Glasgow audience's perception of Empire embodied, and whether support for it necessarily involved a conflict of interests with notions of Scottish patriotism. It might be that popular Scottish sentiment viewed colonial expansion as a gen-uinely pan-British cause, which transcended English assertions of leadership, and that Scottish enthusiasm was focussed on its external benefits in terms of the potential opportunities for careers and expansion overseas. Alternatively, it may have been the case that Scottish popular (as opposed to institutional) enthusiasm for Imperial causes was lukewarm, supporting Senelick's suggestion that music hall's role was often to propagandise against the better instincts of the audience.

One possible explanation for some of the inconsistencies concerning responses to stage Imperialism could lie in the cosmopolitan influences acting on Scottish performers and, in a more limited sense, on the Scottish theatre-going public. The chapters on the industry's development will indicate that from the 1870s music hall in Glasgow had a dual nature, the city being both an important part of the national music hall circuit and home to an independent performing tradition that could claim a national status. Glasgow audiences were used to a wide range of stage depictions of Englishness, and to regular appearance of leading English stars, most of whose appeal relied on class affinity with their audience to offset other cultural differences. The fact that English audiences were supposedly unable to understand Scottish comics before Lauder should not obscure the fact that Scottish audiences were quite used to English accents on the stage, and knew their way through the French windows into the drawing room of musical comedy. Scottish performers in turn gained experi-ence of working with English audiences, and of evaluating their cultural iden-tity away from home. By the 1890s, when support for Empire was approaching its zenith, the highest expression of institutionalised Scottish support for the Imperial ideal involved the voluntary suppression of separate Scottish nation-ality in favour of the popular concept of 'North Britain'. At a time when hotels, railway companies, national newspapers and even the postal system resorted to this appellation, the term itself might be seen to symbolise the dilemma of both the Scottish music-hall industry and the split allegiances of the public. For in the contrasting appeals of Empire and Scottish identity, the broker – given the audience in Glasgow halls, who might have spoken Scots, Gaelic or English, and who might have been Highland, Lowland or Irish – was the performer. Such artists' Scottish identity was usually the touchstone of their stage persona (to English audiences Scottish performers were always Scottish first and working class second unless they chose to negate their background altogether). Given Scottish performers' experience of manipulating their accent and material for consumption (and comprehension) by English audiences, which surely amounted to a cultural self-awareness unusual for the time, it follows that the stage projection of Scottish identity that evolved in music hall was at least partly refracted through the eyes of the returnee from the outside world, through the experience of having been a foreigner in a foreign land. Who better to offer audiences a consensual, shorthand image of what Scottishness amounted to, in the form of a composite of images and associations with which the disparate elements of the Scottish audience could all find something to identify? By being both quintessentially Scottish, on a professional basis, and a cosmopolitan citizen of the wider world, by dint of spending their working lives travelling (and a number of the more eminent toured to America, Australia, Canada and South Africa), the Scottish music hall pro was 'North Britain' encapsulated, with all its contradictions of national identity and loyalist sacrifice.

The idea that the cultural stereotyping of the stage Scot was partly a response to Scottish audiences' own demands for a redefinition of Scottish identity is a possibility that Cameron and Scullion have raised.[36] Whether, as I have suggested, the contribution of Scottish performers as a group was also significant in the form the image took will be explored in this book.

In conclusion, it is important to observe that the temptation to explore themes raised by the existing literature carries with it a danger of assuming that the history and timescale of developments in music hall in Glasgow mirrored that of London. This book will show that often they did not and that, on the face of it, the dissimilarities between the economic and social profile of music hall in Scotland and England are often more striking than the similarities.

## Notes

1  Ian McCraw, *The Fairs of Dundee*, Publication No. 34 (Dundee, Abertay Historical Society, 1994), pp. 44, 59; *Bon Accord*, 13 April 1889, p. 6.
2  Rev. Robert Bremner, *The Saturday Evening Concerts, A Sin and a Snare* (Glasgow, George Gallie, 1857).

3 Thos Chalmers in 1847: quoted in Callum G. Brown, *Religion and Society in Scotland since 1707* (Edinburgh, Edinburgh University Press, 1997), p. 95.

4 W. Hamish Fraser, 'Developments in Leisure', in W. H. Fraser and R. J. Morris (eds.), *People and Society in Scotland, Vol II, 1830–1914*, pp. 236–264 (pp. 241–242).

5 Irene Maver, 'Leisure and Culture: The Nineteenth Century', in Hamish Fraser and Clive Lee (eds.), *Aberdeen 1800–2000: A New History* (East Linton, Tuckwell Press, 2000), pp. 406–407.

6 *Birmingham Daily Mail,* 9 April [1879]; reproduced in *The Comet* in connection with Walter Banks's forthcoming presentation of *Uncle Tom's Cabin* in September 1879.

7 See Fraser, 'Developments in Leisure', pp. 260–261.

8 'The Kirk and Recreation', *The Piper o' Dundee*, 25 May 1892, p. 331.

9 Dagmar Kift [née Höher], *The Victorian Music Hall: Culture, Class and Conflict* (Cambridge, Cambridge University Press, 1996), p. 95.

10 Frank Boyd, *Records of the Dundee Stage from the Earliest Times to the Present Day* (Dundee, W. & D. C. Thomson, 1886), pp. 2–3.

11 Barbara Bell, 'The Nineteenth Century', in Bill Finlay (ed.), *A History of Scottish Theatre* (Edinburgh, Polygon, 1998), p. 180.

12 J. H. Muir, *Glasgow in 1901* (William Hodge, 1901), p. 194.

13 Callum G. Brown, *Religion and Society in Scotland since 1707* (Edinburgh, Edinburgh University Press, 1997), p. 102.

14 See Elspeth King, 'Popular Culture in Glasgow', in R. A. Cage (ed.), *The Working Class in Glasgow 1750–1914* (London, Croom Helm, 1987); Adrienne Scullion, 'Media Culture for a Modern Nation: Theatre, Cinema and Broadcasting in Early Twentieth-Century Scotland', unpublished PhD thesis, University of Glasgow, 1992; Alasdair Cameron and Adrienne Scullion (eds.), *Scottish Popular Theatre and Entertainment: Historical and Critical Approaches to Theatre and Film in Scotland* (Glasgow, University of Glasgow Library Studies, 1996); see also Adrienne Scullion, 'Geggies, Empires, Cinemas: The Scottish Experience of Early Film', in *Picture House*, 21 (summer 1996), 13–19. See also the music hall section in Bell, 'The Nineteenth Century'.

15 Jim Davis and Victor Emeljanow, in their recent survey of London theatre audiences, suggest that, while the advent of the halls undoubtedly provided stiff competition for popular theatres, 'any assumption that there was a massive drift by working class audiences to the music halls … is a complete misreading of history': Jim Davis and Victor Emeljanow, *Reflecting the Audience: London Theatregoing, 1840–1880* (Hatfield, University of Hertfordshire Press, 2001), pp. x, 226–230. Michael Booth similarly argues that the diversity and mobility of Victorian audiences, in a constantly evolving marketplace, makes class-specific views of individual entertainment genres extremely difficult: Michael R. Booth, *Theatre in the Victorian Age* (Cambridge, Cambridge University Press, 1991), pp. 6–13. For discussion of the social complexity of popular theatre audiences in Glasgow in the 1840s, see Tracy C. Davis, 'Let Glasgow Flourish', in Richard Foulkes (ed.), *Scenes*

*from Provincial Stages: Essays in Honour of Kathleen Barker* (London, The Society for Theatre Research, 1994), pp. 98–113.

16  Laurence Senelick, 'Politics as Entertainment: Victorian Music-Hall Songs', *Victorian Studies*, 19:2 (1975), pp.149–180 (p. 150).

17  Gareth Stedman Jones, 'Working-Class Culture and Working-Class Politics in London, 1870–1900: Notes on the Remaking of a Working Class', *Journal of Social History*, 7 (summer 1973–74), 460–508; repr. in Bernard Waites, Tony Bennett and Graham Martin (eds.), *Popular Culture: Past and Present. A Reader* (London, Croon Helm, 1982), pp. 92–121.

18  Stedman Jones, 'Working-Class Culture', p. 116.

19  See I. G. C. Hutchison, 'Glasgow Working-Class Politics', in Cage (ed.), *The Working Class in Glasgow*, pp. 112–121.

20  Stedman Jones, 'Working-Class Culture', p. 100.

21  Stedman Jones, 'Working-Class Culture', p. 102.

22  Peter Bailey, '"Will the real Bill Banks please stand up?" Towards a Role Analysis of Mid-Victorian Working-Class Respectability', *Journal of Social History*, 12 (1978–79), 336–353, p. 338.

23  Elspeth King, 'Popular Culture in Glasgow', p. 180.

24  Stedman Jones, 'Working-Class Culture', p. 108.

25  J. J. Bell, *I Remember* (Edinburgh, Porpoise Press, 1932), pp. 132–133.

26  See Penny Summerfield, 'The Effingham Arms and the Empire: Deliberate Selection in the Evolution of Music Hall in London', in Eileen Yeo and Stephen Yeo (eds.), *Popular Culture and Class Conflict 1590–1914* (Brighton, Harvester, 1981), pp. 209–210.

27  King, *Popular Culture in Glasgow*, p. 169.

28  Cameron and Scullion (eds.), *Scottish Popular Theatre*, p. 39.

29  Alasdair Cameron, 'Popular Theatre and Entertainment in Nineteenth Century Glasgow: Background and Context', in Karen Marshalsay, *The Waggle o' the Kilt*, (Glasgow, Glasgow University Library, 1992), p. 12.

30  Bill Findlay, 'Scots Language and Popular Entertainment in Victorian Scotland: The Case of James Houston', in Cameron and Scullion (eds.), *Scottish Popular Theatre*.

31  See Penny Summerfield, 'Patriotism and Empire: Music Hall Entertainment 1870–1914', in John M. Mackenzie (ed.), *Imperialism and Popular Culture* (Manchester, Manchester University Press, 1986), pp. 22–23.

32  Whilst agreeing with the basic premise, Summerfield suggests that location was less important in determining the social composition of audiences than type, size and capitalisation of the institutions concerned. This judgement seems predicated on the much more densely competitive London music hall. In the smaller pool of Glasgow, where choice was much more restricted, location seems to have determined the other factors.

33  For Hamilton see notebook of Herbert Doughty. Unpublished document.

34  The existence of a small but detailed literature on the professional sub-culture of English music hall has been a great asset here. Most useful have been Lois

Rutherford, '"Managers in a small way": The Professionalisation of the Variety Artistes, 1860–1914', in Peter Bailey (ed.), *Music Hall: The Business of Pleasure* (Milton Keynes, Open University, 1986); and Tracy C. Davis, *Actresses as Working Women* (London, Routledge, 1991).

35 'Bursts' were popular teetotal concerts, offering entertainment that included music-hall acts, in which the audience were given tea and a bag of buns or pastries on entry. When they had finished the buns, they would blow up the paper bag and pop, or burst, it, hence the name.

36 Cameron and Scullion (eds.), *Scottish Popular Theatre*, p. 57.

# 2

# The development
# of music hall, 1850–85

In London, the early music hall of the 1830s and 1840s developed from a number of different, socially distinct genres: the song and supper clubs, a legacy of the permissive eighteenth century, attracted an aristocratic and professional clientele, while tavern and saloon concerts, and the more basic free and easies catered for the various different levels of skilled artisans, shopkeepers and working men and women. At the same time, older pleasure gardens such as Vauxhall and the newer Cremorne, opened in 1832, used the crowd-pulling popularity of star tavern singers such as W. G. Ross to prolong their survival in an ephemeral marketplace.

These different formats offered variations of essentially the same song-based entertainment, and drew on a common pool of professional performers. However, in Scotland the confluence of older seasonal fairground entertainments, which signified what was formerly the crossover between town and rural societies, with new forms developed in response to changing patterns of urban living, produced their own hybrid sub-genres almost as socially nuanced as those of London. While traditional travelling and fairground entertainments remained popular for most of the second half of the nineteenth century, the development of music hall *per se* was essentially urban, or at least disseminated through the influence of urban culture.

In Glasgow, the development of music hall was inextricably linked with a specific area of the town centre, the old entertainment quarter centred on the Saltmarket. By the middle of the nineteenth century the city was entering its most dynamic period as a rapidly expanding industrial centre. Between 1801 and 1861 its population had increased fivefold and was growing at the rate of 7,000 persons a year.[1] As industrial sites expanded westwards along the banks of the Clyde, so the development of the West End and outer suburbs proceeded. At the same time waves of migrant workers (70,000 in the period between 1841 and 1851) arriving to serve the new industries gravitated to the area with the worst and cheapest housing, the tenements of the old city centre around Glasgow Cross. This area, bounded by Argyll Street and Trongate in the west, the Saltmarket to the south and Gallowgate to the east, contained the main concentration of free and easies in the city, and was to become home to the first generation of Glasgow music halls.

First-hand accounts of conditions applying in the Trongate/Saltmarket area in the 1850s by Alexander Brown, writing under the pseudonym 'Shadow', were published in book form as *Midnight Scenes and Social Photographs.* True to its sub-title, *being Sketches of Life in the Streets, Wynds and Dens of the city,* Brown's reports were an early attempt to use social realism to document the living conditions of those on the fringes of Glasgow society, the new underclass, the inner-city urban poor. They provide invaluable evidence of the conditions prevailing in the area that provided the early music hall with its constituency. Shadow's accounts of brothels and shebeens, of low lodging houses, families living in packed cellar dormitories and child prostitutes sleeping in doorways, give a vivid impression of street culture and the wretchedness of life for the poorest in society. To middle-class readers more used to congratulatory broadsheet items announcing that 'the sanitary condition of the city … was never in a more satisfactory condition'[2] such reports must have been shocking. From our point of view they put the appeal of free and easies and music halls into sharp perspective. The following is Shadow's description of a low lodging house in Saltmarket, inhabited by working people, into which he was invited. Entry was through 'a low, damp, earthy-smelling, subterranean sort of passage', giving on to two rooms, which provided living quarters for between six and eight people. One girl asleep had to be up to go to work at four a.m. The first room, containing 'a group of half-dressed people of both sexes collected around the fire-place' gives on to a doorless sleeping room, which Shadow terms 'a wretched hovel'.

> It is small, ill-lighted, and worse ventilated. A penny farthing candle stuck into the neck of a bottle diffuses a melancholy light throughout the room. In a corner is a window, near the roof, just enough grudgingly to illuminate a prison cell. On the floor, at convenient distances and almost at our feet, are placed two beds, in one of which is a young woman, a lodger … In an obscure part of the abode is a large filthy pail, apparently the urinal common to the entire household.[3]

The occupants here were not criminals or moral reprobates but working people whose misfortune it was to be poor. But if in these circumstances the attraction of social gatherings held in warm, well-lit surroundings was understandable, we cannot automatically presume that the free-and-easy, and later music-hall, audience was drawn from the immediate vicinity.

The Saltmarket area was also long-established as the city's entertainment quarter, largely due to the presence of the Fair, and its concentration of pubs and amusements attracted people from many outlying districts, making it the obvious area for the development of new entertainments such as music hall. But while the social composition of music-hall audiences will be examined more fully in chapter 8, there is some circumstantial evidence that at least a sizeable proportion of that for the Argyll Street halls may have been drawn from the immediate locality, and from the areas of dense, insanitary housing described. The fact that the Britannia Music Hall on Trongate, which opened around December 1859, was known to have a strongly Irish audience, reflected in the special popularity of Hibernian artists at the house, would certainly seem to mirror the density of the Irish immigrant population in the surrounding area, which was one of the highest in the city. In 1851, 45 per cent of the population of St Mary's and Tron Parish was Irish-born, and by 1881, even after considerable slum clearance had been carried out, the figure was still as high as 32 per cent.[4] It is also likely that the identification of free and easies and the early music halls with the notoriety of this area, and the poverty of its social milieu, was to be a major factor in music hall's failure to attract a middle-class audience before its relocation to the city centre in the 1890s.

In Glasgow, as in London, various types of amateur concerts and tavern-based music-making had existed from the 1830s and 1840s. A paradox in Glasgow's case was that much of the activity at such events involved precentors, who were employed by churches to lead their congregations' singing, and who were clearly discouraged from involvement in secular entertainments. Stenbridge Ray, conductor of the Barony Choir, was suspended from office after he was found to have been singing in a theatre, but was reinstated on condition that he would give up theatrical engagements. But that did not stop others from this group, who constituted the main body of the city's music teachers and composers, from exploiting opportunities for gainful employment. One account recalled:

> It was a great treat to hear John McDougall, precentor in St. Enoch Church and 'Wull' Zuille, precentor in the 'Hie Kirk' (or Cathedral), singing duets in the Lyceum Rooms; Fraser's Hall, King Street; Haggart's and Pollock's taverns, King Street; the Black Boy tavern, Gallowgate; the Black Bull Rooms, Argyle Street, and other fashionable resorts of the day.[5]

If these tavern-based concerts have an eighteenth-century feel, the impression of performers going between such venues sounds very similar to the circuit frequented by Charles Rice, the early London music-hall performer, who similarly augmented his income as a porter at the British Museum with part-time evening work as a pub singer.[6]

Although in Glasgow the first music halls to call themselves by the term did not appear until the early 1850s, the participatory form of entertainment they purveyed had, in essence, been around for a generation, in the informally organised concerts put on in the backrooms of public houses, known as free and easies. Held under the auspices of a publican or landlord, who provided a room, a piano and the services of a chairman, these were basically communal sing-songs, in which customers were encouraged to stand up and deliver their party pieces, comic songs or sentimental ballads, with which the assembled company could join in. Here participants could drink, smoke, dance and otherwise entertain themselves in a boisterous but convivial atmosphere that for many immigrants and newly arrived city dwellers must have echoed the sort of community life they had left behind in the countryside.

Contemporary first-hand accounts of free and easies concur on the primitive nature of the presentation and surroundings but vary somewhat in their estimation of the moral character – or at least potential – of the proceedings. Notwithstanding the fact that most commentators had their own agendas, the establishments themselves clearly varied considerably in ambience and respectability of clientele. A contributor to the *Abstainers Journal* of 1854 describes how, on entering a Glasgow free and easy

> our ears are at once regaled with *very fine* music from a piano, and a skilful player at the head of the room, in which are seated about 130 well-dressed lads belonging to various handcrafts in the city. We find ourselves in what is called a 'Free and Easy'.[7]

The writer notes the presence of a chairman ('by far too good-looking and well-dressed for such a place') and, despite the smokiness of the room, finds himself impressed by both the ability of the pianist and the singing of a young man called upon to deliver a song. But if the correspondent is open-minded enough to accept the general worthiness of the entertainment, it is because he has other axes to grind; as was usual with temperance campaigners, the target was not the customer but the manipulative publican, who is exploiting the ordinary man's love of music for his own commercial ends. 'Music has its attractions', he concedes, 'but why should it not be rescued from the debasing associations of the public house?'.

Other investigators felt less compunction to acknowledge the good character of those taking part. An article from the *North British Daily Mail* of 1871, some

17 years later, describes a Glasgow free and easy very similar to that mentioned above, the venue being

> a sort of right-angled double room, very low in the ceiling, with deal tables running parallel to each other down the centre. The atmosphere was stifling with the heat of many gaslights and the breath of about two hundred youths who crammed the apartment. It was thick with the smoke reeking from some two or three score of pipes ... As to music, there was a fiddler, a harper, and a harmonious chairman, the last of whom got overcome towards ten o'clock, and was conveyed from his official seat of honour in a most inharmonious condition.[8]

The image of free and easies as low-ceilinged dens was common. Bryce's, at 63 Prince's Street, Edinburgh, was remembered in the 1870s as 'a long subterranean room, where the light of day was unable to penetrate', while White's, at the head of the old North Bridge in the same city, was attained when 'Entering from the pavement with the assistance of a thick brass hand-rail, you descended a dozen steps, and found yourself in a long cellar'.[9]

By contrast to the 'harmonious' chairman, Shadow's account of a visit to the Jupiter in Glasgow's Saltmarket in the late 1850s finds the venue already operating under the temperance banner. Although commonly cited as one of the city's leading singing saloons,[10] along with the Shakespeare, Sir Walter Scott and Oddfellows, the Jupiter is clearly a different type of establishment to those previously described, not least in scale; here the room is sub-divided, with a separate 'snug', or sort of dress box, containing 'a few people, quiet and decent-looking enough', as well as an inclined pit, or 'gods'. Most significantly, there is an admission charge of 3d. This is clearly not a free and easy; on the face of it, it is a theatre or 'geggie',[11] having more features in common with Parry's theatre (previously visited by the correspondent) than with the place described in the *Abstainer's Journal*. The ringing of a bell, use of costume and reference to a 'company' all suggest a professional theatrical enterprise. And yet the content of the performance, its reliance on songs, their style and subject matter, and the level of interaction with the audience, all point to the incipient music hall;

> As we enter, a song is being sung, 'Anything for a Crust'. The artiste, dressed in appropriate habiliments, is vociferously applauded. The curtain drops, and, as before, a scene takes place among 'the gods', who are in number upwards of a hundred or so. They consist chiefly of working lads from twelve to twenty, with a slight sprinkling of another class, of both sexes, not quite so respectable. Fruit, ginger beer, &c., are now handed round. The bell rings and a smartly-dressed young English woman ascends the stage or platform; and, what with beauty and song, enraptures the audience. She pauses, smiles, and sings again, and finally retires amidst vociferous applause.[12]

This would seem to be a proto-music hall, but one already run on very different lines from a free and easy. The Jupiter has a proper auditorium, capable of holding a large, paying audience (there is reference to a 'box-keeper' who takes the money and sells fruit and refreshments). Moreover, the entertainment is performed by professional artists, some of them from England, rather than by members of the audience. In this context, the Jupiter can be seen as a commercial, professionalised Saltmarket version of the free and easy entertainment. Glasgow's two leading music halls in the late 1850s, Brown's Royal Music Hall and Shearer's Whitebait, usually acknowledged to have been the city's first, were much more closely modelled on the free and easy format, with a chairman, admission through buying a drink, and performers who, while professional, would have circulated freely amongst the clientele. Could the Jupiter, which did not call itself a music hall as such, even though the term was current, have represented a variant of the same basic entertainment, but one derived from the popular theatre tradition of the Saltmarket, rather than from the newer pub-based free and easy?[13]

Shadow goes on to describe other establishments in the Saltmarket, 'in all of which intoxicating liquors are used', which sound more like the first free and easies discussed. But these singing saloons, as they are termed, are clearly much grander, more upmarket affairs;

> One of them, in particular, is beautifully fitted up, finely painted, and brilliantly illuminated. These are frequented by the mechanic, clerk, or shop-keeper. The singing, music and dancing in these establishments are esteemed respectable.[14]

The number of different types of venue so far discussed – free and easies, geggies, penny theatres and singing saloons – give an impression of the range of popular musical and theatrical genres available to Glasgow audiences in the 1840s and 1850s.

Glasgow was quickly to develop into the most important Scottish centre for music-hall activity, with more halls than the other principal cities combined for most of the second half of the nineteenth century. But while other Scottish cities did not generally possess purpose-built venues until the 1860s, most by the mid-century had some form of localised music-hall entertainment, often with links to older amusements. In the 1840s Aberdeen had a number of pubs with large rooms attached to them 'designated free and easies', where 'singing, recitations, and music on various instruments were supplied by those attending them, and proved a very attractive accompaniment to the drink'. Presided over by a chairman, on a Saturday these were recalled as having been 'very popular with certain classes of wage-earners, especially young men, who held at that time very few opportunities of meeting together in a social capacity and interchanging with each other the gifts of song, conversation and music'.[15] By 1852 Mrs Liffen's Hall, an annex of the Adelphi Hotel, offered a series of concerts with specially engaged performers, chaired by Sam Cowell, a leading star of the London music halls. Recalled as 'much frequented … the proceedings being of the free and easy character', Liffens was 'quite an after-business resort' which boasted 'the best native oysters from the London markets'. If this has more than a ring of the metropolitan supper club about it, Cowell was succeeded by no less a figure than W. G. Ross, a Glasgow compositor who also became a big star of London 'Caves of Harmony' with his grim ballad 'Sam Hall'. Other favourites, in what was clearly a professional music hall, were the banjo player Little Barlow and Charles Sloman, a well-known London tavern singer. Celebrated as an improviser of songs, Sloman features in the recently published diaries of his friend Charles Rice, a fellow singer in London pub concert-rooms, who marvelled at his ability to combine 'four or five subjects, given by a company, into one extemporaneous run of poetry … remarkable for its metrical correctness'.[16] The fact that Sloman, and his more celebrated colleagues, should be working as far north as Aberdeen in the early 1850s emphasises how wide ranging the network of professional activities had already become by this time. Later in the decade the Brothers Fraser took the city's Mechanics' Hall, offering 'cheap concerts … illustrating incidents associated with Scottish song, by dress and pictorial surroundings', and the same hall was later occupied by Signor Fumarolo, an Italian bass who led 'a clever variety company' in popular concert series that continued until 1860. That these essentially comprised music-hall entertainment is evident from Fumarolo's advertisements in the trade paper, *The Era*: 'Wanted immediately for People's Concerts Aberdeen, a good comic vocalist, an attractive lady dancer, and other professionals'.[17]

Dundee's entertainments similarly possessed the constituent elements of music hall long before its emergence as a distinct genre. Regular visitors to the city's First or Lady Mary Fair in the Meadows in the first half of the century included Ord's and Ducrow's Circuses, Scott's Royal Victoria Theatre, Billy Purvis's Theatre, Scott's Pantheon and Giles Theatre of Varieties.[18] By the 1840s the city's minor theatres – known as Penny Gaffs – included Fizzy Gow's in Lindsay Street, formally the Clarence Theatre, and another in the Seagate, where the poet McGonagall appeared. From the early 1860s Springthorpes, who had presented waxworks since the 1830s, began offering music-hall entertainment in the basement of a church in Bell Street, Dundee, their concert-room being 'one of the kind of establishments which, during a comparatively few years past, have sprung up in most towns to meet a demand created by a growing musical taste, not of the highest kind, among the masses. It was formerly a waxworks, but the attractions offered to ears proved more potent than those which appealed to eyes; and so figures were exchanged for songs'.[19] Unfortunately the unsuitability of the basement location contributed to the fatal panic that occurred at the hall in January 1865, when 20 people were killed.

Given the wide diversity of amusements available, what remains to be explained is why it was the entertainment that began in free and easies and evolved into music hall that became the favourite of the urban working classes, rather than a variation of one of the existing forms of popular music theatre. A possible answer is that it didn't; that music hall was not nearly as pre-eminent in the pantheon of later nineteenth-century popular entertainment as we have been led to believe, and that other forms of theatre such as melodrama and pantomime were far more popular with working audiences than has been allowed for. This theory, suggested by the wide range of recent research into Victorian theatre audiences, including that of Clive Barker and others into those of the Britannia Theatre, Hoxton, is partly substantiated in the case of Glasgow by evidence that will be examined in the next chapter.[20] Alternatively, it may be that free and easies, and through them music hall, should be seen as a variation or evolution of existing forms to new patterns of urban living. This view, that music hall in Peter Bailey's words, 'adapted an older cultural order to the perameters of a new urban world',[21] could be taken to embrace not only existing local entertainments but also other cultural influences brought by immigrant communities newly arrived in the city. Adrienne Scullion has stressed the contribution of Highland and Irish culture to the evolution of the Saltmarket free and easy, as 'in the pubs and shebeens of this community drink gave way to ceilidhs and informal sing-songs and music-making'. She goes on to state her view that 'a particular and significant influence in the evolution towards music halls *per se* came from this ceilidh tradition, which these communities brought with them to industrialising Glasgow' and sees the ceilidh as 'a key factor in the development of what is a uniquely independent Scottish popular theatre'.[22] Although the early predominance of the ceilidh influence sounds very plausible, as does Scullion's suggestion that Glasgow music hall might have developed slightly earlier than its London counterpart, the most distinctive feature of subsequent music hall was the speed with which it came to embody a wide and cosmopolitan range of cultural influences.

The difficulty of establishing precisely which features derived from which genre are anyway compounded by the tendency of older forms to transform or reinvent themselves in response to changing conditions. Elspeth King has written of the rich entertainment tradition represented by Glasgow Fair,[23] held annually at the bottom of Saltmarket until 1870, when it was relocated to nearby Vinegar Hill. Many elements of these older amusements outlasted the original semi-rural fair tradition; freak shows and fairground curiosities were assimilated into city-centre waxwork displays such as those that survived on Glasgow's Trongate until the 1920s; jugglers, acrobats and strongmen continued to be seen in circuses and music hall, while scenic skills used to produce popular panoramas and dioramas were transferred to permanent 'educational' exhibitions and theatres, where elaborate painted front cloths were a popular draw with the public.

If Glasgow's city fathers went out of their way to expunge the taint of the fairground from the city centre, other cities took a less doctrinaire line, with the result that older amusements co-existed with music hall for much of the second half of the century. Indeed, the striking aspect of entertainments in the Northeast is the relative parity of the wide range of competing amusements. In Dundee, gaffs remained a popular feature, both during traditional fairs and as semi-permanent fixtures on sites on waste ground near the city centre. Shows of the 1880s like those run by Giles, Hicks, MacGivern, Clarks and John Young were unmistakably local in provenance: 'Outside the wifie with the basket of whelks did a roaring trade', while the entertainment itself consisted of dramas such as 'The Smuggler's Cave', at the culmination of which

> the 'hero' (Hicks) with his sword jagged a small bladder full of cow or sheep blood and the villain, 'Tally Mug,' made a magnificent 'Deid Fa', so realistically that the 'gods' demanded four encores before they were appeased … The 'property swords' were made of the 'girds' or hoops taken from whale oil barrels and had an unfortunate habit of bending at an inopportune moment; the fair tresses of the leading lady was 'Tow' from Baxters or 'Beasties' Mill.[24]

In Edinburgh booths offering theatre and variety shows remained a familiar feature long after the establishment of larger music halls, and provided a training ground for local performers such as the comedian N. C. Bostock, who gained his early experience in a penny gaff in the Lothian Road.[25] Circuses too remained extremely popular, with John Henry Cooke opening a new wooden arena in Bridge Place, Aberdeen, in 1888. The building later became the Jollity Vaudeville and People's Palace music halls, and a number of other halls were similarly established in former circus premises, including the Alhambra and Southminster halls in Nicolson Street, Edinburgh, and both McFarland's original Alhambra in East Station, and later halls in Lochee Road and Nethergate in Dundee.

But if many strands of the older entertainments like those of Glasgow's Saltmarket resurfaced later in other forms, and overlapped and coexisted in their declining years with the new entertainment, we should not make the mistake of trying to impose a false continuity on the origins of music hall, which was distinctly different in a number of important respects. In Glasgow, geggies like Mumford's and penny theatres such as Parry's and Calvert's may have resembled music halls in terms of interaction between audience and performers and their use of irreverent, broadly satirical material. But on a practical level the cut-down playlets they offered were (in however loose a sense) scripted, and presented songs and music within the context of a narrative framework. Free and easies, like music hall, offered a sequence of separate and unrelated items. A more profound difference may have been that unlike these travelling 'low' theatres, which drew mainly on long-popular patriotic and anti-establishment sentiment for their historical plays and parodies, free and easies had a different social aspect, and arose to cater for a new, more specific working audience, who shared a common urban experience and lifestyle. It seems quite possible that the entertainment they developed was a celebration (if that is the right word) of this new urban culture, and drew on collective memories of the alienating, dislocating experience of migration from countryside to city accumulated over the course of a generation.[26] Moreover, however much the Fair geggies were perceived as 'peoples' theatres', they were nevertheless commercial enterprises in which the paying public were entertained by professional performers. In contrast, the essence of the free and easy was that the audience were active participants who provided their own entertainment, the improvisatory element playing a central role. It could be argued that the distinction was largely notional: that in Scotland, as in England, free and easies soon turned to employing professional singers to lead the entertainment. But the principle of participation remained an important part of the audience's 'owning' of the entertainment.

In viewing the music halls proper of the 1850s, it is hard not to view the entertainment they offered as a parenthesis to the bleak social conditions previously described. In any case, the new halls seem to epitomise the new social function and importance of entertainment in urban society. Short-day working on Saturdays, already common in the west of Scotland by the early 1840s, was extended to factory workers by the Factory Act of 1850,[27] and by the mid-century a new awareness of the importance of constructive leisure was reflected in the popularity of excursion trains and incipient development of seaside resorts.

Traditional Fairdays were increasingly used to take advantage of affordable rail excursions. In 1855 more than 20,000 passengers from Dundee travelled by special trains to destinations including Glasgow, Edinburgh, Perth, Aberdeen and Arbroath, and on the Tay ferries.[28] In commercial terms, the potential for popular amusements was evident and signalled a change in emphasis. The annual Glasgow Fair, organised along the patterns of traditional feasts, offered entertainment on an occasional basis as a treat or break, an exception to the routine of normal life. In contrast the music halls that emerged in the 1850s and 1860s did so in response to an altogether more urgent demand for cheap entertainment, to be available on a continuous basis. Walter Freer, manager of Glasgow Corporation halls for thirty-five years, recalling his boyhood in the 1850s, wrote that 'Youngsters ... like myself haunted the music-halls because they could get neither warmth nor pleasure in their own homes'. In *My Life and Memories* Freer describes one of the first Glasgow halls, Shearer's Whitebait Music Hall in St Enoch's Wynd which opened in 1853;

> As you went in you paid your entry-money, and the price of a refreshment (for drinking in those days was almost as common as breathing) and took your place in the hall beyond. The stage was railed off from the audience, and the owner of the music-hall acted as chairman, announcing each item as it fell due.[29]

The reference to the 'hall beyond' suggests that, as with most early music halls, the premises were probably a conversion, in which a backroom or annexe had been built on to the original public house to increase capacity. As the huge demand for live entertainment became ever more apparent, publicans were quick to appreciate the commercial potential; singing saloons and other licensed premises were adapted and enlarged to increase capacity and provide facilities for live performance. Although entertainment rather than drink was now the main draw, the income from the bar remained a vital component of the new venues' financial success. The fact that music hall had evolved in public houses, and that most of the early proprietors were in the wines and spirits trade, meant that, as a form, it was always associated with the consumption of alcohol. The temperance lobby in particular, despite the strivings of later generations of managers, always found it impossible to disassociate music hall as entertainment from the corrupting influence of alcohol, or to absolve music-hall managers from the charge of being in business to bring about the moral ruin of their fellow citizens.

In terms of format, the entertainment Shearer's offers is very similar to that of a free and easy; the chairman (here the proprietor), is still in charge and although we are in an auditorium of sorts, and Freer calls the platform a stage, the mention of a rail as dividing it from the audience implies that there is not yet a proscenium arch to 'frame' the stage picture, as in conventional nineteenth-century theatres. The major difference is that this is evidently a fulltime concern, employing professional performers; Freer recounts how Shearer's outbid its local rival, Brown's Music-Hall, to secure the services of a leading comedian, Jimmie Taylor, for whom they eventually paid £100 in an open auction. (Taylor, an Englishman better known as Jolly John Nash, went on to perform before the Prince of Wales, later King Edward VII.) The growing cost to managers of employing star performers to attract the public was often cited as an explanation of the importance of bar revenues. Freer paints a vivid picture of the excitement provoked by the episode, an early example of a showman's publicity stunt;

> on the first night of Jimmie Taylor's appearance the Whitebait in St Enoch's Square ...was packed to suffocation. Regulations regarding overcrowding did not exist and the proprietor crammed in as many people as the place would hold ... [he, Freer] left my work at six in the evening instead of seven, and arrived at the Whitebait to find it seething with people.[30]

The sense of occasion suggests an entertainment culture. And as if the heady excitement of the occasion were not enough, the atmosphere in the hall clearly induced thirstiness;

> It makes me sweat even now to think of that terrible night and that terrific jam. The perspiration was rolling plentifully off every mortal in the place, there was no ventilation, and the walls themselves perspired no less copiously than the Whitebait's unfortunate patrons.[31]

It is easy to understand why temperance reformers generally saw music hall as a publicans' device to encourage drinking. And in the midst of all this Jimmie Taylor apparently delivered a song entitled 'The Chilly Man' to enormous success.

By the late 1850s Glasgow was established as the main Scottish music hall centre. In April 1860 the leading theatrical journal, *The Era*, mistakenly attributed a report on Glasgow's music-hall activity to Edinburgh. In correcting the mistake in the next issue, the editorial used the very transparency of the error to excuse it, remarking 'it is generally known, however, that the capital cannot boast of even one, let alone such a number of these popular places of entertainment as was mentioned in our last impression'. The venues alluded to had been detailed some months previously, in January 1860, when a report on the exceptional business that prolonged rain over the Christmas holiday had brought to Glasgow's entertainments, listed them as 'the People's Circus, Washington Friends' Panorama, the African Opera Troupe, the Royal Parthenon, the Philharmonic, the Whitebait, the Shakespeare, the Colosseum, the Odd Fellows, the Britannia, and a host of minor entertainments'. But what were these halls actually like, in terms of ambience? The *Era* survey from April of the same year, 1860, effectively a music-hall crawl of the city, contains little hard information about the audience or surroundings, and yet, by detailing the entertainment and reactions to it, manages to give a surprisingly full impression of the atmosphere at the Glasgow halls. Starting with the newly opened Britannia:

> we were amused by the comic songs of Mr McGown and the duos of Mr and Mrs Stephens. Mr McGregor Simpson electrified us with his Jacobite songs, Madame Henessier charmed us with a ballad, and the Misses Duvalli showed much proficiency in the terpsichorean art. Mr Spiers appeared to manage the musical affairs with much success. Crossing the street, we found ourselves in the Royal Parthenon, being much astonished by the impalement feats of a party of Chinese Jugglers and the graceful gymnastics of the Corelli family. Tom Glen gave us a hearty laugh by his rendering of an indescribably comic ditty, and Mr Burton seemed to have danced himself into the good graces of the numerous audience. Miss Kirby, Miss Howard and Mr E. Lyons proved that they were vocalists of no mean pretensions, and well worthy of public patronage. Having got the length of the Philharmonic, under the care of Mr Brown, we listened to many excellent songs from Mesdames Webb, Sinclair, Constance, Losebini, and Jackson. Mr Moss seemed to have all the power over our risible muscles ordinarily imputed to Momus, and the Mdlles Duvernay dance like some beings less corporeal than we of the nether earth. We afterwards had a glass of Dunville's Irish Whiskey punch, with Mr Shearer of the Whitebait, where we found Mr Lowick in the director's chair, and the house in roars at the comicalities of Messrs Raymond and Warren, who were amusing the company with an election speech of immense power. The Misses Le Brun then exhibited their pretty persons and many graces in a mazy dance, and were followed by a ballad from Miss Wilmott, who, in her turn, was succeeded by Mr Sellers in a comic effusion, and Mr Sanders in a more sentimental and serious one. The accompaniments were well played by Mr Colgan, and all the arrangements appeared to give satisfaction. Turning northwards, we arrived at the Milton Colosseum just as Professor Hall was giving a very good ventriloquial entertainment and we afterwards heard Mrs Ramsdale in a sentimental song, Mr J. T. Curtis in a comic one. Mr Ramsdale followed suit, as did Mr Alfred Wood and his little son in a nigger ditty and a plantation breakdown. Mr T. Bishop wound up with a Jacobite air, which he sang in a highly dramatic manner.[32]

Bar the absence of any reference to clogdancing, a popular favourite, or yet to Scotch comics by name, the entertainment covered has just about everything: from Jacobite airs to black-faced minstrelsy via the exoticism of impalement, a satirical election address, hints at the titillating presence of female dancers, and a convivial glass of (Irish!) whiskey, all wrapped up in the smoothly emollient, see-no-evil style of the music-hall trade press (with not a harsh word said about anyone). At a time when most Scottish cities were yet to possess their first pur-pose-built hall, Glasgow was already the centre of a thriving music hall and entertainment marketplace.

The singing saloons and hybrid pub music halls of the 1850s were soon joined by larger, purpose-built venues, all within walking distance of Glasgow Cross; the aforementioned Britannia in Trongate, probably intended as a com-mercial premises of some sort, was fitted out with a music-hall auditorium shortly after completion, and opened around Christmas 1859. It was followed in 1863 by the Scotia Music Hall around the corner in Stockwell Street, and the Star in Watson Street to the east of the Cross in 1873.[33] The sixties also saw other Scottish cities acquire similar venues of their own. In Edinburgh, William Paterson opened the splendid Alhambra Music Hall in Nicolson Street in April 1861, on the site of the fire-damaged Dunedin Hall. The following year the hall relocated to a new building on the same street, later renamed the Princess's, while by the late 1860s the old Dunedin Hall site was occupied by a new building known as Levy's Southminster Music Hall. In the adjacent port of Leith, a number of raucous tavern-based houses sprang up to cater for the docks and their workers; the insalubrious Leith Royal Music Hall, opened in Riddle's Close in 1865 with John Scotland as lessee, was followed by the Theatre Royal (a music hall despite the name) in 1867, the New Star Music Hall on Leith Walk, and the Assembly Rooms in Constitution Street, which offered variety presentations without the all-pervasive influence of alcohol.[34]

The North-east also saw music hall develop as a commercial entertainment in a remarkably short space of time. The Dundee Music Hall, managed by the MacLeod Brothers, opened in the city in the mid-1860s in the refurbished Merchants Exchange in Castle Street. By 1868 it had a competitor, the Alhambra, situated in the former Sangers Circus building in East Station and managed by William McFarland, who took over the MacLeods' venue the fol-lowing year. In Aberdeen the same scenario seems to have repeated itself; the Bon-Accord Music Hall, managed from the late 1860s by J. C. MacLeod, was superseded in 1871 by McFarland's Alhambra in Market Street. By the early 1870s McFarland had established himself as the dominant north-eastern impresario, a position he was to hold for the next twenty years.

New buildings such as these represented considerable investments on the part of the Proprietors and indicated a coming of age in commercial terms. But

**2**     Britannia Music Hall, Trongate, Glasgow, c.1895

if music hall had emerged from the shadow of public houses to stand as an entertainment – and business – in its own right, the free and easies retained their own constituency. In Edinburgh, where there were only ever one or two larger music halls until the 1890s, free and easies remained a popular feature of city entertainment until the end of the century, with Bryces, the most long-lived, only finally closing in 1896.[35] In Glasgow, although clearance of the city-centre slums began in the 1860s through railway developments and the City Improvement (Glasgow) Act of 1868, it took decades to accomplish. The series of investigative newspaper reports published in 1871 as 'The Dark Side of Glasgow' revealed the Dickensian sub-culture of the Saltmarket described by 'Shadow' in the 1850s, to be largely intact. Just as music halls and theatres were packing in the audiences, so a visit to a free and easy on a Saturday night finds the entrance 'literally besieged', and the place so packed that a waiter whom the reporter tries to bribe to let him in, claims to have himself been waiting twenty minutes to get inside to take orders. Unlike reform-minded writers, the Dark Side reporter feels no compunction to acknowledge the good character, or at least intentions, of the majority of participants. As investigative journalism intended to shock a middle-class readership, the tone is sensational and the pictures painted lurid, with the correspondent revealing both his prurience and his abhorrence of all that he encounters; entering a free and easy around the corner from the first, he witnesses a singer who appears to be a local favourite deliver:

> one of the most disgustingly indecent songs which it has ever been my misfortune to hear. Each verse ended with the refrain, 'Wi'his hymns and psalms, his preaching and his praying, and his hallelujah bands,' and the filthy composition turned upon a scandalous episode in poor Weaver's life, to which we shall not further allude.[36]

In particular, the reporter's description of the women frequenting a mixed free and easy demonstrates the gulf that existed between middle- and working-class culture; for him the presence of women amongst the men, smoke and alcohol clearly crowns the dissolute nature of the scene. Of the women he comments:

> Truth obliges me to confess that they were, with one or two exceptions, plain and even repulsive-looking, and at least half a dozen of them were visibly affected by drink. It would be difficult to exaggerate the coarseness of the conversation and behaviour of the company generally. Ribald jokes, indecent talk, oaths and blasphemies mixed with loud hoarse laughs rose on every side.[37]

If we accept the reporter's as a middle-class voice addressing a bourgeois readership, what is conveyed is the total 'foreignness' of the working-class experience. That this continued to be the case as far as the 1890s is suggested by a piece in

The journal *Quiz*, in which a West End gentleman ventures into the Saltmarket on a Sunday evening; describing the people and locale as if he were in darkest Africa rather than in the heart of the city. The reader is invited to:

> look into their faces! There is the low animal type of man well known in our police courts, and by his side a creature who has almost lost the appearance of a woman, – her face is so battered, and her voice so loud, and grating on the ear.

This enormous gulf of comprehension and experience that existed between the suburban middle classes and the urban working classes who inhabited the inner city areas was no doubt an important factor in the absence of the middle class from Glasgow music-hall audiences before the advent of city-centre variety in the 1890s.

Whatever the debate about its origins, the free and easy was the direct precursor to music hall. There is a correlation between its format – with a chairman, platform, the calling up of artists and communal singing – and music-hall practice. There is also the demonstrable crossover of venues and personnel. Not only did the first Glasgow 'pub' music halls such as Browns and the Whitebait develop directly from singing saloon premises, but early proprietors such as David Brown of the Royal and James Baylis of the Scotia were themselves formerly free-and-easy chairmen or practitioners.

In discussing the Glasgow music halls of the 1860s and 1870s, it is important to place them within the wider context of the expanding role of entertainment and leisure generally. The Victorian public's increasing appetite for entertainment in this period encompassed all forms of popular theatre and amusements. As music hall emanated from the area around Trongate and Argyll Street, so new legitimate theatres appeared, both in the modern city centre and business area around Sauchiehall Street, and in the suburbs.[38] Just as improvements in rail travel brought an influx of touring companies from London's West End to play in Glasgow's legitimate theatres, leading to the disappearance of locally based stock companies and the decline of the National Drama,[39] so music hall as a form quickly moved beyond local and regional success to establish itself on a national scale. By the 1870s Glasgow halls were part of an evolving industry that was both commercially sophisticated and cosmopolitan in outlook. The leading trade paper, *The Era*, founded in 1837, advertised itself as the 'acknowledged Organ of the Theatrical and Musical profession in England, America & Australia, finding its way to every Town in the World in which there is a theatre'. Although Glasgow-published trade papers did not appear until the 1880s, Glasgow periodical and newspaper columns such as the

*Evening Times* 'Dramatic and Musical' section relayed titbits of stage news and trivia aimed at both the profession and the general public. Whilst the 'international' feel of such columns was no doubt contrived, they did reflect both the emergence of an industry with a genuinely national (i.e. British) feel, and a new public fascination with the backstage world of the theatre. As in Glasgow, north-eastern journals of the 1880s such as the *Bon Accord*, the *Northern Figaro* and the *Piper O'Dundee* reflected this new urbanity in approach to public entertainments, and, in their reporting of musical and theatrical events, were to prove important advocates of the case for affordable entertainments. Sketches of Glasgow city life in the 1830s portrayed the theatrical community as a gregarious but essentially self-contained group, with their own professional club meeting in a tavern opposite the Theatre Royal in Dunlop Street. In Edinburgh the theatrical haunt of the 1880s was Mrs Gilchrist's tavern in Mylne Square, known as The Presbytery.[40] By the 1890s leading variety performers, instantly recognisable by their dress, enjoyed local celebrity status and were highly visible figures, promenading in the afternoons on fashionable thoroughfares such as Sauchiehall Street, where their display of the latest fashions was much imitated by shop and office workers.[41]

Becoming by the 1880s a capitalised industry with the potential for a mass audience, music hall's paradox was that its national success was based on responsiveness to local audiences. Although the rail system made a vast pool of artists and acts available, the formula for a successful programme varied from venue to venue, depending on a wide range of social, cultural and specifically local factors. The nature of each audience remained distinct and best judged by the individual proprietor or manager, who booked the acts and learned by trial and error (often to his cost) what went down well with his public.

If music hall in Glasgow as elsewhere was essentially local in character, its commercial inspiration and model was London. In 1856, only five years after Charles Morton opened the Canterbury, the influential London hall that became the prototype for a generation of subsequent venues, London already boasted thirty-three large halls and several hundred smaller ones.[42] An enormous gulf existed between the commercial scale of music-hall activities in London and in the provinces. London trade news and gossip dominated *The Era* and other papers, whilst London managers would pioneer most of the industry's work practices, amongst them the invention of the 'turn' system of playing several venues on one night, the introduction of twice-nightly and matinee performances, and the first use of music-hall agents. Whether the early saturation of the capital with music halls was significant or not, by the 1880s

**Table 2.1** Numbers of Glasgow music halls and theatres

|      | Music halls | Theatres |
|------|:-----------:|:--------:|
| 1868 | 5 | 3 |
| 1875 | 7 | 4 |
| 1880 | 4 | 5 |
| 1890 | 3 | 4 |

Source: 'Music Halls in the United Kingdom' and 'Theatres in the United Kingdom', *Era Almanack*, 1868, 1875, 1880, 1890.

the potential and dynamic for expansion lay in the provinces, and with provincial managements.

By comparison, the scale and sophistication of Glasgow music hall as a commercial activity inevitably remained modest. Until the turn of the century growth in the number of venues was very gradual and characterised by short bursts of activity. Between the 1860s and 1900 the city centre had only a handful of halls, reaching a highpoint for the 1870s of eight in 1878, only for the figure to fall back to five the following year. Throughout this period the number of city-centre venues rarely exceeded four or five (see Table 2.1). Up to the late 1870s Glasgow's music halls generally outnumbered the city's legitimate theatres, after which the number fell away, not to overtake the theatres again until the mid-1900s. Moreover, until the 1890s theatres generally had far larger capacities.[43] However the *Era* figures cited here only list the city's principal halls, and it seems likely that there would also have been a considerable amount of music hall activity centred on smaller pub halls or in venues in outlying areas.

In summarising the general ambience of music hall performances in the 1870s, and the social composition of the audiences they attracted, the most valuable first-hand accounts are reports of two visits made to Glasgow halls by senior police officers in March 1875.[44] The visits were an official response to complaints made by a public deputation to the magistrates earlier in the month protesting at the lewd entertainment being presented at the Whitebait music hall in St Enoch's Wynd[45] (the ramifications of which will be discussed in more depth in chapter 8). While reports in the trade press such as *The Era* from 1860 generally give a flattering impression of the halls, long on bonhomie and short on detail – very much the industry public relations view – the police reports describe who they found present and give their impressions of the character of the venues inspected. The second of these reports, addressed to Captain

McCall, the Chief Constable of Glasgow, constitutes a tour of the city's music halls, with the correspondent calling first at a hall named the Royal Alhambra, where the artists included

> Sam Moore, Scotch Comic, I Forbes, Highland Dancer, Mr & Mrs Clair, Irish Duettists, Edward Trainer, Irish Comic, Johnny Parry, Pantomimist, Professor Pace, Wizard, Lizzie Pace, Ballard singer and M Grant, Nigger – These artists are very much inferior to the usual run of music hall talent and are paid from 15/- to 30/- per week. At the time of my visit the audience numbered about 250, chiefly lads of 12 to 18 years of age, and 10 females, mostly young. The audience were orderly and the different artists appeared to please them ... I saw nothing of an objectionable kind in this hall.

The Alhambra sounds like a minor hall, playing to small houses. The officer next proceeds to the Britannia, where he reports

> I found the hall comfortably filled and the stage occupied by Irish and Martin, who gave a negro entertainment which appeared to give great satisfaction to the audience. All the arrangements in connection with this hall are in my opinion as near perfection as possible, and I never observed anything either in song or gesture by any of the artists while in the stage that could be considered in the slightest degree offensive.

Next came the Oxford, on the corner of Trongate and Old Wynd, where like the Alhambra, he found 'an audience numbering about 200, mostly young men and boys and a few females, of respectable appearance, the stage being occupied by Miss Fanny Watson, serio comic singer'. As at the Alhambra, the artists 'appear to be the worn out members of the profession. I saw nothing objectionable in this performance and there is an entire absence of the ballet'. The officer then moves on to the Royal Music Hall in Dunlop Street, which he found

> nearly half-filled by a respectable audience. The stage was occupied by Miss Ada Hermioni, an excellent singer, & Persivani & Van-de-Velde, Acrobats, & the Gunness [sic] Ballet Troupe (3 in number) who are excellent dancers and gave a few Highland Dances – They wear skirts reaching below the knee and there is an entire absence of the throwing up of the legs so often witnessed in the Can Can dance.

Here the officer goes backstage to inspect the Green Room (the rest area where performers congregate), which had a bar, and where he found 'lady Professionals seated round a table along with young men and liquor before them'. For his last call the officer visited the Whitebait Music Hall in St Enoch's Wynd, where he heard 'a comic song by Mr and Mrs Harold and a Scotch song

**3**    J. A. Wilson, leading Scottish minstrel c. 1890s

by Mr Muir the chairman – the hall was not half-filled when I entered and the performance finished at 10.30pm'. The Green Room again reveals the ladies of the Ballet Troupe (four in number) drinking with 'a few fast young men', and the officer waits to observe the lady artists leave at a quarter to eleven, and 'the young men a few minutes afterwards'. Although the officer missed seeing the Troupe on stage, the manager informs him that their performance 'is confined to Highland Dancing'.

This report provides a unique snapshot of the range of Glasgow music halls as experienced on a single night in 1875. It also contains valuable insights into the preoccupations of the authorities responsible for policing such establishments.

Two features in particular deserve highlighting. The first is the degree to which music hall had been assimilated into the framework of mainstream entertainment. Despite implied criticism of the tone of the two poorer venues, in neither case is the conduct of the audience found reproachable. If the Britannia gets a good report for the evident propriety of its management, older halls such as the Whitebait and the Royal, where the officer clearly enjoyed the entertainment, also earn positive appraisals for 'respectable' clientele. This recognition of standards is the more credible for the officers' underlying disapproval of the moral basis of the entertainment. The official attitude being expressed is clearly that music hall is now a fact of life which must be accepted and dealt with constructively.[46] This approach is consolidated in what was evidently an ongoing dialogue between the police and music hall managements, which, where regarded as effective, were treated with the respect commensurate with their professional status. Captain McCall would later write to Brown's Royal Music Hall enquiring as to the house's practices regarding dancers' stage costumes and their propriety, and receive in return what amounted to chapter and verse on the industry standard as to what was considered permissible: in his reply, the hall's Chairman Harry Harcourt drew distinctions between the various types of performers ('Serio Comic Singers never appear but in Evening Dress ... and as they do *not dance*, short skirts are not necessary'), and on the crucial question of dancers' underwear, explained that, while 'The Burlesque women appear to rival each other in decency ... the line to be drawn in all cases, I would submit, is that "trunks" should be worn nearly to the knee. I may explain, "trunks" are simply "coloured under draws" puffed, as worn by clowns, acrobats etc.'[47]

Interestingly the provision of good-quality entertainment was clearly a factor in the officers' overall appraisal, probably not on aesthetic so much as public order grounds (no doubt better entertainers were more likely to give audience satisfaction, and less likely to have to resort to lewd or questionable material to compensate for indifferent skills).

The second point to emerge from the reports is that the clientele of the two minor halls, in both cases comprised of young men and boys with a handful of girls, seems very similar to the predominantly young, male audience previously described attending a free and easy in 1871 (the 'two hundred youths' referred to on page 28). By the same token it is quite possible to imagine the 'mechanic, clerk or shopkeeper' who attended the smarter Singing Saloon as being present in the audience at the better halls described. This would seem to suggest either that music hall had inherited the free and easy audience, or that, by the mid-1870s, the two forms were competing for a crossover audience that largely consisted of younger working men with enough disposable income to pay for their amusement.

But if the audience in cheaper music halls might have been similar to that found attending a free and easy, what they were watching and joining in with was, by 1875, very different. The policemen's descriptions of the onstage entertainment go some way to explaining the compromises necessitated by the confluence of the free and easy tradition and the more cosmopolitan range of imported English acts that now made up the majority of music-hall bills. Of indigenous turns, we now have formalised 'Scotch' comics, Highland dancers, and a Scotch song from John Muir, chairing the Whitebait music hall as he would have done a free and easy. It is also intriguing to note the officer's approval of Highland dancing as opposed to variants of the more salacious Can Can, presumably on grounds of wholesomeness and propriety. Irish comics and duettists, representing the sizeable Irish contingent in the Glasgow audience, could also be counted an element of continuity. In contrast the presence of 'negro entertainments', wizards, acrobats, pantomimists and ballet troupes all signalled a broadening of performance styles to embrace theatrical skills beyond the relatively narrow range of the free and easy, where performances seem to have been firmly song-based.

Developments in the 1880s saw music hall in Glasgow continue to expand and define itself as a distinct mainstream entertainment. While the impact of the new syndicates on music hall's commercial revitalisation was not felt until the 1890s, by the 1880s the tide was already moving away from individual proprietorships and towards new patterns of commercial organisation. A feature of Glasgow music hall between the 1860s and 1880s had been that the two leading halls remained in the hands of longstanding proprietors. After an initial nine-year stewardship by John Brand, the Britannia was operated by the Rossboroughs from 1869 to 1892, while the Baylises, James and Christina, owned and ran the Scotia music hall between 1862 and 1892. In seeking constructive comparisons with the more complex hierarchy of London music hall, these older Glasgow halls could perhaps be likened to the smaller independent London venues that Penny Summerfield identifies as having been forced out of business in the 1890s by a combination of licensing authorities and syndicated competitors.[48] But, in the event, these Glasgow halls survived and the old managements were not victims of commercial pressures so much as the passage of time and a changing business climate. A similar change took place in the North-east, where William McFarland, the pre-eminent Dundee and Aberdeen impresario, retired from management in 1891. The increasing expense of out-fitting had in any case long made the building of halls prohibitively expensive for most individual proprietors. By the late 1870s new venues such as the Albert Music Hall in Landressy Street, Bridgeton, reopened in September 1879 after refurbishment following an earlier fire, were usually managed by combinations or partnerships rather than by individuals. Commercial innovations were bound to result from the changing financial climate. The Albert, located well to the east of the city centre and business areas, was lavishly appointed, with an auditorium that held 2,000 persons and was 50 feet (15 metres) in height from the stalls to the top of its arched roof, which was illuminated by two 50-jet sun-light burners. No doubt to offset this outlay and reduce overheads the man-agers, Sutherland and Miller, also took a ten-year lease on the Victoria Hall, Anderston, and planned to operate the two venues in conjunction, an arrange-ment that allowed them to share artists.[49] This twinning of halls preceded Moss and Thornton's similar arrangement in the 1890s.

Just as financial and commercial innovations predated the arrival of the syn-dicates, so attempts by managers of the 1870s and 1880s to improve the social profile of music hall had enjoyed some success. On becoming lessee of the Britannia in 1869, Hubert Rossborough had won press plaudits for introducing new standards of dress for the working men who frequented the pit, 'under which clean clothes and a tidy appearance are insisted upon, with very consider-able advantage to the workmen, who are coerced into attending to cleanliness'. At a time when the 'body' of the Whitebait was taken up by a distinctly pub-like free arrangement of sofas and tables, Rossborough's introduction of private boxes and a lavishly cushioned front circle, 'for the better class of visitors who might desire to take their wives and children', looks (whether or not we accept the aspiration as realistic) increasingly like the shape of things to come, an astute acceptance of the rational recreation mantra that 'our concert halls are educa-tional institutes as well as places of amusement'.[50] By the 1880s, the longevity of the Rossborough and Baylis family tenures, and the accession of David Brown to the status of 'Grand Old Man', may well themselves also have been factors in improving the local industry's social profile. With the passing of time such con-tinuity of ownership no doubt helped confer a respectability of sorts on their enterprises, which evidently enjoyed a reasonable relationship with the police, as the reports previously quoted demonstrate. Changes in working practices and presentation intended to raise the social tone of the entertainment are also evident in the early 1880s. Programmes for Arthur Lloyd's Royal Music Hall and the Alexandra, Cowcaddens, show that, by 1882 and 1883 respectively, bills were already concluding with the National Anthem. Moreover, both carry notices directing that the number of each act, corresponding to their listing in the printed programme, would henceforth be displayed on a board placed by the proscenium. So the Chairman, a central feature of the free and easy, still in place (just) in music hall in the mid-1870s judging from the police report's mention of John Muir at the Whitebait, had been dispensed with by the early 1880s. Another link with the improvisatory heritage of the free and easy had been sacrificed to commercial flexibility and timekeeping, although the persistence of pub-based free and easies in Edinburgh ensured that some well-known chairmen such as Bryce's Norman Thomson survived in their roles until the 1890s. However, it was the retrograde Edinburgh, and not Glasgow, that was to provide the originator of the most significant marketing innovation music hall was to experience, the introduction of variety.

H. E. Moss took over the management of the Gaiety Theatre of Varieties in Chambers Street, Edinburgh, in 1877. His father, James, was a journeyman music hall artist, remembered as 'a fair comedian and violinist', who, turning to management, acquired the Royal Lorne Music Hall in Greenock. His son Edward struck out on his own at the age of 25. Faced with the failing Chambers Street hall, which had defeated three previous tenants, he re-arranged the seating and introduced a policy of smaller bills but offering headline performers. In two years he was able to buy the building and embarked on what was to be a momentous career.

As an entertainment genre music hall was, by the 1880s, fully developed, its potential as a putative working-class form having already been diluted by the influx of English performers and a wide range of speciality and novelty acts. The latter were intended to add the theatrical, and no doubt visual, dynamic thought necessary for larger auditoriums. Their often banal contribution skews conventional expectations of a socially conscious entertainment. The sight of a scantily clad lady riding a bicycle around the stage as a thinly veiled pretext for showing off her posterior to several hundred young men carried little social resonance.[51] The view, sometimes expressed, that what could be termed the trivialisation of music hall somehow began with the introduction of syndicated variety shows a misunderstanding of the basis for the form's development. Music hall was, from its very inception, an escapist entertainment promoted for commercial motives. This is not to suggest that by the 1880s it was not still a predominantly working-class phenomenon: on the contrary, those features of the free and easy that survived the adaptation of the original formula to larger music halls were arguably those with most social resonance. Despite the speciality acts, there to add an element of variation to the weekly diet, performances continued to be heavily song-based; Scottish (and for that matter Irish) performers retained their prominence on the bill; and the participation of the audience in communal singing, joining in with the choruses, remained the focus around which everything else revolved. Above all the audience, as vested in the gallery, was king, and in this sense music hall as a social form could be said to have empowered its working-class audience.

The implication of these observations is that music hall's class identity lay in the circumstances in which it was performed, and in its performing culture, which embraced the audience through their participation, rather than in the content of the material. The songs themselves were generally bland and sentimentalised, with material embodying social observation or comment accounting for a small proportion of bills. Of the surviving examples that do address social issues, few engage them as directly as the 'Sequal to Bauldie, Come Hame', about an unfortunate picked up by the police and taken 'Off to Albion Street', causing his wife or companion to ruefully observe

> Man, the police they have got no pity
> On such puir souls as Bauldie and me
> They glory when they make a capture of ony puir chaps that's been on the spree

and to lament;

> If I had only got a half-crown,
> For tae slip into their hand[52]

A more common ruse when raising grievances was the adoption of a faux literary device, such as that used by James Anderson for his 'Pictures in the Fire', in which a number of the singer's preoccupations swim into view, couched in idle 'what if … ?' terms, as he sits by his fireside on a frosty night, staring into the glowing embers. These preoccupations turn out to be a shopping list of practical concerns over such things as food prices ('I thought I saw a baker's shop, where food was very dear') and dissatisfaction with local government ('I thought I saw our Glasgow Green, with the encroachments taking place. / This scrimping of the Green I think it is a great disgrace').[53] But such examples of music-hall songs as vehicles for public debate or expressions of class-based attitudes are exceptional. The range and type of material printed in programmes and carried in Glasgow-published songsheets suggest that the vast majority of songs performed in Glasgow halls, which varied enormously in genre and type, and many of which were 'national' hits sung by visiting English stars, were devoid of anything that could be construed as significant social commentary. While the range of this song material will be explored more fully in chapter 7, it has been discussed here to establish two important points; firstly, that the relative lack of political or social substance in performing material was already a feature of the music hall of the 1880s, and owed little to the later changes introduced by the syndicates; and, secondly, the fact that music hall songs generally eschewed these issues did not necessarily mean that class parameters or shared social outlook of performers and audience were not significant factors in defining music hall's overall ambience, or its status as a working-class entertainment. It was the manner and style of performers, and the stereotypical figures evoked to deliver patter and sketches that embodied the true social orientation of Glasgow music hall. As a popular entertainment format it did not articulate its social agenda but embodied it in its functioning and culture.

This in turn has a bearing on the final area to be evaluated, that of music hall's social standing with the wider public by the mid-1880s. Evidence of this is contradictory but a valid generalisation would seem to be that improvements to public perceptions brought about by managers' efforts since the 1870s had probably reached a ceiling by the mid-1880s. On one hand, music hall was now an established part of urban life, an important entertainment business estimated to attract 40,000 customers in Glasgow per week, which was clearly there to stay. As an 1887 article on Variety Theatre in Glasgow stated:

> For years people have affected to despise it. But with the development of a broader thought, and a consequent refinement of the entertainment presented to the patrons of Variety theatres, much of the antagonism which managers had to contend against has disappeared.[54]

A few years earlier, in 1880, the Aberdeen journal *Bon Accord* had declared that, under McFarland's management, music hall in the city had 'long passed the period of probation' and become 'as recognised an institution as Her Majesty's Opera House itself'.[55] Commercial success had left the generation of managers about to bow out considerably enriched and with some degree of celebrity or social standing. McFarland, whose social position was mitigated by the fact that he had managed theatres as well as music halls (having 'aspired to higher things', as his obituary put it), made a great deal of money from his theatrical ventures and ended his days running a hotel in Southport. In Glasgow, Christina Baylis was able to retire to a large house in Pollokshaws, and H. T. Rossborough reputedly amassed a considerable fortune during his 25-year management of the

Britannia.[56] But the 1887 article went on to suggest that such progress had only served to harden existing attitudes, polarising opinion on music hall, often along religious lines.

In the latter respect a key factor, and a paradoxical one given Glasgow's Presbyterian majority, was the involvement of temperance and other social movements in the city's range of music-hall entertainments, a particular feature of Glasgow's amusement culture and one that set it apart from other music-hall centres such as London. This went beyond the fact of individual music halls embracing temperance values, although, in a city with only a handful of venues, this already gave the promulgation of such values an inordinate influence. The key element in Glasgow's case was the direct involvement of the city fathers and various improving organisations, sometimes acting in conjunction, in the promotion of music-hall-style popular concerts. This reformist presence in the field dated from the first phase of music-hall development – with Abstainers' Union concerts beginning in 1854, followed by Good Templars Harmonic Association events from 1872 – and gathered momentum towards the turn of the century, with the Corporation concert series managed by Freer beginning in the 1888.[57] It created what in effect was the equivalent of a subsidised sector operating parallel to the commercial halls, and one that provided both increasing commercial competition and a bridge to wider acceptance, in the form of a socially palatable version of what was basically the same entertainment.

But if the involvement of civic and reforming institutions allowed for the possibility of qualified social acceptance, the lack of a middle-class audience for music hall by the mid-1880s was self-evident. The police reports from the 1870s previously discussed describe the audience at better halls as including members of the labour aristocracy – skilled craftsmen, artisans and self-employed tradesmen and shopkeepers – but make no reference to what could be termed a middle-class presence, comprised of professional people, the business and managerial classes or white-collar workers. The reasons for this may be complex but, in the case of Glasgow, the situation and type of venues was probably a highly significant factor. With the exception of the Gaiety in Sauchiehall Street, an unsuccessful theatre that turned to music hall in 1876, Glasgow's major halls were all by the mid-1880s still located in the insalubrious area around Glasgow Cross, which was still suffering the residual effects of the notoriety occasioned by the 'Dark Side of Glasgow' articles. Their much repeated claim of 200 brothels and 150 shebeens in one-sixteenth of a square mile had entered Glasgow lore,[58] but was probably no worse than longstanding dread of typhus and the typhoid epidemics associated with such areas, the last of which had been in 1853–54. The damage to middle-class sensibilities was lasting. A guide to Glasgow published in 1872 and reprinted in 1888 referred to 'the horrors of the Saltmarket', and how it was 'almost impossible to describe the squalid hideousness' of the area between Saltmarket and Trongate that stopped just short of the Britannia.[59] The author and playwright J. J. Bell, describing a visit to the Scotia Music Hall in his youth in the 1880s, succinctly encapsulated the seediness of the milieu:

> In those days Stockwell Street was none too savoury. Constables in pairs walked up and down; there were smells of frying fish and drink, scenes of squalor and frowsiness, sounds of blasphemy.[60]

Although the Scotia, where the audience was 'almost entirely working class' was itself innocuous, Bell writing that 'there was nothing about it to suggest unseemliness', its location in such a disreputable area effectively precluded 'respectable' middle-class attendance. In contrast, new legitimate theatres were being built in the area adjacent to the new business and financial centre situated to the west between Sauchiehall Street and Hope Street. The implications for music-hall managements were clear. If the large working-class audiences attracted to the Argyll Street venues constituted, by the 1880s 'a vibrant music hall and popular theatre tradition',[61] the commercial dynamic that had always governed music hall's development was already taking its cue from the changing legislative climate and general increase in interest in theatre to broaden the social base of the audience. In practical terms this necessitated the severing of the last links with early music hall and the old, coarse Saltmarket entertainments and relocating to larger, more modern venues in the city centre, where a middle-class family audience could be cultivated.

To conclude, by the 1880s changes in patterns of ownership and work practices aimed at raising the social profile of music hall were already discernible, prompted by the evident commercial potential of the industry. The entertainment itself had evolved beyond the original free and easy formula to embrace a wide range of imported influences, but retained the participatory elements and strong local associations with its audience.

But although music hall was established as the most dynamic entertainment genre of the time, it still faced considerable competition, even at the lower end of the market. Rival entertainments in Dundee in the 1880s included Cooke's and Newsomes' circuses, Hamilton's Diorama, MacLeod's Waxworks, Sam Hague's and the Livermore Brothers' minstrel troupes, and regular visits by the Kennedy family 'in Scottish song and story'. Moreover, the 'low' gaff theatres were still thriving, as '"shows" of a secondary class were held in the Lindsay

Street Quarry immediately behind St Paul's Mission in the Overgate … at the then vacant spaces of ground in the Seagate'.[62] Elsewhere, too, the street culture of semi-permanent booths pitched on vacant ground was very much alive. In Edinburgh, licences granted by the City Magistrates for public entertainments in 1884–85 included, along with Moss's Varieties and various public halls, side-shows ranging from a 'Fire-King', the 'Tay Whale', and a Giant and Giantess, to performing seals, troupes of performing fish, dogs and monkeys, and booths offering variety entertainments in the Cowgate and Blackfriars Road.[63]

In middle-class eyes fairs had long been associated with the threat of violence and disorder, and of gangs of working-class youths running amok. While music hall was still (to use an unfortunate metaphor) a stone's throw from its disreputable fairground past, it remained damned by association. The careful public relations work of managers could be undone at a stroke by an incident such as the 'riot' at the Bon-Accord Music Hall at Aberdeen in April 1889, when sections of the audience, feeling short-changed when an advertised sketch failed to materialise at the end of a benefit evening that had overrun, chased the orchestra from the pit and set about destroying the music stands and footlights until the hall was cleared by the truncheon-wielding police. The local press condemned the rioters, appalled that 'Young Aberdeen … bids fair to rival a Glasgow-Irish audience or the denizens of Whitechapel', whilst admitting that the management had partly brought the damage to themselves.[64]

The battle was clearly not yet won. It would take a new generation of impresarios led by Moss to hit on the presentational means of rebranding music hall as an upmarket entertainment, and by so doing deliver the knockout blow to older amusements.

## Notes

1 See John F. McCaffrey, 'Introduction', to Shadow, *Midnight Scenes and Social Photographs: Being Sketches of Life in the Streets, Wynds and Dens of the City* (Glasgow, University of Glasgow Press, 1976 [1858]), p. 6.

2 'Health of the City', *Glasgow Courier*, 26 March 1850, p. 4.

3 Shadow, 'No.VII', in *Midnight Scenes*, p. 67.

4 Andrew Gibb, *Glasgow, the Making of a City* (Beckenham, Croon Helm, 1983), p. 130.

5 William Guthrie, 'Glasgow Concert Singers, 1830–70', in *Old Glasgow Club Transactions*, 2:5 (session 1912–13), pp. 353–354.

6 Laurence Senelick (ed.), *Tavern Singing in Early Victorian London: The Diaries of Charles Rice for 1840 and 1850* (London, Society for Theatre Research, 1997).

7 'The Publicans' Dodges', *The Abstainer's Journal*, 20 August 1854, p. 182.

8  'More about Free-and-Easies', from 'The Dark Side of Glasgow' serialised in *North British Daily Mail* between 27 December 1870 and 1871; from p. 31, Cuttings Book, Mitchell Library Glasgow Collection (MLGC).

9  J. Wilson McLaren, *Edinburgh Memories and Some Worthies* (Edinburgh, W. & R. Chambers, 1926), pp. 49, 55.

10  See W. F. Frame, *Tells His Own Story* (Glasgow, Wm Holmes, 1907), pp. 30–31; James E. Handley, *The Irish in Scotland* (Glasgow, J. S. Burns, 1964), p. 124.

11  Geggies were touring fit-up theatres constructed of canvas and wood, which visited rural fairs with heavily cut-down versions of popular classics such as Rob Roy. The most famous Saltmarket geggies were Dupain's, Parry's and Mumfords, which was housed in a wooden building that survived until the early 1900s. Geggies themselves were active until within living memory, Will Fyffe's father being a proprietor of one such company. See Cameron, 'Popular Theatre and Entertainment in Nineteenth-Century Glasgow', pp. 7–12; Jack House, *Music Hall Memories* (Glasgow, Richard Drew, 1986), pp. 10–12.

12  Shadow, 'Jupiter Temperance Hall', in *Midnight Scenes*, No. 10, 'Thursday Night', pp. 84–85.

13  The semantics of what were still evolving genres are confusing. Frame referred to the 'miniature music-halls' of the Saltmarket in the 1850s, stating that saloons such as the Waverley, Oddfellows and Jupiter were 'licensed as music halls', by which he presumably meant that they were licensed for musical entertainment. But it seems likely that, writing in 1907, he was using the term 'music hall' in its generic sense, retroactively. Brown's titled itself a music hall and the Whitebait was usually formally termed 'Concert Rooms', while the exterior of the Jupiter proclaimed it the 'Jupiter Temperance Hall'.

14  Shadow, *Midnight Scenes*, p. 85.

15  A. S. Cook, *Aberdeen Amusements Seventy Years Ago*, contributed to the *Aberdeen Free Press*, April 1911.

16  For Mrs Liffens see William Carnie, *Reporting Reminiscences* (Aberdeen, Aberdeen University Press, 1902), pp. 46–47. For Charles Sloman, who appeared with Charles Rice, see Senelick (ed.), *Tavern Singing in Early Victorian London*, p. 21.

17  *The Era*, 22 January 1860.

18  Ian McCraw, *The Fairs of Dundee*, Publication No. 34 (Dundee, Abertay Historical Society, 1994), p. 53.

19  *Dundee Courier and Argus*, 4 January 1865, p. 2.

20  Clive Barker, 'The Audiences at the Britannia Theatre, Hoxton', *Theatre Quarterly*, 9:34 (summer 1979), 27–41; for a wide-ranging analysis of London audiences, see Davis and Emeljanow, *Reflecting the Audience*.

21  See Peter Bailey, 'Custom, Capital and Culture in the Victorian Music Hall', in R. Storch (ed.), *Popular Culture and Custom in Nineteenth-Century England* (London, 1982), pp. 180–208 (p. 204).

22  See Alasdair Cameron and Adrienne Scullion, 'W. F. Frame and the Scottish Popular Theatre Tradition', in Cameron and Scullion (eds.), *Scottish Popular Theatre and Entertainment*, pp. 39–57, p. 40 and Scullion footnote 3.

23  King, 'Popular Culture in Glasgow', pp. 157–169.

24  George M. Martin, *Dundee Worthies: Reminiscences, Games, Amusements* (Dundee, David Winter and Son, 1934), p. 158.

25  Wilson McLaren, *Edinburgh Memories and Some Worthies*, p. 111.

26  See King, 'Popular Culture in Glasgow', pp.159–162.

27  See Hugh Cunningham, Leisure in the Industrial Revolution, c.1780–c.1880 (London, Croom Helm, 1980), p. 145.

28  Ian McCraw, *The Fairs of Dundee*, p. 56.

29  Walter Freer, *My Life and Memories* (Glasgow, Civic Press, 1929), p. 34.

30  Freer, *My Life*, p. 35.

31  Freer, *My Life*, p. 36.

32  *The Era*, 22 April 1860, pp. 11, 12.

33  See M. H. Hay, *Glasgow Theatres and Music Halls* (Glasgow, Glasgow Mitchell Library, 1980), pp. 16, 17, 22, 101, 116.

34  For Edinburgh music hall dates see Bruce Peter, *Scotland's Splendid Theatres* (Edinburgh, Polygon, 1999).

35  Wilson McLaren, *Edinburgh Memories*, p. 54.

36  'The Free-and-Easies of Glasgow', 'Dark Side of Glasgow', ML Glasgow Room Cuttings Book, p. 30.

37  'More about Free-and-Easy', 'Dark Side of Glasgow', ML Glasgow Room Cuttings Book, p. 32.

38  The Prince's Theatre Royal, West Nile Street in 1863, the Prince of Wales Theatre, Cowcaddens in 1867; the Gaiety, Sauchiehall Street in 1874, the Royalty, Sauchiehall Street in 1879, and the Princess's in Main Street, Gorbals in 1878.

39  See Adrienne Scullion, 'Media Culture for a Modern Nation? Theatre, Cinema and Radio in Early Twentieth-Century Scotland', University of Glasgow PhD thesis 1992, pp. 103, 104; and Alasdair Cameron, 'Study Guide to Theatre in Scotland', Glasgow University Department of Scottish Literature 1989, pp. 7, 8.

40  See John Urie, *Reminiscences of 80 Years, Paisley 1908*, pp. 87–88 for an account of the Garrick Club, whose membership included members of Alexander's stock company, which met at McLaren's Tavern. J. Wilson McLaren, 'Memories of Old Edinburgh', in *Old Glasgow Club Transactions*, 1936–37, pp. 31–32.

41  J. A. Hammerton, 'Snap Shots in Our Strand', in *Sketches From Glasgow* (Glasgow and Edinburgh, John Menzies, 1893), pp. 118–127.

42  Dagmar Kift echoes Peter Bailey in arguing that the Canterbury's importance has been exaggerated, and music hall in general depicted as a product of London culture at the expense of the diverse range of music hall that developed at the same time, or earlier, in provincial centres such as Bolton and Bradford. See Kift, *The Victorian Music Hall*, pp. 17–21.

43  A *North British Daily Mail* article of 6 January 1900 ('Amusements in Glasgow: What the Public Spends on Them') referred to safety laws introduced after the 'Star' panic having restricted the current capacity of the Theatre Royal to 3,500, and that of the Grand Theatre to 3,000. However, prior to these constraints some music

halls may have been as capacious; an earlier account of the Scotia (*Glasgow Sentinel,* 9 January 1869) suggested the hall held between 3,000 and 4,000 people.

44  'Report of Visit to Music Halls on 27 February 1875', by Superintendent Brown, dated 1 March; Report of Lieutenant Andrew, dated 9 March 1875; both addressed to Capt. McCall, Chief Constable; Glasgow City Archive SR22/62/1.

45  See 'The Morality of the City: Important Deputation to the Magistrates', *North British Daily Mail,* 2 March 1875; and Kift, *The Victorian Music Hall,* pp. 115–120.

46  In the report of 1 March 1875, the officer states 'I very much disapprove and regret to see females degrading themselves in such unbecoming performances' but adds that he had 'seen something similar carried on in these halls for many years'.

47  Letter from Harry Harcourt, Director and Chairman of Brown's Royal Music Hall, to Captain McCall, 3 March 1875, Glasgow City Archive SR22/62/1.

48  See Summerfield, 'The Effingham Arms', pp. 221–224.

49  'The New Albert Music Hall, Glasgow', *The Era,* 7 September 1879, p. 4.

50  See 'Britannia Music Hall', in the *Glasgow Sentinel,* 25 September, 23 October, 27 November 1869.

51  See Glasgow Police Report, 1 March 1875.

52  From *Scotia's Music-Hall Songbook,* No. 8, undated but probably from the 1880s; Scottish Theatre Archive (STA).

53  This continues; 'We pay Road and Prison Taxes, also for our Public Park / But what do they do with all the money we are entirely in the dark / I thought these things had altered been for this we much require / And reduced taxation we had got in this picture in the fire'. Other 'pictures' include mention of an explosion at Clerkenwell ('I saw the widows and orphans, their sad faces I did lament / I thought the authorities were to blame for their bad management'), and a plea for a new bathing pond on Lower Green: from *Scotia's Music-Hall Songbook,* No. 8.

54  'The Modern Variety Theatre', *Evening News & Star* (*Glasgow Evening News*), 29 April 1887.

55  'Dramatic Notes', *Bon Accord,* 17 April 1880, p. 3.

56  See Fred Locke, 'Theatres of Great Britain No.3, Glasgow', *The Playgoer,* April 1902, 87–91, p. 90.

57  See King, 'Popular Culture in Glasgow', pp. 170, 177–180.

58  'Dark Side of Glasgow', *North British Daily Mail,* 27 December 1870.

59  See *Tweed's Glasgow Hand-book,* 1872, reprinted as *Glasgow a Hundred Years Ago* (Glasgow, Molendinar Press, 1972), p. 30.

60  Bell, *I Remember,* pp. 131, 132.

61  Scullion, 'Media Culture for a Modern Nation?', p. 104.

62  Martin, *Dundee Worthies,* pp. 157–159.

63  'Licences granted by the Magistrates for Public Entertainments etc, 1884–85', Edinburgh City Archives, Licence Book 1884–95.

64  *Bon Accord,* 13 April 1889, p. 6.

# 3

# 'A time for amusement': the introduction of variety, 1880–1914

Between the late 1880s and 1914 music hall in Scotland underwent a commercial transformation that took it to the peak of its popularity in the years immediately before the First World War. In 1888 Glasgow had three music halls, and activity was centred on the old entertainment quarter around Argyll Street and controlled by long-established proprietors. By 1914 the city's music halls had increased to 18 (as against 6 legitimate theatres), and the focus of activity had switched to the fashionable city-centre area around Hope Street and Sauchiehall Street, where new larger venues known as 'Palaces of Varieties' (the most magnificent – the Empire, Pavilion, Alhambra and Coliseum – built in the last twenty years) were operated by heavily capitalised syndicates. What had been regarded as a tawdry working-class form was, as city-centre variety, reborn as a mainstream popular theatre genre, offering 'respectable' family entertainment aimed at middle-class audiences, or, as the impresario Walter de Frece described them when opening an Edinburgh variety season in 1907, 'people who require a pure and legitimate class of musical entertainment'.[1]

The roots of this transformation in music hall's fortunes lay at least partly in a concerted campaign mounted nationally by the industry in the 1880s and 1890s to improve the moral tone of the entertainment. Intended to counter widespread public perception of music halls as disreputable or immoral places, it resulted in a series of changes to both the presentation and content of the entertainment. The most prominent of these reforms sought to eradicate the elements considered most offensive to respectable sensibilities: music hall's association with pubs and liquor, and with on-stage vulgarity. The resulting changes radically altered the character of music hall as it had been experienced since the 1860s.

Although, as the previous chapter has pointed out, managers had been attempting to improve music hall's social profile from the late 1870s, it was the syndicated managements that emerged in the early 1890s which continued and profited from the process, contributing the bulk of marketing and presentational innovations, and pioneering the formula for what became known as variety.

Viewed on the wider national scale, the motivation for these changes has been much debated. Peter Bailey has suggested that a possible dynamic, and a reason for the new strident emphasis on the respectability of venues in publicity and advertising, was the industry's concern to pre-empt the more drastic action likely to be brought about by the temperance lobby and other campaigners for reform unless public perceptions of music hall were drastically improved.[2] An alternative theory is that the changes were essential to music hall's commercial expansion, which managements realised could only continue if the audience could be broadened to encompass middle-class and lower-middle-class patrons. Thus the conscious raising of music halls' moral and social tone could be primarily seen as a calculated business development, an example of repackaging a product for a different sector of the market. A variation on this would be the suggestion that managers' impulse to make music hall a more respectable entertainment was an intuitive response to the changing social mores of the period; that the older music-hall style was out of step with the more rectitudinous times, and the introduction of a new, more socially accessible genre, variety, was not so much an attempt to attract middle-class audiences, as a reflection of aspirations to upward social mobility within the working classes themselves.[3] This perspective goes some way to explaining early music-hall historians' depiction of the advent of variety as a long overdue act of liberation.

This chapter will explore the key developments that took place in Scottish music hall from the 1880s onwards, focussing on five majors factors; firstly, internal pressure on music hall proprietors to broaden the social range of the audience for purposes of commercial expansion; secondly, external pressure from legislation, local government and licensing authorities; thirdly, the impact of new technology, particularly the introduction of early forms of cinema; fourthly, broader changes in audience taste; and fifthly, the role of individual managers and impresarios.

In examining the first of these – the industry's own commercial incentive to broaden the audience to guarantee its continued growth – one presumption is that managers' primary intentions were to transform music hall into a respectable entertainment that would attract the middle classes. Certainly the overall thrust of the changes, which involved removing offensiveness from the stage, and insulating the better class of patrons from their social inferiors inside

the theatre, was consistent with this purpose. In Glasgow as elsewhere, a funda-
mental part of this process involved disassociating music hall from its former
boozy associations. In general, this proved only partially successful, partly
because drinking played too central a role in music-hall culture (the form had,
after all, evolved in the backrooms of pubs), but also because bar revenue was
still too important a part of halls' income to be foregone. Nevertheless, from the
early 1880s the sale of alcohol in the auditorium itself became less common,
although its consumption there, where permitted, remained a distinctive feature of music hall. However, in the case of Glasgow, as we shall see later in this
chapter, the licensing of the city's music halls to serve alcohol had already long
been severely restricted. It remained a paradox that the wider public, no doubt
influenced by Presbyterian denunciations of commercial entertainments, made
scant allowance for this and continued to associate the city's halls with drink.
One explanation might be that Glasgow's unlicensed music halls and numerous
singing saloons continued to hold sway in the public imagination in the 1880s,
contributing to this perception.

Perhaps as significantly, in the lower parts of halls the former free arrangement of chairs around tables was replaced by fixed rows of theatre seats facing
the stage, followed shortly afterwards by the disappearance of the chairman.
The change in emphasis within the auditorium, where the audience's attention was now (forcibly) concentrated on the stage, rather than distracted by
the competing appeals of drinking and dining, gave the new halls a much
closer resemblance to legitimate theatres than had previously been the case.
The generally improved sense of order and decorum that resulted from the
seating of patrons, who had previously felt free to mill about, also helped to
validate the claims of music hall to be considered as a theatrical form in its
own right. Where these claims gained support, it was usually in socially pragmatic terms, as a lesser of evils. While legitimate drama was all very well,
Aberdeen's *Bon Accord* noted, there was 'a large section of the community
which prefers amusement of a lighter and more varied kind', and for which 'it
must be refreshing to have a place where an entertainment of a diversified
character is presented, and where one may "drop in" and be amused for half an
hour without the tedium of trying to found out the point of a half-finished
play'. Without such an option, 'a considerable portion of the public would, in
the absence of the intermediate quality of entertainment afforded by music
hall – spend their time in the pursuit of some pernicious pleasure'.[4] This establishment of music hall as aesthetically worthwhile, in terms of justifying the
price of admission, was essential to the attracting of a broader audience, even

though it meant proprietors losing the income from catering. It is important to remember that early music-hall managers were regarded primarily as caterers, and that the term seems to have retained its usage in a theatrical context; in 1904 the showman E. H. Bostock referred to himself in advertisements as 'The well-known Amusement Caterer', and as late as 1913 Rich Waldon, impresario of the Royal Princess Theatre was being termed 'one of our oldest and most respected Glasgow caterers'.[5]

Over the same period, from 1880 to 1900, strenuous efforts were made to raise the moral tone of the content of performances. Acts or material found coarse or lewd were banned, with managers usually insisting that artistes submit their songs for approval in advance of engagements. The need for 'clean' material was soon a well-advertised precondition of employment at most Glasgow halls, and by the 1890s many contracts contained punitive clauses involving fines and summary termination of engagement for any performer who strayed from the approved script or outline to cause offence. Not even leading stars were exempt. A standard contract issued in 1894 by the Britannia Music Hall, Trongate, to Glasgow-born Marie Loftus, one of the biggest national stars, stipulated that the management had the right to select which of her songs and material she would perform, that she undertook to obey the stage manager 'in all matters concerning the Stage, Encores, or Addressing the Audience', and should conduct herself 'soberly and respectably'. It also warned that in the event of non-fulfilment she undertook to pay a sum 'the equivalent of three times her salary' in liquidating damages.[6] The Rules and Regulations that accompanied a later Britannia contract, dated 1905 but probably in use since the turn of the century, were even more explicit:

> Any artiste introducing anything Obscene or Vulgar, in gesture or saying, into his or her business, no matter how slight, will be instantly dismissed from the Establishment, and forfeit the whole of their salary. Artistes will do well to carefully read and thoroughly digest this rule, as the Management is determined to have it rigorously enforced.[7]

Despite the unequivocal wording, clauses such as these were clearly intended as statements of intent to artistes and were for discretionary use by managements. It remains unclear whether their application in practice matched up to the severity of their language.

With propriety now a major preoccupation, performances ended with the national anthem and managers used all means at their disposal to broadcast news of these changes to the wider public. By making speeches before the curtain, issuing written statements attesting to the quality of the entertainment, and

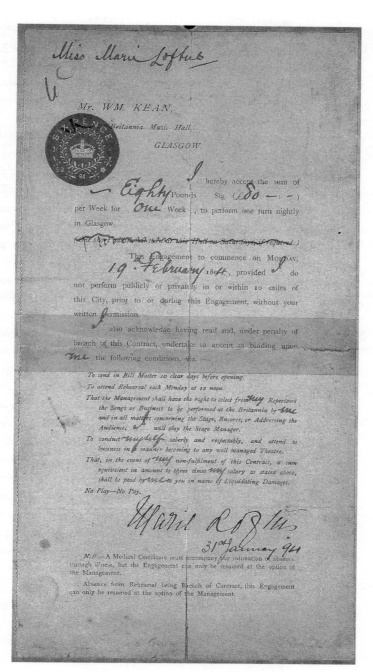

*Miss Marie Loftus*

Mr. WM. KEAN,

*Britannia Music Hall,*

GLASGOW.

*Eighty* hereby accept the sum of
Pounds Stg. (£80 :— : —)
per Week for *One* Week , to perform one turn nightly
in Glasgow.

( ~~One short turn at this Hall on Saturdays if required.~~ )

This Engagement to commence on MONDAY,
*19 February* 1894 , provided *I* do
not perform publicly or privately in or within 10 miles of
this City, prior to or during this Engagement, without your
written permission.

*I* also acknowledge having read and, under penalty of
breach of this Contract, undertake to accept as binding upon
*me* the following conditions, viz. :—

*To send in Bill Matter 10 clear days before opening.*

*To attend Rehearsal each Monday at 12 noon.*

*That the Management shall have the right to select from* my *Repertoire
the Songs or Business to be performed at the Britannia by* me
*and in all matters concerning the Stage, Encores, or Addressing the
Audience,* I *will obey the Stage Manager.*

*To conduct* myself *soberly and respectably, and attend to
business in a manner becoming to any well managed Theatre.*

*That, in the event of* my *non-fulfilment of this Contract, a sum
equivalent in amount to three times* my *salary as stated above,
shall be paid by* me *to you in name of Liquidating Damages.*

*No Play—No Pay.*

*Marie Loftus*

*31st January 94*

*N.B.*—A Medical Certificate must accompany by intimation of absence
through illness, but the Engagement can only be resumed at the option of
the Management.

Absence from Rehearsal being Breach of Contract, this Engagement
can only be resumed at the option of the Management.

Marie Loftus contract with William Kean of the Britannia Music Hall, Glasgow,
31 January 1894

printing their photographic portraits on bills and programmes, proprietors effectively offered themselves as personal guarantors for the moral character of their establishments. The request carried in Britannia programmes of the 1890s that the proprietor, Arthur Hubner, 'will be obliged to anyone who will inform him of any suggestive or offensive word or action upon the stage that may have escaped his notice' was characteristic.[8]

If the actual entertainment offered under variety was not markedly different from that of 'old' music hall, bar the removal of overtly lewd acts and a more opulent presentation, this did not necessarily disprove the sincerity of the commitment to attract a more respectable audience. Managers' inclination, conscious or otherwise, was no doubt to go as far as was felt necessary in assuaging middle-class sensibilities whilst retaining the essential elements of what was already a proven and successful formula. For this reason the changes were largely concerned with front of house, marketing and presentational considerations, while the relationship between performers and audience, soon to be constrained by the formalising influence of twice-nightly performances, first introduced in Glasgow in 1902, was left largely untouched.

The changes so far discussed seem to support the idea of a self-imposed drive towards greater respectability on the part of managers, for social as well as purely commercial reasons. But to this end, one of the most important requirements, the upgrading of existing halls and building of new venues in the city centre, called for the investment of considerable capital. The changes that this brought about in both the management and financing of music hall should not be underestimated as a causal effect in their own right. In examining the changes to music hall's working practices in England, Peter Bailey has rightly drawn a distinction between measures intended to improve the moral profile of music hall, and other changes whose sole purpose was to increase efficiency and profitability (an example being the discouragement of encores to enable the strict timekeeping necessary for twice-nightly performances). In this context the commercial transformation – one might almost say 'professionalisation' – of music-hall management under variety was responsible for many of its defining characteristics and deserves examination.

In the 1890s syndicated managements established themselves as the dominant force in Scottish music hall. At a time when the industry was expanding and changing, their emergence was itself a symptom of the growing sophistication of the web of financial and contractual relations that linked managers, investors, theatres and artists. Limited liability companies had been introduced in 1862 but, perhaps because the established pattern of music hall in the main

Scottish centres had remained relatively stable, controlled by the same handful of managers for a generation, they do not seem to have featured in theatrical finances until the 1880s. However, as early as the late 1870s those new venues that did appear, such as the short-lived New Albert Music Hall by Bridgeton Cross, opened in 1879, had become so expensive to outfit that co-management of halls was already commonplace. By the 1890s the business climate had altered considerably. In Glasgow, the passing of the Baylis and Rossborough proprietorships of, respectively, the Scotia and Britannia Variety Theatres, and the closure of Davy Brown's Royal Music Hall in Dunlop Street signalled the departure of the old guard of managers who had learned their business in free and easies. John Brand, the first proprietor of the Britannia, who ran the venue between 1860 and 1869, had previously been manager of Sloan's Oddfellows, a pub music hall in Argyll Street. James Baylis, who built the Scotia Music Hall in Stockwell Street, and the huge Royal Coliseum at the top of Hope Street (on the site of the present Theatre Royal), had formerly been chairman of Oddfellows and the manager of an upstairs hall in the Cowcaddens called the Milton Colosseum, later known as Milton's Magnet due to its popularity. He had reputedly lost an eye whilst working as a waiter at the Jupiter when a customer threw a soda water bottle at him. Of H. T. Rossborough, proprietor of the Britannia between 1869 and 1889, little is known other than that he apparently made a great deal of money from the venue, which on his death was run by his wife until she relinquished control in 1892. James Baylis's widow Christina similarly managed the Scotia from his early death in 1870 until she bowed out in 1892.[9] Wives taking over their deceased husband's businesses seem to have been a feature of this phase of Glasgow music-hall ownership, perhaps reflecting families' reluctance to give up on a good thing when the head of the household passed on.[10] Mrs Shearer also succeeded her husband James at the Whitebait, being named as proprietor in a licence application in 1875, while Christina Baylis gained a reputation as a formidable and astute manager, despite her lack of previous experience. The best-known Glasgow music-hall impresario, David Brown, was a butcher who graduated from singing in free and easies to owning his own establishment, and was honoured in old age with a 'Man You Know' profile in *The Bailie*, where he was hailed as 'The Shah of Scottish Music Halls'.[11]

But while free and easies were the predominant career path for Glasgow managers, this wasn't the case everywhere. North-eastern music hall managers of the same period were more associated with backgrounds as showmen. The MacLeod Brothers, who opened the first music halls proper in both Dundee and Aberdeen in the 1860s, subsequently exhibited waxworks, and as such were active into the 1890s. The Springthorpes, presenters of popular music hall concerts in both cities in the 1850s and 1860s, and who suffered a tragedy at their Dundee concert hall in 1865 when 20 people lost their lives in a panic, were also associated with waxworks, while William MacFarland, the leading music hall – and later legitimate theatre – impresario in both Dundee and Aberdeen in the 1870s and 1880s, had previously been a manager and advance agent for the Sanger Circus, and began his own career as a showman, exhibiting a diorama of 'The Holy Land' at Dundee's Kinnaird Hall.[12] This experience does not necessarily discount the claims of the free and easy to be seen as direct precursor of music hall: it rather demonstrates how showmen involved in older amusements switched to what was seen as the coming entertainment.

If the founding fathers of music hall in Glasgow provided a direct link with the free and easy culture of the 1850s, and ran their venues as family concerns, the generation who succeeded them were businessmen in a more modern sense, adept manipulators of capital who moved in and out of consortia formed with fellow impresarios for the purposes of financing different enterprises. Although experienced managers in their own right, they differed from their predecessors in the scope of their ambitions, regarding music hall as a commercial activity ripe for entrepreneurial development.

The personification of the new ethos, both as the pioneer of the new financial and presentational methods, and as exemplar of the generational transition, was H. E. (Edward) Moss. The son of James Moss, a middling performer who, like Dan Leno's parents, had appeared at Baylis's Milton Colosseum, Moss had gained early experience at the hall his father subsequently managed, the Royal Lorne in Greenock. In 1877, at the age of 25, he took over the Gaiety Theatre of Varieties in Chambers Street, Edinburgh. Undaunted by the failure of three previous lessees, Moss, by rearranging the seating and securing headline national stars to bring in audiences, quickly made the hall profitable. Two years later he bought it for £14,000.

At the time of their first incursion into the bigger Glasgow market in 1891, Moss and Thornton were yet to emerge as the most dynamic of the new music-hall syndicates. The Glasgow-published *Professional Gazette*'s account of the opening of its new acquisition, the Gaiety Variety Theatre, in 1891 vividly illustrates the promotional style of the new managers. Following lavish refurbishment, the reopened theatre was pronounced 'transformed from a dingy and dusty looking place to a palace' that would in future be 'lighted entirely by electricity'. As reported, the management's intended plans for the venue could have served as a manifesto for the new era of music hall. The proprietors proclaimed that

> the class of entertainment to be provided will be in strict unison with the building; it shall be as refined as it is excellent; a conspicuous feature will be the absence of all that can be construed into vulgarity, the fixed determination of the management being to raise a class of entertainment which has made such rapid strides in public favour during the last few years, and sweep from there all that is tainted or objectionable ... We therefore trust that in an endeavour to purify and raise the tone of the music hall entertainment, we shall command the good wishes and support of all classes of society.[13]

The missionary zeal with which the authors pledge to purge the establishment of the taint of vulgarity was calculated to persuade even the most sceptical of the integrity of the new undertaking. This rather sanctimonious tone was regularly employed by managers on such occasions, as was the natural segue into extending an invitation to those who had never visited a hall to come and see for themselves. If such massaging of public morals for commercial ends seems shameless to twentieth-century observers, it is important to realise that the sentiments were probably quite genuine, and that some managers did regard themselves as men of good character whose job it was to provide a more respectable form of popular entertainment.

At the Glasgow Gaiety's opening, the performance began with the appearance on stage of the full company to sing the 'Queen's Anthem' and went on to comprise a lavish variety bill, although the reporting is careful to stress the refinement of the presentations. Thus, although 'Mdlle Victorina, the modern Hercules' gives 'as remarkable an exhibition of strength as has ever been seen on the stage', lifting 623 lbs, and holding on to a brass cannon while it was fired, catching the cannon ball and breaking chains, her feats were 'all done in a free and easy and graceful manner'.

Gala events such as theatre openings, with their opportunities for formal speechmaking, gave managers a public platform from which to put across the message that things really had improved to a wider audience. The statements delivered on these occasions were conceived as much with a view to their reporting in the following day's press as for their impact on the audience present. At the Gaiety opening, the assembled patrons were addressed from the stage midway through the programme by H. E. Moss himself. In his speech, a model of its kind, he mentioned that he had formerly been a resident of Glasgow, and that, although he had 'travelled about and opened many variety theatres in other towns in conjunction with Mr Thornton', this was their 'first venture in the second city of the empire'. After hoping that the audience were pleased by the decorations (Applause), he passed the credit to the tradesmen responsible and went on to state

> we have not come here with any idea of trying to monopolise the variety business in Glasgow. We want to conduct this place as a first class, West-End variety theatre, and I think there is room for such a place in this part of Glasgow. We have present with us to-night a lady whom I shall not call an opponent, for we shall only work in friendly rivalry with her – I mean Mrs Baylis. (Applause.) She has favoured us with her countenance this evening, for 'Auld langsyne' (Applause).[14]

After various votes of thanks, the report concludes that 'The hall was closed at a respectable hour'. The combination of tact and deference to civic pride demon-strates the assurance which the syndicates could bring to their public relations. Inviting Mrs Baylis, 'Proprietrix' of the Scotia Variety Theatre, to be present was an act of graciousness, cleverly judged to win the approval of the local audience. But the denial of any interest in monopoly was disingenuous; within a year Moss and Thornton had also acquired the lease of the Scotia, which they oper-ated in tandem with the Gaiety, as the leading variety management in the city.

The impact of this arrangement on their rivals was evidently considerable. The proprietor of the Britannia Music Hall, William Kean, was subsequently declared bankrupt in 1897, blaming his loss of £3,500 in the Britannia on the effects of competition:

> During that time the People's Palace, which was closed when I entered upon the lease, opened and Messrs Thornton and Kirk acquired the Scotia in conjunction with the Gaiety and they floated a limited liability company. Between these two I could not get artistes and here I could not get people inside.[15]

Although Kean was an inexperienced manager who lost out to more skilled competitors, the old-style single-hall proprietor was increasingly vulnerable to pressure from better capitalised venues managed by syndicates competing for the same audience. By the 1890s the expense of building new venues, and of refurbishing and capitalising existing music halls in an effort to keep up with the competition, involved considerable capital outlay. The issue had become pressing following the enormous success of Moss's revolutionary Edinburgh Empire Palace Theatre, opened in 1893. Designed by the leading theatre archi-tect Frank Matcham, its spectacular 3,000 seat auditorium, which featured a sliding roof for ventilation, set new standards of comfort and opulence, which other managers soon felt obliged to emulate. Moreover its building had been funded by a limited liability company, an innovation which permitted investors to share both the risk and the profits of such enterprises. Moss, who pioneered the music-hall application of this form of financing, from which grew the giant Moss Empires circuit of variety theatres, provided some insights into its working in a 'Men You Know' profile from *The Bailie* of 1897. After his initial successes in building new Empires in cities such as Edinburgh, Newcastle, Sheffield and Glasgow, Moss found that 'These companies were received so eagerly by investors who knew the projector that, in nearly every case, the capital was applied for four or five times over, and in some cases ten times over'. But a surfeit of hungry investors brought its own dangers; Moss attributed his continued success to the fact that

> he never floated a concern, however good, and promising, overloaded with capital ...The difference between a sound concern fairly capitalised, and the same concern over-capitalised, is that, in the former case, a stress seldom, if ever, arises great enough to bring the dividend so low even of that of an ordinary safe investment, while in the latter case, the same stress of circumstances might wreck the company.[16]

The reliance on consortia of investors, many of whom had interests in more than one venue, was naturally conducive to organisation on a larger scale. While music hall had functioned as a loose national network of sorts since the 1860s, syndicated managements formalised the system through the growth of large circuits of theatres, mostly organised on a local or regional basis. At a time when demand for artists was growing, the circuits were able to wield their combined booking power to secure exclusive rights to leading stars whilst achieving economies in other areas.

One result of the new shared or combined ownership of halls was the introduction of the 'turn' system, by which acts could appear at more than one theatre on the same night. In December 1894 Moss and Thornton would maximise their headlining Glasgow engagement of Little Tich by having him appear at both their venues in the city, the Scotia and the Gaiety, each evening. By 1900 two other Glasgow halls, the Tivoli Variety Theatre (proprietors Bernard Armstrong and Thomas Colquhoun) and the Queen's Theatre, formerly the Star (proprietors Fred Cooke, Armstrong and Colquhoun) were similarly operating in concert, sharing complete bills by means of careful timetabling to allow acts time to travel to and fro between the two venues, situated at Anderston and Gallowgate respectively.[17] By the mid-1900s, following its introduction at the New Scottish Zoo and Hippodrome, and later the Pavilion, twice-nightly performances became standard for the city's larger variety houses.

Smaller consortia often included music-hall managers and professionals, or businessmen from related trades who had some working contact with or commercial interest in music hall. The prospectus for Pickard's Glasgow Panopticon company of 1910 lists six subscribers besides Pickard himself, who were required to state their occupations.[18] All from Glasgow, they include a printer, a contractor, a wright, two theatrical managers and a public entertainer. If the involvement of the theatre professionals is self-explanatory, it is also probable that the participation of the printer and contractor, and possibly the wright, was based on the expectation of future business with the venue.

By the late-1890s the majority of Scottish music halls and palaces of varieties were in the hands of syndicates or consortia. Where independent proprietors survived and flourished, it seems usually to have been a testament to their readiness to resort to innovation in order to stay one jump ahead of the competition. Both the South African Arthur Hubner, whose cinematograph provided what were probably the first film shows seen in Glasgow (at the Skating Palace in 1897) and Yorkshireman A. E. Pickard, who leased the Britannia in 1906, and reopened it as the Panopticon, offering waxworks, mechanical amusements and even a menagerie as well as music hall, fell into the category of born showmen who would have prospered in almost any circumstances.[19] In the event Pickard too had to resort to the formation of a limited company to run the Panopticon in 1910. Another English showman, the Londoner Herbert Crouch, shared Pickard's opportunistic streak. Arriving in Glasgow in 1880, he exhibited 'the first tinfoil gramophone' at 137 Argyle Street, subsequently Crouch's Wonderland, where between 1880 and its closure in 1912 he displayed waxworks, mechanical models and figures, together with human freaks and live variety acts.[20]

The early 1900s saw the addition of a new wave of larger city-centre variety theatres. Moss and Thornton, now known as Moss Empires, was by now established as the leading national syndicate and continued to expand. By 1904 Moss boasted total capital of £1,400,000 (rising to £2,086,000 in 1906) and controlled 22 theatres, a figure which increased to 38 in 1908.[21] The company's initial Glasgow acquisitions, the Gaiety and Scotia, soon proved to be stop-gaps. The Scotia was sold off and the Gaiety demolished to make way for a new Empire Palace, which opened on 5 April 1897, while a second Moss super-venue, the Coliseum, opened in 1905. The Empire, a sister house to the Edinburgh theatre and similarly designed by Frank Matcham, was intended to be Moss's Glasgow flagship. With foyers, shops, waiting rooms, bars, and a magnificently ornate auditorium with seating for 2,500, it represented the ultimate

Crouch's Wonderland, Argyll Street, Glasgow, by Muirhead Bone; Mrs Christina Baylis; and Herbert Crouch

**6**    The Empire Theatre, Glasgow, c. 1900

in variety theatre design and was to remain Glasgow's leading venue until its demolition in 1962.

Other new variety theatres reflected increasing interest from southern circuits and impresarios with national aspirations. In Glasgow, the Tyneside manager Thomas Barrasford opened the Pavilion Palace of Varieties in Renfield Street on 29 February 1904, and two weeks later, in association with Rich Waldon, the Palace Theatre in Main Street, Gorbals (formerly the Grand National Halls). The magnificent Alhambra in Waterloo Street, built by a consortium headed by the London impresario Sir Alfred Butt, opened in 1910. In Dundee, the Livermore Brothers, proprietors of the Court Minstrels, one of the largest touring minstrel troupes, opened the former Jollity Variety Theatre as the People's Palace in 1892. Two years later they acquired a venue in Aberdeen, the first of two in the city, adding their north-east halls to a tour that by the mid-1900s also included Sunderland, Bristol and Plymouth. Increased competition in a burgeoning leisure market was also reflected by a steady growth in the number of Scottish venues. Annual *Era Almanack* lists, which only included larger venues, nevertheless show the number of music halls listed in the four Scottish cities discussed increased from 6 in 1900 to 12 in 1907. In 1903, Barrasford challenged the Edinburgh monopoly of Moss's Empire with his new Tivoli in Stockbridge, a converted roller-skating rink, which presented three-performances a day in an attempt to carve a niche in the existing market. A further incursion came in 1907 when the Liverpool impresario Walter de Frece, later knighted, launched a five-month variety season at the Theatre Royal Edinburgh, thereby breaking another taboo. Reporting the glittering opening, *The Era* could barely contain its triumphalism at the sight of the 'historic house' with 'the "Legitimate" displaced, vaudeville in full swing, and the incense from Havana or humbler cigarette curling roofwards to the shrine of My Lady Nicotine'.[22]

Not surprisingly lesser managements struggled to compete. Zoo proprietor E. H. Bostock, who ran a circuit of Lanarkshire halls, had his first experience of variety management in an acrimonious partnership with Barrasford, with whom he launched the 2,500-seat Glasgow Hippodrome in New City Road in July 1902. After extricating himself by selling out to Barrasford, Bostock later bought the venue back and in 1905 entered into a second unsuccessful partnership, this time with Moss Empires, whom he had approached to forestall them opening a rival venue at nearby St George's Cross. The collaboration faltered when Bostock suspected Moss of supplying inferior acts for the Hippodrome, but on ending the partnership he found Moss's monopoly of leading artists too great to compete against and, losing £100 a week, was forced to close in 1909.[23] Where smaller circuits like Bostock's and Pickard's survived it was invariably at the lower end of the market. By 1914 Moss Empires, with the Empire and Coliseum, dominated Glasgow music hall in much the same way as the Howard and Wyndham company did its legitimate theatre.

Penny Summerfield has pointed out that, whether or not it had been the original intention to pursue the middle classes, the expense of building new variety theatres soon made the extension of the upper social range of the audience a necessity.[24] However, this expense was not only caused by the splendour of the new venues; it also reflected the cost of complying with demands of new safety legislation introduced both nationally and locally from the 1880s.

Indeed, the question of licensing and legislation constitutes the second area we should examine to ascertain the forces that motivated the emergence of variety.

The Theatre Regulation Act of 1843 had ended the monopoly of the Theatres Royal and allowed all types of theatre to apply to the magistrates for a theatrical licence. However, there remained a clear distinction between theatres and music halls, which for licensing purposes were still classed as pubs offering entertainment rather than as theatrical venues. Thus music halls were permitted to allow smoking and serve alcohol in the auditorium, but were not allowed to perform plays. This situation, and music hall managers' attempts to circumvent the legal restrictions placed on them, was recalled in an 1895 article in the *Glasgow Harlequin*:

> Older playgoers will remember the days when the halls, unlicensed for theatrical performances, produced what were euphemistically termed 'ballets', but which imitated pantomime as closely as the letter of the law allowed. 'Tis now twenty years, or even more, I daresay, since the late Mr. Baylis of the Scotia Music Hall was prosecuted on this ground. Several years afterwards, too, when his widow, the well-known manageress, produced what was about the last of these entertainments at the Scotia, she lodged a *caveat* in order to prevent any theatrical manager staying the performance with an interdict. Since then, however, we have had legitimate pantomime in a music hall, but that, of course, was at the Gaiety, a house with a theatrical licence, while in Edinburgh this year the Empire Palace has the erstwhile Lyceum show of 'Cinderella'.[25]

Friction between music-hall proprietors and legitimate theatre managers, jealous of music hall's dispensation to serve alcohol in the auditorium, came to a head in the 1890s, when the theatre managers complained that the increasingly elaborate sketches, often amounting to mini-plays, featuring in music halls were contravening the spirit of the law, and that, in any case, the legitimate drama was demeaned by its performance in the boozy, smoke-filled atmosphere of the halls.[26]

But if the core of the dispute with legitimate theatre is generally regarded as having been music hall's prerogative to serve alcohol, the case of Glasgow seems contradictory. In the first place, the centrality of alcohol to music hall in the city since the mid-1850s seems open to debate. Loudon's Shakespeare, one of the leading singing saloons of the 1850s, was recalled as 'a handsome and well con-ducted place, the artistes being of a very good class [where] Of course, alcoholic liquor was sold, and the patrons were permitted to smoke'.[27] Of course. But in the same period the Milton Colosseum, a popular early hall situated in the Cowcaddens, when the area was 'little short of a howling wilderness, and its inhabitants had little inclination to devote their evenings to harmless amusements', was apparently run with great success on the basis of 'popular prices, good companies, and temperance refreshments.'[28] The area's Wild West image is somewhat dissipated by the notion of an apparently 'dry' entertainment. Some twenty years later, press coverage generated by the furore of 1875, when a deputation of citizens protested to magistrates about the lewdness of acts appearing at a Glasgow music hall, reveals that only two of the half-dozen halls discussed in police reports at the time were licensed to serve alcohol.[29] Moreover, although the magistrates refused to be browbeaten into a wholesale reconsideration of their policy, the offending venue, the Whitebait, lost its licence soon afterwards.[30] It is unclear quite what the rationale was for so severe a restriction of licences that yet stopped short of an outright ban. But the fact that of leading halls the Britannia, at least in its early years, operated on a temperance footing, as did the Scotia under Mrs Baylis until the 1890s, suggests that both these longstanding managements were able to conduct highly successful businesses without offering alcohol. Whether this was due on the owners' part to strong conviction or simple pragmatism, as a means of making life easier with the licensing authorities, is not clear. Certainly Mrs Baylis's great-granddaughter recalled family stories of the Scotia's patrons being issued with metal pass-out tokens, to enable them to adjourn to adjacent pubs for a beverage during breaks in the performance, a practice that was widespread in England. Overall, the impression is of an accommodation between the Presbyterian outlook of the city fathers and established managers whereby music halls were tolerated providing they were run along strictly approved lines, which effectively meant without alcohol.

The same arrangement seems to have existed in 1891 when, in discussing Moss and Thornton's application for a licence for the newly acquired Gaiety, the Glasgow JPs' Court found themselves in an awkward position when Moss requested a spirit licence as well as a theatrical licence. Despite fulsome testimony to the managers' unimpeachable record in other cities, concern emerged that the granting of such a licence was bound to invite similar applications from the city's established music halls, the Britannia and Scotia. The implication was that no music hall in the city was currently licensed to serve alcohol, and that awarding such a licence to Moss was to risk setting a precedent. Given the Moss combine's reputation as purveyors of respectable entertainment, there is a certain irony that in this case it was they who were seeking to overturn the status quo by effectively requesting permission to reintroduce alcohol to Glasgow music hall. Particularly striking in *The Era's* report of the proceedings is that

Bailie Martin, the main supporter of Moss's application, who moved that both licences be granted, seemed to be arguing for a relaxation of previously held attitudes and an increased liberalisation on the part of the authorities. As reported, Martin stated that

> He would like to know if in all the theatres of the city – for he had only been in once in two years – there was such a thing as people getting drunk and disorderly. If opportunities were afforded already for getting a little drink, and the people conduct themselves decently he did not see how they should object to a handsome, fine, attractive place of amusement such as this. There was a time for everything under the sun, a time for amusement, a time to sing and a time to dance, and he was glad an opportunity was being given to the people to have a place to hear music and see dancing.[31]

If the avowed respectability of Moss and Thornton's scheme would partly account for this enthusiasm, there is also a definite plea for a shift in emphasis and, by implication, a recognition that times have changed.[32]

If the licensing position regarding alcohol shows signs of having been conducted within a framework of values already well established by the 1870s, the question of safety as an issue of municipal concern seems to have first arisen as a result of a specific incident: the panic at the Star Music Hall in Watson Street, Gallowgate, on 1 November 1884, when 14 people were crushed to death.[33] Genuine theatre fires were a common occurrence at the time, and had caused the destruction of four Glasgow theatres in the previous fifteen years.[34] But the Star disaster, although not unprecedented (61 people had died in a similar panic at the Theatre Royal in 1849, and 20 died at Springthorpes in Dundee in 1865), was widely reported in the press and the loss of life shocked the public, sparking off a wider debate about safety in places of entertainment. As a result, on 6 April 1885 Glasgow magistrates issued regulations specifying safety features to be incorporated into the construction of new or renovated theatres and music halls, together with public safety and fire prevention measures to be introduced into all existing venues. These covered provision and widths of exits and aisles, and maximum widths of rows of seating, as well as installation of electric alarms linked directly to fire stations, provision of gas stop-cocks and fire hydrants, secondary lighting and attendance of firemen and police officers.[35]

Thereafter the 1890s saw music halls brought within the scope of national building and safety legislation for the first time. The Glasgow Police (Further Powers) Act of 1892 allowed for the licensing of music halls (which as a form had previously fallen outside the definition of theatre provided in the 1843 Theatre Act) by a magistrates committee, and for the provision of by-laws.

Printed for public display in Glasgow venues, as specified by the terms of the act, these by-laws are an extension of the 1885 regulations. Interestingly, although music hall was now recognised as a theatrical rather than catering genre, in licensing terms a distinction continued to exist between theatre and music hall. While by-laws regarding construction and public safety were identical for both, music halls retained the right to sell alcohol and tobacco in the auditorium: consequently the posters detailing corporation by-laws came in two versions, one for display in city music halls and the other for theatres. In addition, the Public Health (Scotland) Act of 1897, which subjected halls to further by-laws concerning safety, was followed in 1900 by the Glasgow Building Regulations Act, which set out new standards for construction, fire-proofing and the provision of emergency exits for the city's theatres, music halls and public buildings.[36]

Taken collectively, the legislative and licensing framework discussed does not suggest that variety was prompted by direct or concerted pressure to reform from this quarter. As has been demonstrated, by the early 1890s alcohol had already been proscribed for most or all Glasgow halls for the preceding twenty or so years. Moreover, Corporation venues were by the 1890s heavily involved in promoting their own popular concert series, suggesting that civic authorities were far from intimidated by the moral threat posed by popular entertainment. However, the need to comply with the by-laws and safety legislation that began to appear in the mid-1880s and 1890s, echoing increasing consciousness of these issues amongst the middle classes, added considerably to the expense of building and maintaining theatres and music halls, and was undoubtedly an important factor in the shift towards management by consortia rather than by individual proprietors. When the People's Palace Variety Theatre in Bridge Place, Aberdeen, was destroyed by fire in 1896, the theatre's rebuilding, in admittedly lavish style, cost its owners the Livermore Brothers £15,000. In a bizarre postscript, the fire itself was commemorated in verse by McGonagall, in his most excruciating vein:

> The fire broke out on the stage, about eight o'clock
> Which gave to the audience a very fearful shock;
> Then a stampede ensued, and a rush was made pell-mell,
> And in the crush, trying to get out, many people fell.[37]

The advent of new technology and, in particular, early film, a third area that might have been expected to influence variety's development, was certainly utilised to help define the identity of the new genre, but only in a relatively

superficial sense: notwithstanding its commercial innovations, the variety formula itself was essentially backward-looking, a product of the 1880s. Music
hall's eager adoption of film on its emergence in the mid-1890s rather reflected
a general preoccupation with gadgetry and technological developments, itself a
symptom of an almost obsessive pursuit of novelties of all kinds. This fascination with technology had several aspects. In the first instance variety made a
point of distancing itself as far as possible from the old disreputable, 'traditional'
music hall of the 1860s and 1870s. Promotional material for variety theatres of
the 1890s and 1900s put enormous emphasis on their state of the art features.
As well as electric lighting, the Glasgow Empire and Pavilion (1897 and 1904
respectively) both featured sliding roofs, which could be opened to cool the
auditorium in summer, while Hubner's short-lived but luxurious Hippodrome
on Sauchiehall Street (on the site of a subsequent ABC cinema) offered advance
booking by telephone, and stressed that urgent cables and telephone messages
could be delivered to patrons during the performance. Hippodrome programmes also went to great lengths to inform the audience about the hydraulics
employed in flooding the stage tank with water for the aquatic parts of the
entertainment.

These features extended to backstage and technical specifications, the new
variety theatres being equipped with full-depth stages and flying facilities, in
stark contrast to the basic circumstances afforded by older halls. The scale and
appointments of the new venues were also conducive to a more ambitious
scenic presentation than had formerly been attempted, although this should be
seen in relative terms; in many variety theatres acts still appeared on a bare stage,
in front of painted drops depicting totally inappropriate subjects or scenes.
However, the splendour of the new palaces of varieties increased the burden of
expectation on managers to continually come up with bigger and better entertainments. Although singers and songs remained the core of the entertainment,
and vocalists and comics remained the archetypal music-hall stars, a vast range
of acts was needed to help stave off audience boredom.

Here too modernity was a key element, with performers quick to advertise
any technological advance or claims to quasi-scientific or educational status.
Amongst the more bizarre presentations were aquatic 'tank' acts such as the
Diving Norins, and The Finneys, who billed themselves as 'Great Scientific
swimmers in their Crystal Tank Performance'. Magic lantern shows, panoramas
and dioramas had long proclaimed the educational value of their depictions of
military actions, scenes from foreign lands and biblical subjects. Poole's
Myriorama presented its sequence of scrolled canvas paintings and tableaux

with a linking narration delivered by a presenter in evening dress equipped with a pointer stick, after the manner of an illustrated lecture.[38] But the 1890s saw an increasing number of acts drawing on technological innovations, reflecting the interests of the time. Illusionists such as the 'Great' Dr Walford Bodie, master of mesmerism and pioneer of bloodless surgery, exploited public fascination with recent scientific developments. Originally an electrician from Macduff, and not a doctor in anything, Bodie made a considerable career from capitalising on the mystique that still surrounded electricity at the turn of the century. Part of his act in the mid-1900s featured the simulated electrocution of a member of the audience in an electric chair of his own design, and his repertoire also included routines involving X-rays, magnetism and hypnotism, which Bodie claimed enabled him to effect miracle cures.

Elsewhere performers used technological developments to spice up well-worn 'turns'. One sharpshooting act appearing in Glasgow in the 1890s gave itself a novel twist by purporting to demonstrate the lifesaving properties of a bulletproof coat.[39] Similarly, *The Submarine*, a sketch presented at the Alhambra in 1912, realistically depicted the drama that took place inside a submarine when, having dived and been involved in an underwater collision, the crew are told that a technical problem means that they are trapped. *Henri de Vries Submarine F7*, which appeared at the Olympia, Bridgeton, in April 1914, showed 'a British submarine in action attacking a German dreadnought' and publicity similarly advertised its educational value in illustrating the workings of the new technology to the public.[40] It was in this context, the desire for whatever was 'of the moment', that music hall seized on the possibilities of film.

From their first appearance in the mid-1890s, early bioscope systems were quickly taken up by music halls as novelty presentations. A display of Edison's kinetoscope at the Empire Palace, Edinburgh, on 13 April 1896 was regarded as distinctly unimpressive. Aberdeen's first screening came on 30 September, this time featuring the Lumière Brothers' system, at the Livermore Brothers' Alhambra. In Glasgow the pioneer was Arthur Hubner, who before acquiring the lease of the Britannia in 1897 had introduced regular screenings at the Skating Palace in Scott Street the previous year.[41] These early films were several minutes long and featured subjects such as the departure of the paddle steamer *Columba* from Rothesay pier, and the Gordon Highlanders leaving Maryhill barracks.[42] By the turn of the century most Scottish variety theatres featured a cinematograph, bioscope, palacescope or other system, with advertising often stressing the topicality of the material. In 1898 Hubner's Britannia, now the 'home of cinematographic displays', was presenting imported scenes of 'the

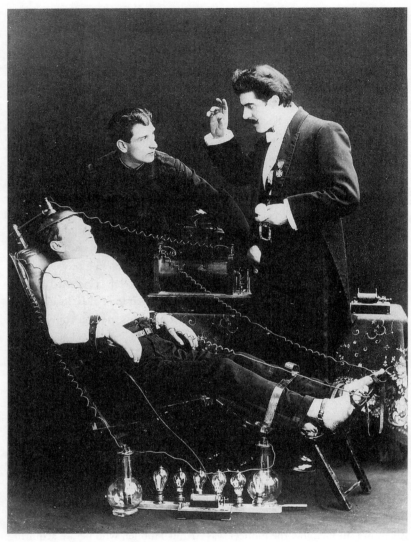

**7**     Walford Bodie's Electric Chair

present Spanish-American rumpus, scenes in Cuba and the blowing up of the "Maine"', while at Christmas of the same year E. H. Bostock had secured a hand-coloured version of Cinderella from Paris.[43] In 1909 came the introduction of the Cinematograph Act, the first year's application of which saw Glasgow magistrates grant 57 licences, many being for short-run exhibitions or displays in music halls or on concert programmes.[44] The first cinemas proper, known as picture palaces, appeared in the late 1900s, and by 1914 there were at least twenty purpose-built cinemas in Glasgow, many offering films interspersed with live acts in a format known as cine-variety, which will be examined later in this chapter.[45] The period following the First World War was to see many larger music halls revert to cine-variety, usually as a prelude to conversion to use as full-time cinemas. This fate befell the Coliseum, Savoy (Sauchiehall Street) and Olympia, Bridgeton, all practically new buildings. Cinema itself grew rapidly in popularity in the period up to the First World War, even as music hall was reaching its own high water mark as a mass entertainment, before declining and being overtaken by the new medium in the interwar years.

However, although the emergence of film and the introduction of variety were almost contemporaneous, their development was largely independent. While variety offered the early film processes an important showcase, it never had exclusive claims on the new medium, which was from its inception both portable and highly versatile. The first bioscope screenings in Scotland had after all taken place at fairgrounds, in large canvas booths or tents under the auspices of travelling showmen such as the Greens and Pooles.[46] And by 1901 the dissemination of film was already so widespread – through lectures and demonstration screenings in public halls, at fairground 'penny gaffs' and through variety – that one Glasgow church group was showing 'moving pictures' to children at a Sunday School soiree.[47] Rapid improvements in the technical and artistic standards of films, together with their growing popularity and obvious commercial appeal, made it inevitable that they would soon progress beyond guesting on variety bills to purpose-built venues of their own. Film's lasting contribution to music-hall culture, the cine-variety format, offered what amounted to a subordination of live performers to the requirements of the new medium, and as such was really more of a precursor of cinema than a distinct music-hall genre in its own right. However, it did play an important role in bringing variety acts before new audiences in areas that had not previously supported a music hall. In this respect film's influence was closely bound up with the expansion of music hall in the 1900s, and also forms part of our fourth area of investigation: the debate as to whether the advent of variety might have reflected changing public attitudes or taste as much as commercial opportunism on the part of managers.

Certainly the period from the 1890s saw a new recognition of the value of entertainment as an integral part of everyday social activity. This marked a shift in attitude on the part of certain establishment institutions, sections of the middle classes and broadsheet newspapers, and conferred a social rationale or legitimisation of sorts on entertainments that had previously been excluded from 'serious' consideration. Music hall was the chief beneficiary of this new more relaxed outlook. Guidebooks for visitors to Glasgow from the 1870s and 1880s had given details of the principal theatres and their histories but made little or no reference to music halls.[48] By the 1900s attitudes had been transformed, and the city's wide range of entertainment venues was now cause for civic pride rather than embarrassment. In one popular survey published in 1909, in a section entitled 'Glasgow and its Amusements', readers were reminded that 'It was not so very long ago ... that Glasgow was almost as parochial in its tastes as many Scotch villages are now. No doubt this was largely, if not entirely, due to the want of opportunities.'[49] A contrast was drawn between the situation fifty years before (when Glasgow possessed 'only one theatre, no music hall, no football club, some cricket, a little golf') and the current embarrassment of riches, 'when within the city there are no fewer than a dozen commodious and well-equipped theatres and music halls'. Of music halls specifically, the 1909 survey noted:

> While the Glasgow theatres do well, the music halls, generally speaking, do better ... Ten years ago the Empire in Sauchiehall Street and the Britannia in Argyle Street were the only variety halls in the city. Now we have the Empire, Coliseum, Pavilion, Palace, Zoo-Hippodrome, Gaiety and Panopticon.

However, the implication of a divide between metropolitan as opposed to country values was highly apposite. The new, more relaxed approach necessarily involved the setting aside of longstanding Presbyterian objections to entertainment of almost any sort, prejudices which nevertheless continued to hold sway in other parts of the country. As one disgruntled manager stated in a Glasgow journal of 1897,

> It is incomprehensibly strange ... how great a feeling exists against the stage even yet in Scotland. ... In the smaller towns, such as Paisley, the church and chapel influence is felt far more than in the cities. I have seen so much of the man who drinks ginger ale in public and whisky in private, who taboos the theatre and the music hall, cries down these places of entertainment from the pulpit, from the fireside at home, behind the counter and the desk, at the corners of the street, and yet when in town is an early applicant at the pay-box of the Empire.[50]

But in Glasgow and other urban centres, where the new enthusiasm extended to most aspects of leisure and organised sports, theatre of all types became increasingly popular and fashionable with the wider public. Theatrical news now permeated beyond the established entertainment columns in newspapers and journals, which had been around for thirty years, into more generalised town and general news columns.

Reference is increasingly to theatres and music halls as amenities rather than as causes of dispute or moral contentiousness.[51] Similarly, the significance of theatres as commercial concerns becomes more apparent, with press speculation on the location of new venues touching on many of the issues of infrastructure and catchment areas aired in such debates today.[52] The following excerpt from the *Quiz* of 1898, although couched in incidental terms befitting the 'Town Tattle' column, demonstrates the maturity of press concerns:

> I HAVE more than once argued that the immediate neighbourhood of Partick Cross is an excellent site for a theatre, which would be certain of large patronage. The Subway, Underground and Suburban Railways converge in close proximity, in addition to the car service, so making the position a very central one. Now the suggestion is so far anticipated by Mr. Richard Waldon, of the Princess's Theatre, having secured ground near to Govan Cross where he intends to erect a theatre. From Partick Cross to Govan Cross by Subway is but a matter of a few minutes.[53]

The underlying presumption here, that the acquisition of a theatre, or at least access to one, was a natural stage in a town or suburban areas' development, is significant. Whether a music hall, even a modern palace of varieties, would have received such an unqualified welcome at this point is more open to question. However, variety's drive to expansion undoubtedly exploited this interest in leisure, and between the turn of the century and the First World War new venues appeared not only in the city centre but also in outlying and suburban areas. The opening of a new variety house in Partick in 1910 provides a chance to observe variety's social progress by this point and its functioning on a less extravagant scale at local level.[54]

The Star Palace, 203 Dumbarton Road, opened with a special performance on 2 July 1910. The invited audience, 'a large and select gathering' included a Baillie, who presided over the occasion, a Deputy Chief Constable, their wives and a handful of other dignitaries. The performance comprised a variety concert followed by a moving picture show, both of which were 'repeatedly cheered'. At the end, in replying to Baillie Hay's vote of thanks, the manager, Mr Lazenberg, hoped that the ladies and gentlemen present had enjoyed themselves and stated that the management 'had brought artistes, the best possible to be got, and if they were to visit the Empire they could not have a better class of artistes. He was bringing that class of artistes that they might say they had something new in Partick – something that had come to stay (Applause)'. A local paper similarly concurred that the Star Palace was 'filling a long felt want', and found the theatre 'so attractive that one does not wish or require to go further when once a visit has been paid'.[55]

The proceedings, which ended with a vote of thanks followed by refreshments, were a scaled-down version of the Gaiety opening described earlier in the chapter. With all formality observed and eminent local figures attending to confer approval on the new venture, they suggest that variety had, at some level, been assimilated into respectable society. However, as the account of the 'variety concert' indicates and advertisements confirm, the Star Palace was not a music hall in the full sense: as the 'Star Palace and Variety Theatre' it offered cine-variety, a combination of films and live acts (in this case usually three), given twice-nightly and supported by a small orchestra or piano. Moreover, managers evidently realised that parity between the film and live elements was likely to be short-lived. Although the Partick venue was a conversion, plans of other new purpose-built cine-variety halls such as the Maryhill Star Palace, opened in the same period, similarly reveal a shallow stage and only rudimentary facilities for live performance. The future of such venues was already clearly felt to lie in film.

A possible inference of the evidence examined is that the variety of the 1890s took its cue from the spirit of the times; that managers, perceiving the new more permissive climate, and a huge potential audience, tried to meet the public halfway by providing music hall with a 'makeover', which improved its presentational aspects without altering the entertainment itself. One of the attractions of this theory is that it encompasses managers' impulses on both an intuitive and a business level. As to the other side of the equation, the question of whether the public's own moral perspective had significantly altered since the middle of the century, indications are that attitudes to music hall had not so much consciously changed as softened with familiarity. Evidence for this lies principally in the fact that the entertainment itself changed very little in the transition. On the much-vaunted eradication of vulgarity, there is a strong suggestion that, in the case of risqué material, explicitness was simply replaced by innuendo. Despite managers' morality clauses and public statements, much of the performing material delivered between the 1890s and the First World War, especially in songs, continued to rely on an underlying sexual frisson for its effect. Returning to the example of Marie Loftus, an excerpt from a *Quiz* profile of 1894 conveys something of the nature of the double standard in operation under variety. After praising her gowns and predilection for large hats, the article continues,

As for her songs! They are difficult to write about. A man in the pit last night said he thought some of them were 'no verra proper'. But he was a bigot. Let him learn that Marie has had in her audiences more than one real live councillor from George Square, and let him repent quickly that a comment so inapropos ever fell from his lips.[56]

The twinkle in the eye and mock outrage of the 'bigot's' dismissal encapsulate a common attitude to such songs. People could see in them what they wished. Those present in the audience would have little doubt of what was being alluded to by the manner of its delivery, especially in the hands of an expert practitioner (and after all, the very nature of music-hall performance lay in the triumph of delivery over content). Equally, on the printed page the texts of such songs were often surprisingly mild, or at least ambiguous, and those who wished to could afterwards disavow themselves of having been present at anything remotely unseemly. As with double entendres, there was nothing you could put your finger on. The premise was that of the in-joke, a conspiracy in which both audience and performers colluded.

The fine line being negotiated between outward propriety and inner meaning was much the same as in the 'old' music hall of thirty years before. The difference lay in social context and perceptions. By the 1890s music hall had been in existence for nearly fifty years. While audiences might continue to blush at, or occasionally even be shocked by, what they saw or heard at music hall, they could hardly claim to be surprised. Nor was the entertainment any longer regarded as dangerous or subversive, except by a diminishing but still vocal religious minority. Music hall/variety was rather part of the mainstream of popular culture, a successful form whose songs encapsulated the mood of the day and whose influence had permeated many other entertainment genres. And it was by these vicarious means, through exposure to its songs and annual visits to pantomime, if not necessarily by actual attendance, that the wider public had, over the course of a generation, become conditioned to music hall's value system, which felt comfortable and familiar. Material that had once been considered beyond the pale was, by the 1890s, still racy but nevertheless within the limits of acceptability for the broadminded. This process of incremental shifts in public mores, amounting more to cultural acclimatisation, was to continue beyond the point where the variety format could continue to reinvent itself. By the 1930s George West, star of the Royal Princess's pantomimes, would regard innuendo-based songs, with lyrics such as 'All the folks they do the shimmy, stamp their feet and shake their "Jimmy"' as a stock in trade.[57]

In conclusion, the emergence of variety is not attributable to a single cause, but was rather the result of a number of inter-related factors. While chapter 8 will deal with music-hall audiences in more detail, it seems important here to touch on issues of social constituency, as a means of establishing quite what variety was and who it was aimed at.

As part of this it is important to appreciate that music hall existed in a highly competitive marketplace, and may itself have been under increasing pressure from rival entertainments in the 1880s and 1890s. Chief amongst these was popular theatre, whose attractions for working audiences have often been over-looked. An account of the gallery at a Glasgow theatre in 1885 describes how 'Decent working-men with their wives, and maybe an elder son or daughter are here in strong force', as well as 'fishwives ... [who] keep one in mind of their presence by the very powerful smell of "caller herrjn"' which emanates from their clothing', and factory girls who had saved the sixpence for admission from their dinner and overtime.[58] Notwithstanding the 'decency' of most present, the impression is of a robust atmosphere, with a fight breaking out at one point and the audience vocal and enthusiastic participants in the drama, all of which tends to support evidence that working-class audiences patronised a wide range of entertainments. In addition to theatre, these included such seasonal attractions as the amusements of Glasgow Fair, pantomime, outdoor military spectaculars mounted by the New Barracks Carnival, the New Scottish Zoo, and Hengler's Circus, not to mention concerts and 'bursts'.

No doubt part of the attraction of theatre was the prospect of a good story as an alternative to the repetitiveness of the music-hall format. The audience in the passage quoted were attending a melodrama, the sort of piece described as 'three murders, an abduction and a leap-for-life'.[59] Another highly popular genre was 'sensational' drama, in which the storyline provided the pretext for a spectacular stage effect, usually involving an earthquake or man-made disaster such as a train crash. Several Glasgow theatres regularly featured this sort of piece, a genre in which the Royal Princess's in the Gorbals specialised (a 1900 advertisement for *In The Shadow Of Night* claimed that for the Act 4 representation of 'The River Thames at Midnight', 'The stage is flooded with real water in order to realise this scene').[60] But theatre's attraction went beyond scenic spectacle and full-blooded moral drama. Music was also integral to many types of drama. Most theatres kept orchestras, which played overtures and selections during scene changes, and many popular genres incorporated songs and ballads into the action. Moreover, despite the kudos associated with the legitimate theatre, most Victorian and Edwardian drama was narrative-driven, intellectually undemanding and therefore accessible to a wide range of social classes (factors that were to lead play-goers who wished to see something more challenging to raise a subscription in 1909 to allow Alfred Wareing to found the Glasgow Repertory Theatre, which performed Chekhov, Ibsen and Shaw at the Royalty Theatre[61]). Just as Irish material tailored to local immigrant sensibilities remained a key element of Glasgow music hall well into the twentieth century, so Irish domestic drama (what W. S. Gilbert termed 'The pathos of Paddy as rendered by Boucicault'[62]) was a staple of theatre nationally between the 1860s and 1900s. But whereas the music hall content, however sentimentalised, had a core of genuine cultural resonance for its working-class immigrant audience, the works of Dion Boucicault and his imitators were rural celtic fantasies, picturesque and remote enough from contemporary urban experience to captivate also the middle classes. The denouement of Boucicault's *The Colleen Bawn* (1860) takes place in an underground 'Water Cavern', where the eponymous maid (usually played by Mrs Boucicault) is thrown from a rock into the water by the crippled villain and left to drown, only to be rescued by the play's wise-cracking rogue of a hero, Miles Na-Coppaleen (played by Boucicault himself in one of his most winning performances). Combining scenic spectacle, pathos, romance, cliff-hanging suspense and a thrilling (and highly moral) resolution, it was one of the definitive scenes of Victorian popular drama.[63] It was also hokum, but Queen Victoria, a great admirer, saw the play four times and Irish melodramas were continually revived by Glasgow theatres such as the Metropole, which as late as 1899 was offering short repertory seasons of Boucicault's plays.[64]

These were just three of a large number of different genres and sub-genres that included touring west-end productions such as those from Drury Lane, 'society' pieces, historical action-adventures, 'military' dramas and comedies, crime thrillers, suspense 'shockers', supernatural mysteries, pantomimes, burlesques and farces.[65] While by the late 1880s music hall's influence on new genres of popular theatre was clear, so too was the fact that the older halls and the entertainment they offered, essentially unchanged since the 1860s, were appearing increasingly old fashioned. In this context, on purely theatrical grounds, it is hard not to conclude that, had variety not been introduced in the 1890s, the arrival of musical comedy, which allowed for the integration of elements of music hall's extrovert performing style with a storyline and elaborate production numbers, would surely have prompted some similar initiative aimed at repositioning music hall in the more fashionable mainstream.

In these terms variety in its incarnation before the First World War can be defined in two ways. Firstly, it was a dynamic new system of combined theatre management, in which the importance of finance reflected the large capital investment in theatres and artists necessary to attain a mass audience. Certainly most of the innovations and new working practices that shaped variety and gave it its identity resulted from this new business culture. In this respect music hall remained the generic entertainment form, while variety was primarily a marketing initiative in which the medium was the message.

However, if this describes what variety became, it doesn't explain its underlying motives or the social resonance it evidently enjoyed at some level, given its huge success. A second definition could see the new genre as a less planned, more spontaneous development, in which managers intuitively realised that the time was now right for music hall if only the social barriers to wider attendance could be removed. This reading – variety as an intuitively evolved commercial response to the changing needs of the audience – also calls into question the extent to which managers were really intent on pursuing a middle-class audience. It seems likely that they were instead attempting something less ambitious: to install middle-class values or notions of respectability (not necessarily the same thing) in music hall, so that upwardly mobile sections of the lower classes would feel they could attend music hall without compromising their social aspirations. This idea of variety reflecting the changing needs of the existing audience, who wanted a more respectable aspect to their nights out, seems very plausible. It also comes closer to reconciling the many contradictions in public attitudes towards music hall/variety, which reflected the entrenched nature of religious and social prejudices. The theory is also consistent with evidence that in reality the switch to variety actually did little to convince or convert those sections of 'respectable' society not already predisposed to attend. As a boy in the 1900s Tom Honeyman (b. 1891), later Director of Glasgow Museums and Art Galleries, visited music halls in secret because his parents, liberal-minded temperance campaigners who approved of legitimate theatre (and enjoyed amicable contacts with variety performers through the Good Templars concerts), nevertheless felt that music hall and pantomime posed a moral threat.[66]

If the Honeymans' objections were based on unshakeable conviction, it was also true that whole swathes of the middle-class constituency, and many church-goers and non-conformists from all sorts of social backgrounds, would never have considered going to a music hall of any kind. But what variety probably did achieve, by observing the letter, if not the spirit, of contemporary mores regarding notions of respectability, was to furnish those who wanted to attend with a social pretext of sorts. In other words the existing audience felt better about itself. Other groups, including sections of the middle classes, echoing the mixture of urbanity and condescension that had characterised the *Bailie*'s intermittent coverage of music hall since the 1870s (that it contained nothing to scare the horses, but equally nothing much to get excited about) were more inclined to visit on an occasional basis, now that venues were in the main city centre and the circumstances of the experience closer to that of legitimate theatre. For their part managers did not care if middle-class patrons' appreciation was often 'ironic' in the sophisticated modern sense, and the idea of young middle-class men going slumming persisted into the 1940s, when dinner-jacketed parties would 'go on' to catch the end of a variety show at the Queen's Theatre in Watson Street.

As to the role of the Glasgow authorities, if anything the restrictiveness and stability of the city's licensing regime between the 1850s and the 1890s seems to have contributed to the feeling that, by the end of this period, public sensibilities were mature enough to warrant a relaxation of previous controls. In this respect Bailie Martin's assertion that, to put it broadly, everything has its day, may well have been the best encapsulation of the opportunism that variety represented. Although as a form variety gave music hall a corporate face, and consolidated the impression of a nationally organised network, of which Glasgow was the northern outpost, accusations of an imposed homogeneity are probably misplaced. Moss Empires was the only circuit with a genuinely national (i.e. pan-British) aspect, all others being regionally orientated. Moreover, the block booking of artists apart, the system of financially linked but semi-autonomous theatres grouped into circuits or 'tours' usually functioned more like confederacies than centralised organisations. Above all, audiences remained intensely local in their identities, a fact that was well appreciated by managements in their choice of artists. Moreover, as will become apparent in subsequent chapters, what might be termed city-centre variety never achieved a complete monopoly in Glasgow, which continued to foster a wide range of different types and subgenres of music-hall activity.

## Notes

1  'Edinburgh Variety Theatre', *The Era*, 6 April 1907, p. 23.
2  Peter Bailey, *Leisure and Class in Victorian England: Rational Recreation and the Contest for Control, 1830–1885* (London, Routledge & Kegan Paul, 1978), pp. 164–167.
3  Bailey suggests that managers' own aspirations to upward social mobility may have been as significant as purely commercial motives for reforming the image of music hall.

4  'Dramatic Notes', in *Bon Accord*, 17 April 1880, p. 3.

5  *Glasgow Programme*, 29 August 1904, and 11 August 1913; Mitchell Library Glasgow Collection.

6  Contract between Miss Marie Loftus and Mr Wm Kean, Britannia Music Hall, Glasgow, 31 January 1894: by kind permission of the Raymond Mander & Joe Mitchenson Theatre Collection.

7  Rules and Regulations accompanying Britannia Music Hall Memorandum of Engagement to the Norman Bros, 17 July 1905; by kind permission of Mr and Mrs Robert Bain.

8  Britannia Music Hall programme, 1897; MLGC.

9  For Rossborough see Fred Locke, 'Theatres of Great Britain No. 3. Glasgow', *The Playgoer*, April 1902, p. 90; for Mrs Baylis see House, *Music Hall Memories*, and *Glasgow Evening News*, 8 December 1954; for the fullest account of the Baylises, see 'Death of Mrs Baylis', *Era*, 8 January 1898, p. 22.

10  For female managers, see Tracy C. Davis, 'Female Managers, Lessees and Proprietors of the British Stage (in 1914)', *Nineteenth Century Theatre*, 28:2 (winter 2000), 115–143.

11  *The Bailie* No. 39, 16 July 1873.

12  For MacLeods see the *Northern Figaro*, 6 December 1885; 'Death of Mr William McFarland', *The Era*, 23 April 1898, p. 22.

13  *Barr's Professional Gazette and Advertiser*, 7 February 1891. This journal changed its name several times, and appears variously as *The Professional and Authors' Journal* (1885–88), *Barr's Professional Gazette and Advertiser* (1888–1901) and *Barr's Monthly Professional Writers' and Singers' Journal* (1903–06); all at MLGC.

14  *Barr's Professional Gazette and Advertiser*, 7 February 1891.

15  Statement of Wm Kean, Sederunt Book, pp. 20–33, National Archives of Scotland, West Register House.

16  'Men You Know', *The Bailie*, 7 April 1897, p. 1.

17  See Queens and Tivoli advertisements in *Glasgow Programme*, 3 September 1900.

18  Glasgow Panopticon Limited Prospectus, June 1910; SSA. The company was to be formed under The Companies' (Consolidation) Act, 1908, to raise £12,000 capital.

19  For Hubner see *Educational Film Bulletin*, September 1946, SSA; for Pickard, 'The Panopticon', *Glasgow Programme*, 16 July 1906, MLGC.

20  See *The Eagle*, 18 February 1909, p. 13; MLGC.

21  See the full-page Moss advertisements in the *Era Annual Advertiser* (formerly the *Era Almanack*) for the relevant years.

22  'Edinburgh Variety Theatre'.

23  See E. H. Bostock, *Menageries, Circuses and Theatres* (London, Chapman and Hall, 1927), pp. 166–173, 182–191.

24  See Summerfield, 'The Effingham Arms and the Empire'.

25  The *Glasgow Harlequin*, 24 December 1895, p. 4. The Gaiety referred to was a theatre in Sauchiehall Street that Charles Bernard acquired in the 1880s and began operating as a form of variety venue, but with a full theatre licence. The term 'ballet' covered a multitude of sins, and was sometimes used to refer to more licentious

entertainments offered at venues such as the Garden of Eden in Sauchiehall Street, which J. J. Bell recalled from the 1880s as a place where the girls danced behind an iron fence.

26  J. B. Howard's evidence, 4304–4316, 18 May 1892, *Minutes of Evidence taken before the Select Committee on Theatres and Places of Entertainment*, London 1892.

27  Guthrie, 'Glasgow Concert Singers, 1830–70', p. 348.

28  'Death of Mrs Baylis', *The Era*, 8 January 1898, p. 22.

29  In the letter entitled 'A Professional on Music Halls', in *North British Daily Mail* 13 March 1875 (p. 5), the correspondent refers to 'the two halls licensed to sell strong drink'. In 'Glasgow Magistrates Licensing Court', *North British Daily Mail*, 24 April 1875, Mr McKechnie, the advocate representing David Brown's licence application, stated 'that there were in Glasgow these two licensed music halls, one of which (Mr Brown's) had been licensed for 25 years, and the other (the Whitebait) which had been licensed for 27 years'. The subsequent defence of 'drinking in a public hall like this' makes it clear that the license was for the sale of alcohol.

30  'Glasgow Magistrates Licensing Court'.

31  'The Glasgow Gaiety Licence', *The Era*, 28 February 1891, p. 18.

32  Other civic leaders shared Martin's belief that the 'time for amusement' had come, if not his permissive approach, judging by Liberal councillors' involvement in the consortium that ran the People's Palace, an attempt to provide a 'respectable' popular variety hall for the working class that operated between 1892 and 1897: see King, 'Popular Culture in Glasgow', pp. 166–167.

33  'Terrible Disaster in the Star Music Hall, Glasgow', *The Professional and Author's Journal*, No. 3 (24 January 1885); MLGC.

34  The Prince of Wales Theatre, Cowcaddens, Glasgow, was destroyed on 13 January 1869; the Alexandra Theatre, Cowcaddens, on 25 March 1870; the Royal Albert Music Hall, Bridgeton, Glasgow, on 19 January 1876, and the Theatre Royal, Cowcaddens on 2 February 1879.

35  Magistrates and Council of Glasgow (Police), *Regulations for Theatres and Music Halls, Churches, Schools, and Public Halls, and Inspection of Drainage*, 6 April 1885; Glasgow City Archive (GCA). Further rules and regulations published in the *Glasgow Herald* of 7 September 1887 seem to consolidate the earlier regulations whilst incorporating public morality clauses of the existing Theatres Act.

36  See also R. E. H. Read and W. A. Morris, *Aspects of Fire Precautions in Buildings* (London, HMSO, 1983), pp. 11–16; and John Lindsay, *Review of Municipal Government in Glasgow* (Glasgow and Edinburgh, Wm Hodge, 1909), pp. 29.

37  William McGonagall, 'Burning of the People's Variety Theatre, Aberdeen', taken from 'Yet Further Poetic Gems', pp. 54–5, in *McGonagall: A Library Omnibus* (London, Duckworth, 1986).

38  Myriorama shows also incorporated models and stage effects, together with music, variety acts and, in later years, a bioscope. For details of the Poole family and the myriorama see Janet McBain, *Pictures Past* (Edinburgh, Moorfoot Publishing, 1985), pp. 12–16, and Jim Poole's obituary in *The Guardian*, 21 January 1998.

Poole's myriorama is also mentioned at the beginning of chapter 18 of James Joyce's *Ulysses* (London, Penguin, 1984), p. 609. For an illustration of Poole's myriorama at Henglers' Cirque see *Quiz Supplement*, 29 March 1894.

39  'The Manard Team in their Scientific Shooting Act. Introducing the BULLET-PROOF COAT. Worn by Miss Julia Manard': see Britannia Music Hall programme, 9 July 1894; People's Palace, Glasgow (PP).

40  For *Submarine F7* see *The Entertainer*, 26 September 1914, p. 6.

41  Fairground shows probably preceded Hubner's Skating Palace shows of 1896 by many years; in a letter to the *Glasgow Herald* on 1 September 1937 a correspondent stated that he saw moving pictures at the East End Exhibition of 1888.

42  See *Educational Film Bulletin*, September 1946; SSA.

43  For *Cinderella* see Bostock's letter to the *Glasgow Herald*, 2 September 1937.

44  See 'Forty years of Films in Glasgow', *Glasgow Herald*, 31 August 1937.

45  See Callum G. Brown, 'Popular Culture and the Continuing Struggle for Rational Recreation', in T. M. Devine and R. J. Finlay (eds.), *Scotland in the Twentieth Century* (Edinburgh, Edinburgh University Press, 1996), pp. 210–229 (p. 212).

46  See McBain, *Pictures Past*, pp. 8–12, and Scullion, 'Geggies, Empires, Cinemas'.

47  Tom Honeyman (b. 1891), later Director of Glasgow Galleries and Museums, recalled being present at one such as a boy in 1901, when the film excerpts included footage of the Boer War, causing the Minister, a pacifist, to stop the screening; see Jack Webster, *From Dali to Burrell: The Tom Honeyman Story* (Edinburgh, B&W, 1997), pp. 13–14.

48  See *Tweed's Guide to Glasgow and the Clyde*, 1872 edn, republished as *Glasgow a Hundred Years Ago* (Glasgow, Molindar Press, 1972).

49  'How Glasgow Amuses Itself', in *Glasgow Today* (Glasgow, Henry Munro, 1909), p. 48.

50  'A Manager's Opinion of Scotland', *The Stage News*, 24 March 1897, p. 28.

51  See 'Amusements in Glasgow: What Public Spend On Them', *New British Daily Mail*, 6 January 1900, p. 2.

52  Such columns now monitored the performance of recently floated theatrical concerns. The *Quiz* of 23 June 1898 (p. 212) stated that 'If anyone ever had a doubt about the success of the Empire Palace ... that doubt must now be thoroughly dissipated, the dividend lately declared for the first year's work being of too decided a character to permit of any further dubiety. It is now time for fellows, who hesitated at the right time to buy shares, to say they must now try to pick up a few'. Similar items also appear in the *Glasgow Programme* in 1911/12 concerning the success of the first year's operation of Butt's Alhambra.

53  *Quiz*, 17 February 1898; MLGC. For similar speculation regarding the siting of the Empress Theatre at St George's Cross, see *Glasgow Programme*, 11 August 1912.

54  'New Star Palace', *Partick and Maryhill Press*, 8 July 1910, p. 4. See also Star Palace advertisement in *Glasgow Programme*, 30 January 1911, p. 8.

55  *Glasgow Programme*, 8 August 1910, p. 8.

56  'Marie Loftus', *Quiz*, 15 November 1894, p. 16.

57 From William Lindore Duff, 'Diary of an Ordinary Working Man', unpubl. ms; quoted by kind permission of Mrs Aileen Monaghan.

58 'Tramp', 'Among the "Gods" in the Gallery', *The Detective* (London and Glasgow), 27 August 1885; MLGC. The only thing to diminish this account is that it is part of a series with sensational overtones; others include 'Fast Life at Rothesay; Or, The Sodom of Buteshire', and 'The Queens Park; Is it a Nursery of Vice on Sunday Evenings?'.

59 Mark Allerton, *Frivolous Glasgow* (Glasgow, Frederick W. Wilson, 1903), pp. 106–107.

60 1900 Playbills; MLGC.

61 See Jan McDonald, *The New Drama 1900–1914* (London, Macmillan, 1986), pp. 44–49.

62 W. S. Gilbert, *Patience*, Act 1: 'If you want a receipt for that popular mystery'.

63 See Richard Fawkes, *Dion Boucicault* (London, Quartet, 1979), pp. 112–118. Boucicault was still performing Myles's spectacular 'running header' into the lake ('created by twenty small boys shaking yards of blue gauze') well into his sixties.

64 Theatre Playbills for 1899, Metropole bill for 14–19 August; MLGC.

65 For the sheer range of commercial entertainments on offer, see Cunningham, *Leisure in the Industrial Revolution*; for popular theatre genres see Booth, *Theatre in the Victorian Age*.

66 See Webster, *From Dali to Burrell*, p. 15. Tom Honeyman Snr was International Secretary of the Order of Good Templars.

# 4

# Performers I: the Scottish 'pro's

This chapter on Scottish music hall performers will examine artists' social backgrounds and patterns of career development, defining their different types and spheres of activity. The last section will use case studies of individual performers to explore three themes: the transforming nature of a music hall career, particularly for women artists; the increasing importance of seaside entertainments from the 1890s; and the significance of semi-professional performers in Glasgow music-hall culture.

First, a note on methodology. The shortage of documentation and statistical data on music-hall performers has meant that evidence for this study is largely reliant on individual biographies and case histories. Although this provides a rich sample of contemporary experience and one that is perfectly valid on its own terms, particularly given the shortage of published academic work on Scottish music hall, the drawing of wider conclusions from the examples of a relative handful obviously needs to be approached with caution. Moreover, biographical material on performers from before the First World War is notoriously difficult to come by. What exists mostly pertains to stars, and is usually heavily anecdotal, short on detail and often inaccurate. Biographies of journeyman performers, which by their nature would be more representative of the experience of the majority of music-hall professionals, are very scarce. Therefore for the purposes of this investigation, which is primarily concerned with the lot of ordinary performers, the main sources of information have been newspaper columns, sketches and obituaries contained in Scottish-published theatrical journals, together with those written primary sources that exist, and letters and oral testimony from surviving family members.

Although Scottish performers, like their English counterparts, came from a variety of social backgrounds, a survey of the biographical sketches and profiles that appeared in the Glasgow-published *Professional* in the 1880s suggests that the majority were from skilled or semi-skilled industrial occupations, and started out in an established trade before gravitating to the stage. The Scotch comedian James Houston (b. 1828) had been an apprentice engineer, and the singer and music-hall proprietor David Brown a butcher, while the songwriters Tom McAusland and John Pettigrew (b. 1840) were, respectively, a printer and gardener. Among Edinburgh music-hall performers, R. C. Pillans, later a great pantomime favourite, had been a printer's apprentice, while James Lumsden, whose career began in the 1850s and who appeared in North America in 1898, had previously been a brass-finisher. Of the later generation who came to prominence in the 1870s and 1880s, R. C. McGill had worked in a Govan ship-yard, and W. F. Frame completed an engineering apprenticeship, while the author and topical vocalist John Ferguson was a painter and paper-hanger, and the songwriters Peter Lloyd and William Preston were respectively an ironfitter and a shoemaker. This broadly concurs with similar research on English artists' backgrounds carried out by Lois Rutherford,[1] and indeed much the same seems to have held true for later Scottish performers who emerged in the period between the turn of the century and the First World War: Harry Lauder (1870–1950) was originally a Hamilton miner, while Fred Collins (1877–1931) and Jack Lorimer (1883–1920) were both painters and decora-tors, and Tommy Lorne (1890–1935) worked in a print works.

Most performers seem to have started out as professional performers on a part-time basis, supported by a day job. The obituary of W. H. Lannagan (b. Bridgeton 1850), the 'Scotch Lion' who died in 1889 at the age of 39, describes how after having grown up looking after his invalid mother, he 'was apprenticed to the bricklaying trade, and having taken a notion of the stage, for a number of years wrought hard during the day and went to concerts at night'.[2]

The most common route to a career on the halls was through successful ama-teur appearances at local benefits or temperance concerts. George Ripon, vocal comedian, began his professional career in 1879 with the Good Templars' Concerts at his native Partick, 'afterwards appearing at Hamilton, Paisley and all the other Towns in Scotland where concerts were given of the same class'.[3] Similarly, an 1885 profile of the young Scotch comic Daniel C. Pollock (b. Paisley 1862), reported that, after having contributed songs to local newspa-pers;

he came out publicly as a singer, and has met with good encouragement in Glasgow, Kilmarnock, Ayr, Stirling and Edinburgh. While at James Willison's ben-efit at Paisley, he was warmly complimented by that gentleman on his abilities as a Comic Vocalist. Last year he entered the competition for the gold medal at the

Harmonic Concerts, Glasgow, and although nearly twenty were present at the 'test' concert, Mr Pollock was among the lucky 'four' who were to make a finale tie for the medal: but unfortunately he was debarred on the ground of having his name advertised as a professional. Undoubtedly he has made a good start which augurs well for a successful future.[4]

Benefit concerts for other performers and, in particular, open competitions acted as both a training ground and showcase for aspiring professionals, many of whom performed their own original songs and material. The Scotch Comedian R. C. McGill, later manager of the Edinburgh Saturday Evening Concerts, clearly had an outstanding record in such competitions;

The first prize he won being a silver cup for comic singing in the Town Hall, Renfrew; the next was a silver medal given by the renowned Irish comedian, Pat Kinsella in the Clyde Music Hall, Govan. Shortly after he won a splendid oil painting for sentimental singing, and a silver watch for comic singing – both on the one night![5]

Such lists of booty were a standard feature of performers' biographies. These competitions were as often held for songwriting as for performing. If by 1886 Peter Lloyd had already been successful in several competitions, 'his latest being a handsome prize given by *The Amateur*, 1886, for the Best Irish Comic Song',[6] then C. R. Armstrong (b. Anderston, Glasgow 1857), the 'World-Renowned Song-Writer' who since the early 1870s 'had written Songs, Sketches and Duets, for nearly all the principal performers, Double and Single, in Variety Halls',[7] had, by the same period, amassed a vast number of such medals and gifts.

This system of concerts and benefits had been in existence since the 1850s, when James Houston had been invited to perform at a prestigious Grand Festival held in Glasgow's city hall by Robert Napier's engineering works. From the 1870s and 1880s the professional aspects of concert entertainment was to become increasingly diverse and sophisticated, with the inauguration of the Glasgow Good Templars' Harmonic Association in 1872, and the subsequent rise of the Abstainers' Union Saturday night concerts. Although the Abstainers' Union concerts were to become 'the big musical events at that time'(the 1880s), at which 'none but the very best artistes appeared', the Good Templars' competitions and concerts were a positive influence for aspiring performers, of which the comic singer W. F. Frame wrote that their establishment 'meant greater opportunities to younger artistes like myself to air their ability'.[8]

In contrast to the increase in concert activity, by the early 1870s the other established proving ground for would-be music-hall performers, free and easies, were entering their final period of decline. Although long usurped by music halls as the focus of the entertainment they had originated, free and easies continued to exert a strong residual influence. Willie Frame, who billed himself as 'The Man U Know', described the typical Glasgow free and easy at the time he was beginning his music hall career in the late 1860s as 'a happy-go-as-you please sort of entertainment, and a capital preparatory school for budding amateurs'. Evoking the city's professional milieu of the time, he wrote that;

> Amongst others, the favourite houses were the Crystal Palace in Nelson Street, Now Albion Street, and Sam's Chop House, up the wide pend close in Argyle Street opposite Miller Street. The latter was a two-night a week house. Old Harry Gray was the pianist there. He was a genius of a musician, and quite a draw for rising professionals like myself. It was a veritable treat to sing to his playing. Many of the 'stars' from the halls visited that house.[9]

This image of amateurs and professionals alike congregating at such sessions, where aspiring performers could hope to rub shoulders with (and learn from) established 'names', who would drop in to deliver an impromptu song or two for the fun of it, suggests that, despite the growing importance of the 'star', an egalitarian spirit still pervaded many aspects of music hall. It also confirms that, although by the late 1860s free and easies were no longer competing with so much as complementing music halls, they were still an important influence on performers' development, and remained central to the culture of the profession.

The passage also illustrates another theme to emerge strongly from Frame's autobiography, which will become recurrent: the ease with which performers moved between the different types of work already discussed, which were clearly anything but mutually exclusive. The fact that an artist secured engagements at the better class of city-centre concerts, or enjoyed a run of music-hall dates did not necessarily preclude him or her from appearing again at less well-paid concerts or expenses-only 'bursts', or for that matter from calling in at free and easies to meet colleagues and perform gratis or for drinking money, to keep a hand in and maintain a public profile when work was scarce. Given the vicissitudes of career and adversity, bridges were rarely burned.

Put in this context a music-hall debut, which generally followed success in local concerts, did not usually mean the end of involvement with concert or other types of work, or automatic advancement in the profession, but rather the opening up of another source of employment. But if concerts were a parallel rather than subsidiary source of work for most jobbing 'pro's, this was rarely by choice. For those lucky enough to be chosen, music hall offered by far the largest financial rewards available, and a successful debut could launch a young performer on a national career in a way that piecemeal success in concerts could not hope to equal. Such debuts usually came in the form of trials, one-off appearances in which the new act would be added to the advertised bill as an 'extra turn'. Both Frame and Harry Lauder gained their first experience of music hall in such circumstances at the Scotia Music Hall in Stockwell Street. Both were considered promising enough to receive a week's booking but, being immature performers, neither managed to break through professionally until later in their careers.

But spectacular debuts by seemingly fully formed artists did occur. After a short engagement at the Britannia Music Hall, Trongate, the comic W. H. Lannagan went on to Moss's Varieties in Greenock 'where the reception was so great that, for twelve nights, the hall was packed to suffocation'. Lannagan was subsequently engaged at Dundee, Aberdeen, Edinburgh, Newcastle and Shields.[10] James Curran (1863–1900), already well-known as a parodist and professional song-writer whose friends 'had often advised him to go into the profession', made a belated debut as a performer at the Britannia on 24 March 1890, at the age of 27. The *Professional* reported that

> The house was crammed and his reception was something terrific; his burlesque songs and parodies fairly caught on, and he was recalled again and again. When Jamie had 'done' the large number of seven songs he thought to get away, but it was no good, the audience 'hauled him back again'.[11]

Although Curran did not go on to become a leading 'star', for others similar early success did rapidly lead to the development of a national career. The Partick-born comic vocalist George Ripon made his music-hall debut at Jarrow in 1879, only months after his first success in the concerts already mentioned, and thereafter 'made such rapid strides in public favour that in a very short space of time he had appeared at all the principal halls in the United Kingdom, and had never any difficulty in getting return engagements at an increase of salaries'.[12] Compared to Frame, who made his first music-hall appearance in 1867 but seems to have remained primarily involved in concert work and touring parties until the 1880s, this was a meteoric rise. Moreover, Ripon clearly broke through into the career fast-track that was the national music-hall circuit almost at his first attempt. By the mid-1880s he was performing in London, while Frame, who was to achieve the greater stature in the long term, becoming a household name in Scotland, did not make his London debut until 1889. The writer already quoted went on to write of Ripon that

In his line he is certainly the best provincial entertainer we have got at the present day [1885], and as a proof that he is an artiste possessed of legitimate talent, he can easily sing five or six songs in evening dress, and make each one go successfully without very much effort.[13]

The rather suave, insouciant image of the ascendant young professional 'star' seems in marked contrast to the more idiosyncratic appeal of the older 'pro's. John Muir, the famous chairman of the old Whitebait Music Hall, formerly a free and easy, in St Enoch's Wynd, was recalled from the 1860s as

a stolid man, of the most serious type – to look at – of the Lowland Scotchman. He had been in his early life a kirk precenter, and somehow never got over the grim decorous primness of the part. He seldom smiled, and when he did so it was of the iciest description. Once in a while he would be seen to laugh, when something excruciatingly funny occurred in the entertainment, perhaps; but it seemed to be under protest, for he would immediately put up his hand and modestly cover his mouth. He did not speak much in his official capacity, except when there might be a particularly warm encore for some favourite. Then would he rise to his feet, raise his right arm from the elbow joint, make a kind of deprecatory movement with his mallet, and exclaim, in a voice of deepest sadness: 'The leddy will appear again, gentlemen!' ... nothing was enjoyed more than, in the event of a stage-wait, or any matter of that sort, to get John on to the stage himself to sing one of his inimitable Scotch ditties. To hear him sing 'Green grows the rashes,' with his sad-toned voice, and the pump-handle action of his right arm, was something to remember.[14]

If tyro performers such as Ripon were the model artistes of the 1880s and 1890s, the residual influence of the free and easies was still apparent in these decades through older performers, and those who populated the lower half of Glasgow bills. The songwriter Tom McAusland, who wrote over 300 songs for comics such as W. F. Frame, J. B. Preston, Harry Lauder, and Bob Sloane, gained his first experience in free and easies in the early 1870s. His obituary from 1900 gives a good impression of the robust, all-round attributes of the earlier generation:

Tom was a great favourite at the 'Free-and-Easies', although he certainly was not possessed of what one would call an 'A1' voice – there are very few comic singers gifted with such a thing – but if the quality of his voice was inferior, the quality of his songs was all there. If we remember correctly, he fulfilled two engagements at the Britannia Music Hall, and appeared at the Good Templars' Saturday Evening Concerts on several occasions – not to speak of various trade re-unions in and around Glasgow. When anyone was in trouble, and required a helping hand, Tom was always ready to come forward and do a 'turn' on their behalf.[15]

This unsigned appreciation written by a friend (probably the music publisher and proprietor of the *Professional*, David Barr) conveys a sense of the different ethos that had pervaded the precursors of the music halls. The informal atmosphere of free and easies had been conducive to members of the audience 'having a go', with the spirit of the rendition being as important as the delivery itself. In the more professionally competitive climate of the 1880s and 1890s, an act's polish and finish were evidently much more important. It is hard to know for certain, but some evidence suggests that by the 1880s the standard of performance (or at least delivery and technique) had risen appreciably, or at least acquired a greater degree of sophistication. In this context, many lesser artists who had a background in local concert work nevertheless failed to make the grade in music hall. Whether this was because of poor material or presentation, or simply lack of talent it is impossible to know. In McAusland's case, it is conceivable that he became too busy with songwriting to perform regularly. But the fact that, despite his aforementioned popularity in free and easies, he failed to progress in music hall beyond the two appearances at the Britannia, even on the back of his celebrity as a songwriter, suggests that his style of performing may have been out of step with the times. As the obituary half implies, it was no longer possible to get away with an 'inferior' voice that was not 'A1'. One can imagine that rough and ready, somewhat disorganised performances which, under the guise of spontaneity, went down a storm in the more informal surroundings of a free and easy, were exposed on the expanses of the larger music-hall stage.

If performing in music halls was now the preserve of professionals, the introduction of popular amateur nights from the 1890s might have been expected to re-establish the rights of members of the audience to participate onstage. In fact, in some respects they had the opposite effect. Far from being supportive of their own, gallery audiences were often highly critical, making little allowance for the amateur status of the talent. Moreover, most of their entertainment value on these occasions seems to have derived from ridiculing the trial turns, who, lacking the experience or technique to project in a large auditorium, often found the occasion intimidating, and either failed to do themselves justice or had their acts truncated by the stage manager when they lost the audience's interest. A veteran performer recalled how, at the notoriously rough Paisley Empire in the 1900s, 'many [amateurs] were lassooed round the neck and dragged into the wings, or a shower of old biscuit tins dropped on them from the flies'.[16] If this sort of response seems like rough justice, it probably deserves to be considered in the context of the school of hard knocks that characterised most other aspects of working people's lives. Moreover, this tough proving ground did produce many famous artists, notably Stan Laurel and Jack

# Queen's Theatre,

## WATSON STREET, GLASGOW CROSS.

## FRIDAY, 25th OCTOBER, 1901.

## 11TH GRAND

# COMIC SINGING CONTEST

## A CHANCE for AMATEURS to ENTER THE PROFESSION.

On Friday Evening, 25th inst., there will be held a Competition for Amateur Comic Singers. The Winner (who shall be judged by the audience) will receive an Original Comic Song, Words, Music and Sole Singing Rights.

## CONDITIONS OF CONTEST.

1.—All Competitors must be genuine Amateurs.
2.—They must be attired in appropriate costume.
3.—Each person on entering the Theatre will be provided with a numbered coupon, and each Amateur will be numbered correspondingly at the sides of the Stage. After the contest the audience are requested to put a cross opposite the number of the Amateur whom they think is the best, afterwards putting the coupons in boxes provided for the purpose at the doors. They will be taken charge of by the Management, carefully counted, and the result announced the following Night.
4.—These Contests will take place every Friday Night and when a Competitor has won three times he will be given a week's engagement to sing the prize songs.
5.—The songs to be given away will be written by the best London Authors and Composers.
6.—Competitors must send in their names not later than Thursday Night.
7.—Every Competitor must have a pianoforte or violin copy of the melody they intend to sing.
8.—Expenses will be allowed to all who appear.

This is an Entirely New and Original Contest, which affords Amateurs a splendid opportunity of entering the Profession.

Wanted Ladies who can Sing and Dance, Double Turns, Single Turns, Comedians, &c. for Competition to be arranged (Amateurs only) apply stating style of business to Manager Queen's Theatre, Glasgow.

Queen's Theatre, Glasgow, Grand Comic Singing Contest advertisement, 1901

Buchanan, who both made their stage debuts at the Friday amateur nights held at the Panopticon in Glasgow's Trongate. And although these events often served to emphasise the gulf that had opened up between 'good' amateurs and professionals, they also went some way towards reaffirming the primacy of the audience, and the local community base of music hall, as will be explored further in chapters 7 and 8.

At this point in their development, after a first appearance at a music hall, performers' careers began to diverge according to degree of luck, talent and dogged fortitude. Depending on their subsequent fortunes, it seems that Scottish music hall performers could generally be divided into two economic categories; those who, achieving local success, went on to work in other parts of Scotland, the north of England and London, as part of the lucrative national variety circuit; and secondly those who enjoyed some local success, but not enough to sustain them in a full-time career for any length of time.

The first group would include those Scots who became national (in this context British) stars, such as Marie Loftus, Arthur Lloyd, W. F. Frame, and later Harry Lauder and to some extent Tommy Lorne. It would also include others who built up considerable careers within Scotland, as well as those performers and acts who, without ever achieving celebrity, earned what was regarded as a good living touring Scotland and other parts of Britain on the large circuits. If this seems a broad category, lumping stars together with journeymen 'pro's, the common factor was fulltime employment as a performer.

The second group included those artists whose careers were conducted on a part-time or semi-professional footing, albeit with short-lived attempts at full-time employment. By definition these acts remained more local in orientation and outlook. In the case of Glasgow, although there is not yet any statistical data on the size or composition of the music hall community, initial impressions are that these part-timers or semi-pros could have been the largest single group of performers based in the city. If this was the case, the presence of a 'floating' community of performers with day jobs would go some way to explaining why so few artists register on official statistics, a possibility to be explored in the next chapter.

The lifestyles and work patterns of performers varied enormously depending on which category they belonged to and on their place within it. Scottish performers who became national stars generally achieved or confirmed this status in London, which, with over 300 halls, was by far the largest centre of music-hall activity. Their pattern of work alternated between London seasons, where they played in music halls (often four or five a night) or long runs of pantomimes, and provincial tours which took in most principal cities of the UK.

Below the established stars came other leading Scottish professionals, for whom a London season was an important rite of passage. Most promising performers who had built a reputation in the Scottish halls gravitated at some point to London, which, as the principal focus of the industry, could provide them with opportunities for wider exposure and, possibly, the breakthrough that would lead to them becoming a star in their own right. Scottish trade papers reporting the progress of favourite performers in the metropolis in the mid-1880s suggest that a sizeable contingent of Glasgow professionals (or Scottish performers who had made their reputations there) were playing in London at the time. The *Professional's* Roving Jack wrote in June 1886:

> As I promised the readers of the Professional that I would have a turn round the halls where the Glasgow 'Pro's' were engaged, I have done so, and devoted a full week to having a look in at the different 'shops' that I found the name of artists from the 'second city' on the programme. In the Royal Holborn I found Tom Berrick, the black tit-bit, and as I anticipated Tommy has suddenly jumped into the front rank amongst the best of single 'Nigs' that perform in London … Messrs. Lally and Doyle are showing at the Trocadero and Foresters'. 'The men with the level eye' have 'knocked the stuffin'' out of a lot of double Irish comedians that have appeared in town for sometime back. The O'Malley's are considered two of the best items on the programme at the two halls at which they appear, namely – The Star Bermonsey and the Temple Hammersmith. Messrs. Sandford and Kenyon have made a pronounced hit at the Royal Standard Theatre of Varieties.[17]

Prominent amongst the group was George Ripon, whose career was continuing to flourish:

> Mr. George Ripon has as we before stated become certainly the rage of London. 'George' has already worked the following halls – Middlesex, Marylebone, Bedford, Collins's and South London, and holds re-engagements for all of them; he is at present performing nightly at four halls, Harwood's 7.30; Royal 8.30; Varieties 9.30; and Star 10.30; pretty stiff work to be sure; on the night of my visit to latter hall at George's finishing song midst the applause I could distinctly hear someone shouting 'Bravo Glesca!' some enthusiast from over the border.[18]

The presence of vocal expatriates in the audience suggests that Scottish performers in London might have attracted, or been utilised to attract, a specific London Scottish audience in the same way that, for instance, Irish artists were regularly booked for Glasgow halls such as the Britannia which had a strongly Irish clientele.

Those performers who were successful and found regular work in and around London either remained there, often securing lucrative work touring the large circuits, or returned to Scotland with their reputations enhanced.[19] Moreover, a good London debut, if well reported in the Scottish trade press, could often lead to a breakthrough at home; notwithstanding the fact that Glasgow was a thoroughly integrated part of the music hall circuit, success in the capital clearly carried a special cachet for Scottish managers. When in the 1870s Tom MacLagan returned to Scotland after his London success at the Lyceum as Faust in the burlesque *Le Petit Faust* opposite Emily Soldene, 'engagement followed engagement, no concert or festival being complete without his services', after which 'lengthened engagements followed at Whitebaits, David Browns and Moss's Edinburgh'.[20] Frame also wrote how, on returning to Glasgow after his London appearances in 1889, 'I was soon engaged to appear at the Scotia, where I became a great favourite. Mrs Baylis, who was the proprietrix, had always great confidence on my drawing powers, and "topped" the bill with me on every occasion'.[21] So although Frame had been prominent in Glasgow as a performer from the 1880s, even managing his own music hall there for 18 months from 1886, it took this London triumph to secure top billing on his home territory.

For those Scottish performers who went on to become major stars, issues of ethnic identity were often far from straightforward. Marie Loftus (b. 1857) was a Glasgow-born performer who became one of the leading stars of British music hall between the 1880s and the First World War. Reputedly discovered by Mrs Baylis, Loftus made her debut dancing on the stage of the Scotia before going on to conquer the wider world. However, although the 'star' exploited her local origins to the full on her regular return visits to Glasgow, the extent to which her Scottish identity was apparent to audiences elsewhere is less clear. A famous pantomime principal boy in Augustus Harris's lavish productions at Covent Garden and Drury Lane, Loftus was also celebrated as a singer of motto songs. If their titles, such as 'I'm so Shy', 'To Err is Human, to Forgive Divine' and 'A Thing You Can't Buy With Gold' suggest universal themes, her professional advertisements in the *Era Almanack* also carried a note that she 'Will take a few good Scotch Songs'. However, it was also the case that although Loftus was Glasgow-born, her parents were Irish, she achieved her first success with a song entitled 'Kilkenny Kate', and, at least in the early stages of her career, she was known as 'The Hibernian Hebe'. Moreover, she evidently retained close links with the Irish community. Present at a meeting of the Glasgow Branch of the Irish National League in 1889, she supported a motion of condolence and sympathy with the relatives of the late Irish comic Patrick Feeney, and contributed £1 to League funds.[22] In other words Marie

# MARIE LOFTUS,

### AN IDEAL PRINCIPAL BOY.

Now appearing with enormous success as

## " Robinson Crusoe,"

# THEATRE ROYAL, GLASGOW.

**MARIE LOFTUS (the Sarah Bernhardt of the Music Halls).**

AGENT ........................................................HARTLEY MILBURN.

Marie Loftus Advertisement, *Era Almanack*, 1900

10    'Au Revoir to Marie Loftus', *The Era*, 5 October 1907. Marie Loftus departing
Waterloo Station en route to South Africa

Loftus, 'The Sarah Bernhardt of the Halls' was a British star who could also
claim to be Scottish by birth and Irish by extraction, which evidently made her
a very exploitable commodity, not least in her extensive tours of overseas
dominions. Loftus's Irish identity, which may have accounted for her special
rapport with Glasgow audiences, illustrates how complex issues of performers'
ethnicity had become by the late 1880s.

Another performer who drew on multiple cultural personae was the comic
George French (1876–1938). Born in Edinburgh and brought up in Dundee,
where his mother was ballet mistress at the Theatre Royal, French appeared
extensively in pantomimes in Scotland and Ireland as a boy. Briefly a rising
national star, chosen to appear in the 1912 Royal Music Hall Command
Performance, French was a gifted character comedian, one of whose most popular creations was a madcap Geordie footballer. Dressed in a black-and-white-
striped Newcastle United strip, donated by some of the club's star players, the
character became a great favourite with audiences in the north-east of England.
However, as well as being an 'Eccentric Comedian' and 'Character Humourist',
French was also sometimes an 'Anglo-Scottish Comedian', whose Scottish songs

included 'In the little Pub we use Just Round the Corner' (on the sheet music for which he was depicted dressed as a kilted Scotch comic), and his biggest hit, 'Maggie frae Dundee', a comic song and patter number in which he was besotted with a girl who worked in a Jam factory.[23] The fact that French could encompass different authentic regional archetypes must have been a great asset in a music hall industry which, though nationally organised, was also intensely regional in the character of its audiences.

The migration of successful Scottish performers to try their hand in London, albeit temporarily in many cases, was a well-established convention by the 1870s. Louis Lindsay (b. 1834), the veteran negro comedian and vocalist, who had toured all over Britain with minstrel troupes as a boy, played at Drury Lane and several London halls before going on to appear before Queen Victoria in 1868. Similarly James Houston had appeared at a London music hall in 1862, where he admitted that he 'did not make a very big hit – for the audience did not understand me very well – still, I got a good reception'.

This issue of the comprehensibility of Scottish acts by English audiences is a complex one. However the assertion, sometimes made, that no Scottish performer before Lauder had succeeded in London was demonstrably untrue. Notwithstanding Frame, in many ways Lauder's direct precursor, who had himself enjoyed a considerable success in London during his visit in 1889, Scottish performers had in fact been successful in the capital from the very inception of music hall. W. G. Ross, formerly a Glasgow compositor, was one of the leading stars of London supper clubs and music halls in the 1840s and 1850s with his grisly ballad 'Sam Hall', which described the final journey of a condemned man *en route* to execution at Tyburn. And Tom MacLagan, billed as 'The Great', was similarly one of the biggest draws at Charles Morton's Canterbury Music hall in London in the mid-1850s. While Ross's Scottish background does not seem to have featured in his career, MacLagan's strong Scottish accent was commented on as a drawback for London audiences. A safer general assertion is probably that the Scottish identity of these earlier performers was largely incidental to their performance, while it was integral to – and indeed was the defining feature of – the later 'Scotch comic' persona perfected by Lauder.

Those full-time performers who remained based in Scotland, which in professional terms usually meant Glasgow, were a combination of mature 'pro's who had ventured further afield earlier in their careers and subsequently returned, and rising younger artists who were still establishing themselves locally. Their work comprised the various types of concerts discussed earlier, together with engagements in both the city's music halls and those of its environs, and of other Scottish cities and towns. If these performers could be called resident, the term must be qualified; although their sphere of activity was more locally based, many probably spent a great deal of time either touring or travelling to fulfil engagements. Some may have been based in Glasgow or its environs in only the loosest, professional sense of a forwarding address.

The groups that have been discussed above comprised the first category of performers, full-time artists who stated their theatrical occupations on census returns. The second category, part-time or semi-professionals, did not generally register as performers on census returns, as most cited their day jobs in the occupation section. It has proved extremely difficult to research this group, whose careers were generally unsuccessful or intermittent, due to the scarcity of documentation or background information on their lives. Before attempting to assess their place in Scottish music-hall culture, we should first examine the financial basis of performers' careers generally, in order to appreciate the difficulties experienced by this second group.

Music hall's hierarchy was firmly based on financial reward. The vast sums that the biggest stars were said to command were legendary, and the subject of great speculation both in the popular press and in the business itself. In 1887 a *Glasgow Evening News* article claimed that a lady serio comic had recently been paid £50 a week by one city manager, that another singer of 'questionable songs' had received £60 pounds a week, and that 'Continental specialities are paid at from £20 to £40'.[24] Such figures were subject to considerable disparities. A surviving contract reveals that Glasgow favourite Marie Loftus was paid £80 a week for her engagement at the Britannia in 1894, while in May 1896 the English star Vesta Tilley was reported to be earning £160 a week at the Scotia. A *North British Daily Mail* article of 1900 claimed that top comedians could earn £30 or £40 a week during the Glasgow pantomime season, which could last for up to four months. By 1913 Lauder's salary 'was rumoured to be £400 for twelve evening shows, with probably extra for the matinee'.[25] The fact that such figures, apart from their obvious inconsistencies, were in all likelihood often considerably exaggerated did not detract from their hold on the public imagination.

What is perhaps more significant in trying to determine the rationale of the profession as a whole is that, compared to the financial expectations of many working trades or occupations, a less stellar career in music hall could also provide a good living. Lois Rutherford has written (of the mid-1900s) that 'even many less established acts fell within the contemporary lower-middle-class income bracket'.[26] Looking further down the scale, the 1887 article on Glasgow went on to state that

Few music hall artists are paid less than £2 10s., and those at that money are 'curtain raisers' only. The average lady serio can boast of from £5 to £7 a week; a very poor 'turn' being paid not less than £3 or £4. When one thinks of the prizes that are in store for those who adopt the music hall stage, the wonder is that there are not more talented men and women choose it.[27]

The key factor was regular employment; the securing of consecutive weeks' bookings on a regular basis meant, in turn, that acts were generally good enough to progress to a higher level of work, and thus better wages. Even a re-engagement at the same venue following a successful appearance often secured an increase in salary as a matter of course. The problem for most part-time professionals was stringing enough work together to make the leap to earning a full-time living from the stage.

If the more realistic aspirants to a career in music hall realised that the highest rewards were probably out of their reach, reserved for the few performers of genius – the Marie Lloyds, Harry Lauders and Dan Lenos – then there was at least the more attainable prospect that a successful career culminating in regular work in the larger theatres could 'set them up'.

Barney Armstrong was a successful variety performer who went into management, and was proprietor of the Tivoli and Queen's variety theatres in Glasgow at the time of his bankruptcy in 1906. In his personal statement Armstrong revealed that the capital of £500 that he put up to become co-lessee of the Tivoli in 1898 'was money I had saved from exercising my profession as a variety artiste', for which he had earned 'about twenty pounds a week', while his wife, also a variety performer who was still working frequently, could earn 'from eight to ten pounds a week'.[28] It may well be that, the question of vocation aside, this was the level of financial reward that most would-be performers aspired to when they entered the profession.

The problem for performers who graduated from amateur concerts and benefits to the lower rungs of the profession was not necessarily finding paid work but getting engagements for a full week, rather than one-off concerts. Statistics relating to the salary levels of the lowest-paid performers are hard to come by, but what exists tends to suggest that the minimum figure quoted in the *Glasgow Evening Times* article of £2 10s. was overstated, and that wide disparities existed between salaries even at the bottom end of the profession.

Correspondence relating to an aborted three-week tour by a concert party of venues in the south of Scotland in 1903 quotes the going rate for a soprano for such work at the time as £3 10s. a week, with a pianist commanding £2 10s. ('both good'), while one of the party's artistes, a contralto, was engaged on a salary of £2 a week plus expenses. In the case in question the promoter, one Alexander Mathieson, sued a Glasgow music agent, J. F. Calverto, for compensation for damages arising from the tour's cancellation, which he claimed was caused by the projector hired from Calverto proving unserviceable. Letters from artists to the solicitors concerned, enquiring after the progress of attempts to reclaim monies owed, illustrate the precariousness of life for those at the bottom end of the professional scale, for whom the implications of such cases went beyond straightforward loss of salary. Catherine Morgan wrote that 'it has spoiled me a good deal for this season, by not standing to a month's engagement which I came to fulfil',[29] while the letter of another of Mathieson's party, skirt dancer Miss Jeanie Hendry, to the solicitor stated that 'You will understand that when I took on Mr Mathieson's engagement I was out extra expenses and also lost several other good engagements through fixing with him for the three weeks running in September'.[30] Instances of performers being let down by employers who either proved to be insolvent, reneged on previous agreements or simply disappeared were so commonplace as to constitute an accepted occupational hazard. As such they seem to have been treated philosophically by many artists.

Small semi-rural concert tours such as that planned by Mathieson were an important source of work. Frame spent two years at the outset of his professional career touring the south of Scotland and coastal towns with a similar party, comprised of himself, two other artists and a pianist. However, for a picture of an exclusively urban semi-professional career centred on Glasgow we shall examine that of Norman McLeod (c.1874–1947), whose family have been able to augment what documents exist relating to his career with stories passed down to his grandchildren.

Born on Skye in about 1874 and probably brought up in Glasgow, as a young man McLeod worked at the Tower Ballroom as an MC, which may well have been his introduction to performing. He began his stage career, which was as a strongman, at some point in the 1890s, prior to his marriage in 1900. After first appearing on his own, McLeod went on to form a succession of double-acts, the titles of which all embodied his Christian name; The Two Normans, The Norman Brothers, and Norman and Louie. Most of this early work was in benefits and concerts in small public halls rented for the occasion. A surviving bill for one such event, a Grand Concert held at the Woodside Halls on 17 December 1900, confirms that the Two Normans were themselves the promoters.

The extensive programme for the evening comprised over twenty artists, and included singers, Indian club jugglers, Scotch comics, eccentric comedians,

THE TWO NORMANS

# GRAND CONCERT

WILL BE HELD IN THE

## WOODSIDE HALLS,

## On MONDAY, 17th DECEMBER, 1900.

Mr. ROBERT EDWARDS, Esq., in the Chair.

The Two Normans have great pleasure in intimating that they have secured the services of the following well-known talented Artistes, viz.:

## Mr. A. H. WRIGHT,
Tenor and Descriptive Vocalist.

Mr. JAMES ARCHIBALD, Mr. JAMES CAMERON,
Eminent Tenor.            Tenor.

MADAM JACK, Popular Soprano.

Miss INA CAMERON,     Miss ROBINSON,
Soprano.                 Soprano.

# BILLY CAMPBELL,
Champion Ball Puncher of America, and Winner of the Championships of the United States and Canada.

## JACK HARVEY,
Champion Clog Dancer. Winner of the Consolation Cup in the Competition for the Championship of the World.

## VERNO,
Juggler and Club Manipulator.

Mr. FRANK RODGERSON,     Mr. JAMES HAMILTON,
Baritone.                  Basso.

## Miss MURRAY,
Highland Dancer, who has performed before Her Majesty the Queen.

### Miss LIZZIE HILTON,
Serio-comic and Hungarian Top Boot Dancer.

## M'GREGOR TROUPE INTERNATIONAL DANCERS.

### ALF GLEN, Female Impersonator.

BROTHERS CLARK,     J. C. MUNRO,
Highland Dancers.            Scotch Comedian.

## D. L. VERRIN,
Eccentric Contortionist Act.

### WILLIE LEAMORE, Variety Artiste and Dancer.

## BILLY PRICE,
Indian Club, Axe and Fire Club Manipulator.

W. K. SUTTON,     ERNY SADLER,
Negro Comedian. The India-rubber Man.     Eccentric Comedian.

# 2 NORMANS 2
Champion All-round Athletes.
See their Marvellous Feats of Strength.

Mr. D. FORRESTER,  -  -  -  -  Pianist.

DOORS OPEN AT 7.    COMMENCE 7.30.     TICKETS, 6d.

# AN ASSEMBLY
Will follow immediately after. Ticket, admitting Lady and Gent., 1/.
Mr. NORMAN YUILL, M.C.

**12**    The Norman Brothers, with Norman McLeod on the left

negro comedians, contortionists, Hungarian top boot dancers, a female impersonator, clog and highland dancers, a champion ball-puncher of America, and a troupe of dancers. Topping the bill were the Two Normans themselves ('Champion All-round Athletes'), one of whom, McLeod's partner Norman Yuill, also acted as MC for the evening. With tickets priced at 6d and with so many acts featured, it seems likely that payment for such performances was nominal. Most who appeared were probably grateful for exposure, regarding the occasion as a showcase opportunity.[31]

By March 1904, now appearing as the Norman Brothers, hand-balancers, with a new partner, George Kirk, McLeod secured an engagement at the Britannia Music Hall, Trongate. Having given 'entire satisfaction', they were then rebooked for another week's engagement in January 1905. Their salary for this second engagement was £2 10s. for the week, but as the contract is made out to the act itself, rather than to either individual, the implication must be that McLeod and Kirk were expected to split this between them (the impresario Fred Collins was, as half of The Two Emmetts, similarly offered £2 10s. a week to tour Scotland at the turn of the century, a figure which his granddaughter and biographer also interpreted as 25 shillings per man[32]). As these 'Brit' appearances represented, as far as we know, the highpoint of the Norman Brothers' short career, this level of financial reward, well below the figure suggested by the *Evening News* article from 1887, puts the pressures involved in continuing on a semi-pro basis into sharp perspective. Even if successful at a music hall and invited back, one could only perform at the same venue occasionally, possibly two or three times a year if that. To earn a full-time living required a broader base of regular work, which many aspiring part-time professionals never managed to secure.

While there is no record of Norman McLeod's activities beyond 1905, there is some evidence to suggest that he continued his stage work, probably with Bostock's Scottish Zoo and Circus in New City Road, Glasgow, where his partner George Kirk had gone shortly after their amicable split.[33] Kirk himself, however, changed direction and under the name of 'Spuds' became a successful clown, touring England and abroad with Bostock's Royal Italian Circus. After marrying into the Pinder circus dynasty, he eventually went to South Africa, where he ran his own circus for some years. If the implication of McLeod's career was that, after a foray into circus, he eventually lost impetus and gave up, Kirk's surviving letters to his friend paint a vivid picture of the life of touring 'pro's. From Sheffield Hippodrome, Kirk wrote:

> When we were playing the South London Theatre I had Gavin Shanks over once or twice, you know who I mean, the *Bottle*, I dont think he is doing too good, he told me he was waiting on pantomime opening, as he is engaged to play the horse, the first night I met him he was boosed, did you read in the paper about a dancer dropping dead in one of the London Caberets, well it was big Alf Nolen, from the sawdust, he was in the time of Burly & Burly, Jack Burly is in America, and Douggie is supposed to have turned a great Christian and gave up the stage, tell Jimmy Adair I hope he gets his position in Canada.[34]

'The sawdust' was a euphemism for the circus business. Although written beyond the period of this study, in the early 1920s, the excerpt demonstrates the extended network of contacts through which professional intelligence and gossip were transmitted, and how even peripheral, part-time performers such as McLeod kept abreast of events in the south.

Norman McLeod has been discussed in depth because his career, and in particular his period with George Kirk as the Norman Bros, seems to have been representative of that of many semi-professional performers, in its relatively short span, in the partners' entrepreneurial willingness to become involved in promotion to generate work for themselves, and in the subsequent variation in their respective professional fortunes.

To complete the picture of the performing milieu, the other professional group that requires examining here is songwriters. The fact that music hall artists generally performed original material meant that there was a constant demand for new, up to date songs and patter, particularly on topical themes. If the number of individuals able to support themselves solely by writing material for others seems to have been limited to a handful, certainly in Scotland, there were also a large number of lesser practitioners who advertised their services in the small ad columns of the Glasgow trade papers. Most of these seem to have been old or semi-retired 'pro's' trying to earn a living by reworking their old material for others to use. Below these existed an informal network of elusive, almost Dickensian figures whom Lauder in his autobiography termed 'Trongate Poets', who sold songs or 'gags' to artists on an ad hoc basis, often in bars.

Most aspiring songwriters in the 1880s and 1890s honed their skills in competitions and local newspapers before graduating to the pages of Barr's *Professional* and *Amateur*, Glasgow-published songsheets that took work by postal submission. Leading writers made their living by selling material to artists on an exclusive basis, well in advance of any wider publication. The question of where copyright resided in such cases seems to have been open to different interpretation. A recently published biography of Fred Collins, a contemporary of Lauder who wrote some of his early material, stated that in the late 1890s 'artists, on purchasing songs for which they paid between £1 and £5, could legally put their names on them'.[35] Although this sounds contentious it is clear from contemporary comment in the theatrical press that writers saw themselves as exploited, given that a song bought for a few pounds could earn the performer a fortune. In this event it seems often to have been the case that writers had to rely on the moral conscience of the individual performer concerned to ensure that they received some further part of the proceeds of successful material. In concluding, we shall examine three themes to emerge from

The Great Northern Troupe, with Effie Stuart centre

13

this chapter. The first is the transforming influence that a music-hall career could exert on the course of individual lives. In a time when people's expectations were very largely conditioned by their circumstances of birth and social position, life on the halls offered the potential for escape, wealth and travel, particularly for women. In her work on actresses, Tracy Davis has put the economic attractions of a stage career into perspective, writing: 'Fields of employment

14    Effie Stuart, 'The Wee Scotch Lassie'

over which women exerted a controlling prerogative were usually low-paid, often seasonal, and susceptible to sudden termination when market conditions changed. For adventurous women who were prepared to travel, the theatre was no more of a risk.'[36]

Although there had always been limited opportunities in legitimate theatre, the growing popularity of music hall in the second half of the nineteenth century led to an enormous demand for new acts, making a stage career a much more plausible proposition for those with the talent and chutzpah to seize their opportunity. One who did was Euphemia Galloway Kiddie (b. Dundee 1880), the daughter of a shoe maker who, having won many medals and cups for her Highland dancing as a girl, in 1895, at the age of fifteen, joined a music hall act, the Great Northern Troupe. On leaving it some years later she embarked on a solo career, and as 'Effie Stuart, the Wee Scotch Lassie', appeared at theatres and music halls in London before her marriage in 1907.[37]

Like Effie Stuart, Flora MacDonald (born 1893, probably in Dennistoun, Glasgow) was a prizewinning girl Highland dancer, whose father often accompanied her on the melodeon. By the time she met and married the pianist and songwriter Dalton Payne in 1912 at the age of 19, she was already an experienced performer and had spent a season with a party of entertainers at Montrose. Together as MacDonald and Payne they played all over the UK, touring to South Africa in 1915, and to Australia and New Zealand in the 1920s.[38]

An even more exotic case of broadened horizons is that of Ethel Davis (b. London 1887), whose parents were butler and housekeeper in a Mayfair household. On her father's death in 1900 her mother took the family back to her native Ardrishaig, but Ethel seems to have left home at some point in the mid-1900s, journeying via London to the Continent, where family postcards from 1910 onwards find her appearing on the stage in Paris and Brussels. By 1914, when she returned for a visit to Lochgilphead, only to be trapped by the outbreak of war, Ethel was mistress to a Belgian count by whom she had a son. With the coming of peace, her lover having been killed in an accident in 1917, she began working as a solo dancer in Scottish music halls under the name Estelle Davis. In the 1920s she again left for the Continent, leaving her son in Scotland, and thereafter travelled extensively, finishing her extraordinary career living in Argentina married to a Moroccan circus proprietor.[39] Although all three women were to varying degrees successful as performers, their examples serve to illustrate the range and diversity of experiences opened up by a music-hall career.

A second theme to emerge is the increasing importance of seaside entertainments as a source of work from the late 1890s onwards. Although minstrel troupes had been active since the 1860s and were long-established visitors to many seaside resorts, the introduction of pierrots in the late 1890s sparked a general increase in the popularity of al fresco entertainments. The evidence of crossover between music-hall performers and such groups suggests an evolving

15    Flora MacDonald, aged 12

pattern of seasonal work, as well as a new area of entrepreneurial activity. A case in point concerns the veteran Joe Wesley, who played the Britannia music hall in Glasgow in the week commencing 19 February 1900, and was held over for the following week. He then reappeared leading a troupe known as the

Flora MacDonald and Dalton Payne, c. 1912

**16**

Britannia Minstrels, playing the same hall in the week commencing 21 May, after which they appeared at Largs in the beginning of June, performing on the foreshore. The local press reveals that the same group had appeared at Largs the previous summer as the Oriental Minstrels. This pattern of a May booking at

**17**     Joe Wesley's Minstrels, Largs 1904

**18**     Fred Hellis (seated centre) with 'Jock McNab' and friends, c. 1911

the Britannia before opening at Largs was repeated the following year, 1901, and Wesley's troupe remained regular visitors to Largs, playing through until September on and off for many years.[40] Other members of Wesley's 1900 and 1901 companies went on to front similar groups elsewhere. These included Jack Belton, who was running his own entertainers in Ayr in 1909, and 'Professor' Fred Howard, who subsequently led a group at the Royal Aquarium, Rothesay. Of performers mentioned in this chapter, both Dalton Payne and Estelle Davis appeared with Leslie Lynn's party at Millport, while Flora MacDonald played a season at Montrose in 1911. From the 1900s until the late 1950s such entertainers' groups were to constitute an important training ground for aspiring variety performers.

The third theme, perhaps the most important, concerns the significance of part-time and semi-professional performers to the continued vitality of community-based music hall in Glasgow in the early twentieth century. Following the disappearance of free and easies in the 1870s and 1880s, popular amateur nights, talent contests and Come-As-You-Please evenings seem to have replaced them in providing opportunities for members of the audience to 'have a go'. In the case of Glasgow, in keeping with this ethos, and in addition to younger aspiring full-time professionals, there may have been significant numbers of part-time performers happy to keep their performing on an occasional basis, as a hobby to complement their day job. An example might be Fred Hellis (b. Glasgow 1885), who appeared at the Star Palace, Partick, in January 1911 at the age of 25. Billed as 'Partick's Own Favourite Ventriloquist', Hellis played various Glasgow halls and social functions and continued to work as a children's entertainer into old age, combining his performing with a fulltime job as a foreman plater at Napier Miller's shipyard at Old Kilpatrick.[41]

Semi-professional activity is also readily detectable in the large numbers of neighbourhood variety concerts held in public halls rented for the occasion, often offering lengthy bills, such as those promoted by Norman McLeod. This blurring of distinctions between amateur and professional, performer and manager, seems reflective of the enduring sense of community that existed in Glasgow music hall at this secondary level, in smaller theatres and halls beyond the city centre. Instances of family ties and associations reinforce the impression of a relaxed performing culture that overlapped and embraced both artists and audience. In a society where people were conditioned to joining in communal singing in pubs and on works outings, and to being called on to deliver a song or party piece at gatherings, those talented enough to earn a living through performing were regarded as achievers on a par with successful footballers and ballroom dancers. Hellis's daughter clearly remembers Jack Buchanan being a regular caller at their house in Old Kilpatrick. Danny Williams, father of Dave Willis, the great Scottish star of the 1930s and 1940s, was a Glasgow meat porter who, when called upon, would perform 'a very clever and amusing sand dance' at athletics club socials.[42] Dave Willis himself was to make an early appearance aged 10 at the Panopticon, Trongate (previously the Britannia) in around 1905, assisting his brother Claude in his magic act.[43] Dave's son Denny followed him on the variety stage as a successful comic and pantomime star. The product of this milieu seems to have been a localised, community-based music hall, with its own distinct working-class value system, that continued to produce a vibrant strain of Scottish variety performers up to the early 1960s. The amateur night, where the audience still exercised its prerogative in choosing the winner, was a mainstay of this constituency. Amidst the various commercially driven innovations that characterised the development of mainstream variety, it represented a major point of continuity, a bridge to an older music-hall culture. Early twentieth-century performers making professional debuts by means of an 'extra turn' – such as Tommy Lorne's at the Bijou, Cowcaddens, prior to a solo debut at the Tivoli Anderston in 1904, or George Clarkson's trial at the Star Palace in Dumbarton Road, Partick, in 1917 – were undergoing the same process of selection experienced by Lauder in the 1880s and Frame in the early 1870s. In fact Lorne, who was to be the great Scottish star of the 1920s, experienced an early career of amateur contests followed by rural touring that mirrored the apprenticeships of previous performers in the same mould of fifty years earlier. Having explored Scottish performers' career structure, the next chapter will examine the music hall community in Glasgow.

## Notes

1   See Rutherford, '"Managers in a small way"', p. 95.
2   'Death of W. H. Lannagan', *Barr's Professional Gazette and Advertiser*, No. 172 (6 April 1889), p. 4.
3   'Our Professionals & Authors. Mr George Ripon', *The Professional and Authors' Journal*, No. 44 (7 November 1885), p. 4.
4   'Mr. Daniel C. Pollock', *The Professional and Authors' Journal*, No. 43 (31 October 1885), p. 4.
5   'R. C. McGill, Scotch Comedian', *Professional*, 28 December 1889.
6   'Peter Lloyd, Glasgow', in *The Professional and Authors' Journal*, No. 74 (5 June 1886), p. 3.
7   'C. R. Armstrong, The World-Renowned Song-Writer', in *The Professional and Authors' Journal*, No. 113 (5 March 1887), p. 4.

8  Frame, *Tells His Own Story*, pp. 76, 34.

9  Frame, *Tells His Own Story*, p. 31.

10  'Death of W. H. Lannagan', *Professional*, No. 172 (6 April 1889).

11  'James Curran', *Professional*, No. 196 (5 April 1890), p. 4.

12  'Our Professionals & Authors. Mr George Ripon', *The Professional and Authors' Journal*.

13  'Our Professionals & Authors. Mr George Ripon', *The Professional and Authors' Journal*.

14  *The Victualling Trades' Review*, June 1906, p. 381.

15  'Death of Tom McAusland', *Professional*, 22 September 1900.

16  Neil McFadyen, 'Fire! Cry that Ended the Death-Rush for Exit', *Sunday Mail*, 20 October 1935, p. 10.

17  'Notes from Roving Jack', *The Professional and Authors' Journal*, No. 77 (26 June 1886), p. 4; see also No. 103 (25 December 1886), p. 4.

18  *Ibid*.

19  One who stayed was Jack (or 'Jock') Lorimer, 'The Hielan' Laddie' (1883–1920), originally from Forres, who after a considerable success at the Palace, Shaftsbury Avenue, in 1904 based himself in Brixton, where his son Maxwell (later famous as Max Wall) was born in 1908. See Max Wall, *The Fool on the Hill* (London, Quartet, 1975), pp. 14–17.

20  'Death of Tom MacLagan', *The Era*, 16 August 1902, p. 18.

21  Frame, *Tells His Own Story*, p. 80.

22  For the Glasgow INL meeting see 'Tit Bits', *Barr's Professional Gazette and Advertiser*, No. 176 (1 June 1889), p. 8. For biographical details of Loftus see 'Marie Loftus at the Empire', *Glasgow Programme*, 13 November 1905; Roy Busby, *British Music Hall* (London, Paul Elek, 1976), p. 115; and *Who's Who in Variety*, p. 52.

23  For George French see Clive Shippen, 'Tonight Playing The Halls', *Evergreen*, spring 1996, pp. 76–82.

24  'The Modern Variety Theatre', in the *Evening News and Star* (*Glasgow Evening News*), 29 April 1887.

25  *North British Daily Mail*, 6 January 1900: I am grateful to Callum Brown for this reference; Marie Loftus Britannia contract, dated 31 February 1894, quoted by kind permission of the Raymond Mander & Joe Mitchenson Theatre Collection.

26  Rutherford adds 'middle class acts on £10–£40 a week were possibly within the upper-middle class income bracket; and stars were on a par with Edwardian barristers and cabinet ministers'; Rutherford, 'Managers in a Small Way', p. 109.

27  'The Modern Variety Theatre', *Evening News and Star* (*Glasgow Evening News*), 29 April 1887.

28  SRO CS 318/57/3.

29  Letter to Paterson and Salmond, 26 October 1903, CS 248/4062, National Archives of Scotland, Edinburgh.

30  Letter to Paterson and Salmond, 23 November 1903, CS 248/4062, National Archives of Scotland, Edinburgh. Jeanie Hendry subsequently toured with the fiddler James Scott Skinner, and was a member of his music-hall act The Caledonian

Four. See James Scott Skinner, *My Life and Adventures* (Aberdeen, City of Aberdeen, 1994), pp. 51, 64–70, 75.

31 Handbill, The 2 Normans' Grand Concert, Woodside Halls, Monday 17 December 1900; collection of Robert Bain.

32 Josette Collins Marchant, *Journey Through Stageland: the Collins Family of Glasgow* (Wigtown, G. C. Book Publishers, 1996), p. 10.

33 Biography of Norman MacLeod based on the transcript of an interview with Mr and Mrs Robert Bain, recorded 4 November 1995.

34 From the collection of Robert Bain.

35 Marchant, *Journey Through Stageland*, p. 9.

36 Tracy C. Davis, *Actresses as Working Women* (London, Routledge, 1991), pp. 17, 18.

37 Information supplied by Effie Stuart's daughter, Mrs Mary Barrow.

38 Information supplied by their daughter, Mrs Rita Wallace.

39 Information supplied by Michael C. Davis.

40 See Britannia MH programmes; *Largs and Millport Weekly News*, 9 June 1900, p. 5; 23 June 1900, p. 5; 4 June 1904.

41 Information supplied by Janet W. Baxter, letter of 14 April 1996 and in conversation.

42 Letter from Ruby W. Brown, February 1996.

43 *Sunday Mail*, 22 July 1934; quoted in Vivien Devlin, *Kings, Queens and People's Palaces: An Oral History of the Scottish Variety Theatre 1920–1970* (Edinburgh, Polygon, 1991), p. 7.

# 5

# Performers II: the music-hall community in Glasgow

A s the centre of the music-hall industry, London was home to a large population of performers, whose professional sub-culture and general ubiquity about the city lent them a dubious celebrity with the wider public. Performers basing themselves in the capital tended to gravitate towards a number of areas with sizeable colonies of 'pro's – most notably Kennington, Brixton, Canonbury, Stoke Newington, and latterly Streatham and Golder's Green.[1] The scale of the commercial and booking operation brokered from London was evident from the cattlemarket ritual involved in finding work, which for most performers involved trawling the agents' quarter by York Corner, immediately south of Waterloo Bridge. The comic George Mozart recalled that:

> The meeting of hundreds of music hall artists every Monday morning in the 'eighties was one of London's novel sights. The public house at the corner was called 'The York.' The pavements surrounding it were always crowded with artistes anxious to get booked to open, very often the same night.[2]

As the centre of the Scottish music-hall industry, Glasgow had its own agents' area, commensurately smaller, situated by a clutch of agents' offices on the corner of Sauchiehall Street and Renfield Street by Lauder's bar. But beyond that, the numbers and types of performers active in the city have not been examined. This chapter will focus on the music-hall community in Glasgow, attempting to assess its size, composition and character. For practical reasons to be discussed, it will not attempt a full enumeration of the city's floating music-hall population, but will offer an informed interpretation of some sources that might prove the basis for subsequent research, drawing on information on performers' lifestyles contained in the previous chapter. The approach is intentionally exploratory and selective.

The first section will examine census and valuation roll returns, seeking indications as to where performers and back-stage workers lived, as well as possible insights into their lifestyles and patterns of work. The second will use the same sources to try and reach some broad conclusions on the size of the city's music-hall population. In both sections an underlying theme will be the extent to which performers were resident in the city or transient, and whether indeed such definitions are helpful.

Given the considerable literature that now exists on music hall, surprisingly little research has been done on performers in centres outside London. Tracy Davis's work on actresses includes some statistical data on actors and actresses in provincial cities, including Glasgow.[3] But as her work mainly explores issues of gender and sexual politics, these statistics are expressed in ratios of male to female artists and percentages of actors and actresses to the total population, giving little indication as to the size of numbers being discussed.

The most visible category of music-hall performers in the city was music-hall professionals fulfilling engagements at Glasgow music halls or variety theatres (again, for the purposes of this chapter the terms music hall and variety are treated as interchangeable). Mostly from England, but also coming from Ireland and English-speaking dominions overseas, these arrived for engagements lasting usually one or two weeks, such bookings being no more than another in a well-trodden round that took in towns and cities all over Britain (the exception was pantomime, which required artists brought from the south to remain for the duration of the run, which could be as long as four months). These visiting 'pro's stayed in theatrical 'digs' run by landladies who were often themselves former performers or who had family or professional connections with 'the business'. The Directory of Professional Apartments in the *Professional* of January 1885 lists 28 landladies in Glasgow, a figure that reflected the current height of the pantomime season (by the summer months the number advertising had fallen to less than half this). Most of these premises were near or adjacent to principal theatres and halls; in Great Clyde Street and Stockwell Street (by the Scotia Music hall), Gallowgate (the Star Music hall), and Main Street, Gorbals (the Royal Princess's Theatre and Palace Music Hall).

Census entries give a good impression of the mixture of performers who used these digs, as well as hinting at the extent of their transience. The 1881 census shows that at 78 Stockwell Street, a few doors down from the Scotia Variety Theatre, Dominique Gerletti, 'Fireworks artist', had staying in his tenement household, in addition to his two sisters Susan (machinist – shirts), and Mary (general servant domestic), 'James Shields, lodger, Unmarried, Comic

Singer – music hall', and William and Mary Langley, married, who were respec-
tively 'Pantomimist' and 'Danseuse – Music hall'. All three were from England.
At no. 116 was Christina Baylis, widow 'Proprietrix Music Hall', the Scotia's
longtime owner, whilst at no. 132 lodging with David Oswald was 'Jane Smith,
Ms, ballet dancer, Lanark, Glasgow'. A few hundred yards away at no. 18 Great
Clyde Street, staying with John McEwan, a butcher, and his wife and daughter,
were 'William J. Ashcroft, married, Music Hall Proprietor, Ireland', and 'Marie
Gerwul, Unmarried, Concert Singer, England'. Also lodging in a tenement at
no. 18 were Robert Rush and Edgar Martin, both 'Unmarried, Comedian,
England', and John Rodgers, 'musician, England'. At no. 15, staying with
Mabel McCrone, a widow who let apartments, were Matthew Lampe 'Dancer
(clog), Ireland'; James Bridewell, also a clog dancer, from England; Clark W.
Dearlove, musician, John Wright, vocalist (both from England); as well as
Margaret Byrne, widow, Ireland, and Alfred Byrne, unmarried, from London,
who were both musicians. Also staying in lodgings at no. 15, this time with Mrs
Bryson (another of the landladies advertising in the *Professional*) were Edward
Lewis, Jessie Lewis (a married couple), and James Creek, all comedians from
England, while round the corner in Ropework Lane, staying at no. 24 with
John Gilbert, his wife, son, and two daughters, were Charles Stewart and Henry
Newman, who both described themselves as 'Vocalist, America'.

These entries are quoted at length because they show the considerable diversity of types of performers active in Glasgow at the time; acts from London,
probably playing in pantomimes, as well as obvious music hall 'turns' such as
the clog dancers; a music-hall proprietor from Ireland (scouting talent or possibly working in Glasgow); musicians, possibly working in theatre or music-hall
pit bands; and what sounds like a double-act from America. In fact, the professional world being a small one, we can identify several of the names mentioned:
Ashcroft, who billed himself as 'The Solid Man', was a well-known Irish performer and manager who worked extensively in Scotland, while the 'firework
artist' Gerletti presented entertainments at Purvis's pleasure gardens in
Dunoon, employing both James Houston and Willie Frame.[4]

The surrounding social milieu is also of interest. Neighbouring tenements
were inhabited by a wide range of small-business- and tradespeople. The occupants of no. 78 Stockwell Street, for instance, which seems to have comprised
some twenty or so households off the same close, included washerwomen,
bookbinders, broom-makers, tailors, and various different manual and factory
workers including cotton mill weavers. Skilled craftsmen and merchants were
also present. No. 15 Great Clyde Street numbered amongst its occupants a

watch and clock maker, a cabinet maker, a letter press printer and a spirit merchant who employed some nine adults and boys in his business. However, if this smacks of relaxed social integration, we should not necessarily take it as indicative of the context in which music hall was more generally regarded. Theatrical digs, which continued to function in much the same way in many British cities until the 1960s and 1970s, only dealt with the itinerant, transient population of touring artists who were visiting the city for short periods. These performers came and went on a regular weekly basis. They undoubtedly attracted public attention, frequenting theatrical bars and dressing as they did in what was considered outlandish fashion, and in a style that was often discernibly foreign to Scots, and they certainly contributed to the formation of whatever public perception of music-hall artists was current. But ultimately, although highly visible, they formed only the most superficial point of contact between music-hall performers and the wider public.

For a more representative context in which variety performers were regarded, we should focus on the community of indigenous, Glasgow-based music hall artists, if there was such a thing. If visiting acts chose to stay in digs close to theatres or halls for reasons of expediency, there was no reason to expect that performers based in Glasgow should have been concentrated in specific areas rather than dispersed about the city. In the event, there is evidence from both the 1881 valuation rolls and census returns that suggests there were marked concentrations of artists, musicians and backstage workers in several specific areas of the city. Furthermore, although these areas overlap to some degree with those in which the digs were located, they also differ significantly, suggesting that Glasgow music-hall performers shared enough of a collective sense of identity as to constitute a community in their own right.

As with the theatrical digs, these areas with high concentrations of music hall artists correlate fairly closely to the presence of theatres, and centre on Main Street, Gorbals, in the south side on one hand, and the Cowcaddens area between Garscube Road and St George's Cross on the other. This latter area, and in particular the lattice of streets either side and to the north of New City Road, is interesting because, although not populated by theatrical landladies (none of the 28 listed in the 1881 *Professional* is located here), it was close to a group of theatres situated on the northern edge of the city centre. By the 1880s these included the Prince of Wales (later Grand) Theatre on Cowcaddens (1869), and the Theatre Royal, formerly the Royal Colisseum music hall, at the top of Hope Street. In following decades these were joined by Bostock's New Scottish Zoo and Circus (1897) later known as the New Olympic Theatre and

Hippodrome, in New City Road, and the Alexandra music hall on the corner of Hope Street and Cowcaddens, while to the west the Empress Theatre opened at St George's Cross in 1910. Perhaps as significantly, the other new variety theatres opened as part of a turn-of-the-century boom, in particular the Pavilion in Renfield Street (1904), were only a short walk away.

This area first suggested itself through the frequency with which references to its streets appeared in the 1881 valuation rolls listings for people with theatrical professions or occupations. But as valuation rolls only include householders who own their property, or heads of households living in rented property, and it seems likely that the great majority of music hall performers lived in short-term rented accommodation, this does not necessarily imply that the same area was also populated by these more representative performers and their families. However, examining the 1881 census returns for certain streets that look promising from the valuation rolls does produce evidence of a wider music-hall population. These census returns, including as they do all persons staying in rented accommodation, give a much fuller impression of the range of occupations of inhabitants of a given area.

One example was Maitland Street, situated just north of Cowcaddens behind the Prince of Wales Theatre. At no. 73, which was evidently a theatrical close, there are separate valuation roll entries for William Packer, musician, Edwin Sennet, comedian, and Abraham Jacobs, scenic artist. In addition the census shows that also at no. 73, lodging with Peter Saunders, retired seaman, his wife and grand-niece, were Harry Flinders and William Jones, respectively theatrical carpenter and propertyman from England. Around the corner in Stewart Street at no. 38 was William A. Mara, age 56, described as 'comedian' originally from Ireland, his wife Matilda, an actress from Edinburgh, and their two daughters, one a widow from Dumfriesshire, and the other unmarried, both also actresses. If the two backstage workers were probably passing through with visiting companies, the family group seem likely to have been a working household.

A second pocket around Main Street also reveals further details of theatrical residents when the valuation roll is checked against the fuller account provided by the census returns. In this case the 1881 Census shows that staying at 16 Nicholson Street were Joseph Lunds and Elizabeth Miles, both vocalists from England, while at 48 Norfolk Street, also adjacent to Main Street, the head of the house was Michael Donnelly, 'stage manager', whose lodgers were Edward and Emily Towers, 'Music Hall artists, England'. A stage manager offering digs to visiting performers, probably appearing at his own place of work, was also typical.

Unfortunately, the inherent weakness of a valuation-roll-led survey means that we should be wary of drawing premature conclusions from such results. It is quite possible that those performers who tenanted property (almost certainly a minority) did so in different areas to those inhabited by their colleagues, who lived as lodgers or sub-tenants on more casual agreements. In any case, the work involved in combing census returns for these areas to confirm whether they also held concentrations of theatricals living in rented accommodation has been too time-consuming a proposition for this survey, especially as establishing this would not preclude the possibility of other concentrations of performers elsewhere. For a more reliable guide to the distribution of Glasgow's music-hall performers, we must wait for the availability of a census database that will enable groups of individuals to be extracted according to their stated occupation.

In attempting to evaluate the size of the city's music hall population, comprising performers, musicians, backstage workers and impresarios, the same limitation – lack of resources to make a detailed study of census returns – means that here too estimates will have to be based on valuation rolls, in this case those for 1861, 1881 and 1911 (see Table 5.1). Examining these figures, the first thing that is apparent is the small number of performers who register. The two largest occupational categories, 'Musician' and 'Artist', are both variable factors; cross-referencing sample musician's entries with census returns does not give any indication as to what area of music players were involved in, although it seems reasonable to assume that, given the number of theatres and music halls active (4 music halls and 5 theatres in 1880; 14 music halls and 7 theatres in 1911), a majority might have been expected to have been employed in pit bands. The term 'artist' has been included on the basis of its sometime use in the theatrical sense, in addition to the later 'artiste'. But, again, cross-referencing of one or two entries with census returns has not produced clarification as to the type of 'artist' being referred to in any given case. However, it seems unlikely that all those listed were commercial artists, especially as the marked increase in the category over the three surveys, from 26 in 1861, to 49 in 1881, to 58 in 1911, accords with a dramatic increase in numbers of musicians and, coincidentally, the sharp rise in numbers of Glasgow halls from the mid-1900s.[5] Given that this scale of increase in commercial or fine artists seems highly unlikely, it seems more probable that at least a proportion of this category were music-hall 'turns' who used the term euphemistically for official purposes, as covering a multitude of sins. However, as both categories are clearly to some degree flawed for our purposes, to preserve the integrity of the totals (nominal though they are, given the limitations discussed) a sub-total is given omitting both.

**Table 5.1** Theatrical presence on Glasgow Valuation Rolls

| Head of household occupation | 1861 | 1881 | 1911 |
|---|---|---|---|
| Actor | 3 | 6 | 4 |
| Actress | – | 1 | – |
| Artist | 26 | 49 | 57 |
| Artiste | – | 1 | – |
| Comedian | 2 | 6 | 11 |
| Elocutionist | – | 1 | 1 |
| Music Director/Conductor | – | 1 | 4 |
| Music hall artiste | – | – | 2 |
| M.H. Keeper | – | 1 | – |
| M.H. Lessee | – | 1 | – |
| Musician | 57 | 60 | 167 |
| Scene Shifter | – | – | 1 |
| Scenic Artist | – | 3 | 4 |
| Singer | 27 | 8 | – |
| Stage Carpenter | 1 | 1 | 1 |
| Stage Manager | – | – | 4 |
| Theatre Attendant | – | – | 6 |
| Theatre Lessee | – | 1 | – |
| Theatre Manager | – | 1 | 5 |
| Theatre Proprietor | – | 1 | – |
| Theatrical Employee | 1 | – | 1 |
| Theatrical Lessee | – | 2 | – |
| Theatrical Manager | – | 1 | 8 |
| Theatrical Outfitter | – | – | 1 |
| Vocalist | 2 | 6 | 14 |
| Variety Agent | – | – | 1 |
| Total | 119 | 151 | 292 |
| Total excluding 'artist' and 'musician' categories | 36 | 42 | 68 |

Source: Glasgow City Archives (formerly Strathclyde Regional Archives). The author is very much indebted to Andrew Jackson for his help in extracting entries from the database by occupational categories.

Elsewhere there are instances of categories changing meaning or going out of fashion. Thus the 1861 roll features 27 singers, a figure which declines to 8 in 1881 and disappears completely in 1911. In contrast the 'Vocalist' category rises from only 2 in 1861, to 6 in 1881 and 14 in 1911, suggesting a change in popular usage. Furthermore, if we are to accept that, with more halls active in

1911, the number of performers could be expected to be larger, then where did the equivalent of the remainder of the 'singers' of 1861 go? Possibly to the 'artist' category?

As has already been suggested, the small number of performers featuring in the valuation rolls probably reflected the fact that most stayed in rented accommodation, or in digs or theatrical houses where only the head of the household was included. However, the question of how large the Glasgow-based community actually was, and how long performers, Scottish or English, stayed before they had exhausted the local outlets for work or before their careers took them to other parts of the country, remains to be answered. As one of the principal music-hall cities in Britain, it had seemed reasonable to expect that Glasgow and its surrounding areas had enough halls and theatres to support a sizeable population of performers and backstage workers. A letter from the manager of Brown's Royal Music Hall in 1875, effectively a briefing paper for the Chief Constable, states that in Glasgow 'There are five halls, employing on an average from 40 to 50 professionals weekly – including Bands men, money & cheque takers, waiters, bill posters, board men etc.'[6] As the total includes the band and backstage and front of house workers, the number of performers engaged at any given time looks modest.

But music-hall bills changed weekly and the turnover of acts was very large – one reason for the continual importation of artists from England and abroad. Tracy Davis's statement regarding the city's actors that 'it is clear that Glasgow's English-born performers were far out of proportion to the English representation in the general population in 1881' may prove an understatement when applied to music-hall performers.[7] It could be that a detailed examination of census returns would reveal the vast majority of performers in the city at any given time to be visiting English professionals.

Support for this view is contained in a letter to the *North British Daily Mail* in 1875.[8] The author, who signs himself 'An Old Professional', writes to protest against 'the morality craze which at present seems to be taking a section of the public by the ears', namely the petition and protest over the perceived flouting of decency at the Whitebait Music Hall (see page 73). After defending standards in Glasgow halls, he goes on to blame recent events on visiting performers (as opposed to local ones), asserting that 'not fifty professionals to the thousand are Scotch men and women. The majority come from a more moral [?] kingdom than puir auld Scotland, although she gets the blame for all done on this side of the Tweed'. The author then provides the following breakdown, by implication a list of performers active in Scotland if

**Table 5.2** Scottish music-hall performers

Present List of Music Hall Artistes, allowing for several hundreds coming and going yearly. These are only recognised professionals. There are perhaps twice as many more not on regular list:—

| | |
|---|---|
| Sentimental Singers – Male and female – one half of which number are now comic and serio-comic | 247 |
| Comics – male | 303 |
| Serio-Comics – female | 273 |
| Negro-Comedians – male and female and companies | 114 |
| Gymnasts – male and female | 136 |
| Dancers – several in each company, such as sisters, &c. | 70 |
| Ballet Troupes – 5 to 20 in each company | 30 |
| Wizards and Ventriloquists | 40 |
| Jugglers – some companies with 2 to 4 members | 25 |
| Dog and Monkey Troupes | 14 |
| Pantomimists – (this is the real pantomimist) | 32 |
| Duettists – 2 to each company | 151 |
| Irish Comic Singers | 34 |
| Each company counted as one, not as individuals. | 1469 |

I am, &e.,

AN OLD PROFESSIONAL

*Source:* 'A Professional on Music Halls', *North British Daily Mail,* 13 March 1875, p. 5.

not Glasgow (see Table 5.2). The list gives a striking impression of the range of different types of act. On examination, its figures and categories closely resemble those contained in the lists of London Music Hall artistes in the annual *Era Almanacks* of the period, and indeed seem likely to have derived from that source, being in all probability based on a totalling up of artists from the categorised lists they provide. But the fact that some of the categories and totals are different, suggesting at least some adjustment, and, above all, are cited in a specifically Scottish context, by a Scottish performer, certainly lends them credibility.[9] If the letter asserts the primacy of English artists, against which Scottish performers were 'less than fifty to a thousand' (i.e. under 5 per cent of the profession), it also acknowledges that twice the number on the 'regular' list were also in constant work.

The most likely explanation is probably that the figures represent the total for the UK profession as a whole, 'active' in the Scottish context to the extent of passing through Glasgow and other Scottish cities in the course of normal circulation. Although not Glasgow-based, their sheer numbers may have constituted a majority of performers in the city at a given time, depending on the time of year. But taking literally the proportion of native Scottish performers as 'less than fifty in a thousand', and applying it to the wider figure of 4,500 fulltime performers (the 'regular' list times two), the total of Scottish music hall turns would amount to some 225 ('acts not performers'). Moreover, both the 'regular' and expanded list are stated as containing fulltime professionals, and would therefore not include the part-time and semiprofessional performers who seem to have been particularly active in Glasgow. In addition, examination of the *Era Almanack*'s listings of acts makes it clear that the actual number of performers was probably substantially higher, given the large number of acts involving multiple performers (of the nearly 100 gymnasts and acrobat acts in the 1875 *Almanack*, about 40 per cent seemed to be family acts, while most of the others were sister or brother combinations). On a rough reckoning, the actual number of acts specified – hypothetically 225 – could probably have been expected to have increased by a factor of three.

Quite where this leaves the composition of the Glasgow community is unclear. Continuing on the hypothetical plane, the above figure, based on the 'Old Professional's 1875 letter, of 225 multiplied by three gives a putative total of 675 full-time Scottish performers, not counting part-timers. Of these, a proportion could be expected to be away working in London or in the north of England at any given time. Others could be expected to be living and working in other Scottish centres, particularly Edinburgh, although it seems fair to assume the largest concentration for the greater Glasgow area, the main population and music-hall centre.

But this remains a hypothetical model. What is perhaps more significant is that the Scottish correspondent, in quoting what were effectively national statistics, illustrates the cosmopolitan outlook of both the industry and individual performers, who on this evidence clearly saw themselves as part of a nationally organised industry.

If this suggests that there is a reasonable case for the existence of a sizeable Scottish music-hall community, and that it seems likely to have centred on Glasgow as its professional base, the disparity between the valuation roll figures for performers, a mere handful, and what we take to be the larger numbers active in the city will not necessarily be clarified by combing the census returns. The problem of performers' seeming invisibility goes beyond this to include two important factors: problems resulting from their mobility and generally ambivalent attitude to declaring their occupation, which may in some cases have been a response to public attitudes towards performers, and the fact that much of their available work was conducted on a seasonal basis.

The first of these problems particularly concerns those semi-professional performers who feature heavily in concert bills at Glasgow halls from the 1890s onwards, who usually fail to register on statistics through their use of their day jobs when citing occupation on official forms. One such was probably Robert Drummond, who often described himself as 'vocalist', although his son's birth certificate of 1905 stated his occupation as 'bread storeman', while the valuation roll for 1911 lists him as 'Comedian'. Norman McLeod similarly gave various occupations, including 'Drayman', on official forms, whilst active performing his strongman act in the Two Normans in the evenings. This trait seems to have extended to related trades. Abraham Jacobs, of 73 Maitland Street, Cowcaddens, is described on the 1881 valuation roll as a 'scenic artist', but on the census of the same year stated his occupation as 'Painter – journeyman house'. In evaluating the reasons for this, it is important to consider the possibility that this may have reflected a wider pattern of short-term working common amongst those in certain trades.

In other areas the problem in tracing locally based as opposed to visiting performers is one of seeming invisibility. Music-hall artists, or for that matter any theatrical occupations at all, are conspicuously absent from listings in Glasgow Post Office directories. On the rare occasions when they can be found, what look suspiciously like music-hall artists are entered under professional categories that have only an oblique relation to their stage profession. In the Post Office directory for 1903–04 'Florence, speciality dancer' is listed as a Teacher of Dancing. Of other entries,

Johnstone, D.B. (Singing), 16 Burnbank Terrace
Johnstone, Miss Janie B. (Singing) (address as above)

sound more like a professional double act than the Teachers of Singing they are listed as, although there is no way of checking this, and the area remains one that is extremely difficult to research.

Moving on to the question of seasonality, it is important to appreciate the extent to which Glasgow's theatrical population fluctuated according to the opportunities for work. During the summer these evidently became scarcer, as halls and theatres closed for the holiday period, and as if this wasn't enough, other competition sometimes intervened to further drive performers out of the city, as the following extract from the *Professional* of July 1888 illustrates;

Business is very flat just now with Professionals. Only one Theatre and one Music Hall working in the great city of Glasgow, consequently there are a deal of artistes 'out of shops'. The whole cry is the Exhibition, this mammoth show is all the rage, besides its many wonders inside, there are plenty of outdoor sports on the grounds, so that the place is visited daily by thousands, and the pile of money taken is something enormous. Rumours went afloat that the Royal Music Hall would be opened shortly but rumour is not always correct. Many professionals are seen parading our Streets in a slow meditating mood, and now and then drink from the fountains on the street, instead of going in for two penny worth. 'The light of other days have faded' sure enough. No doubt some Pro's were fortunate enough to get short engagements in Edinburgh, Leith, and Belfast, while others were content to do a 'turn' in a wooden booth in New City Road.[10]

At the other end of the scale, Christmas pantomimes represented a highpoint of activity. Although most city-centre productions, which utilised huge casts and ran for up to four months, were centred on legitimate theatres rather than music halls (although palaces of varieties increasingly mounted their own pantos from the 1890s onwards), the large numbers of people involved represented a sizeable influx of professional talent, and also drew extensively on the local music-hall community, not least for its star performers. Amongst the English contingent were dancers and Corps de Ballet drafted in from London to augment the local forces, and in Compton Mackenzie's 1912 novel *Carnival* the young heroine Jenny Pearl is sent to appear in a Glasgow panto as part of a child quartet by her dancing school mistress.[11] The following extract from *The Amateur* of 1896 describes the dispersal of a typical Glasgow company, showing how its members were drawn from the parallel worlds of theatre, musical comedy and music hall, and were both local and imported from London for the season:

And so pantomime is practically over at last, and the many people who for nearly three months have contributed to the gaiety of our city are being scattered all over the country. What a flight of the muses! By the closing of 'Sinbad' and 'Alonzo the Brave' over 400 theatrical people have been dispersed. Where do they go? you ask. To find where the mass of them get to would require the organisation of the Census Committee, but in the case of the principals they have usually made their arrangements in advance, and the more talented of them begin touring engagements at once. Miss Loftus and Mr. Sheridan, for instance, will be at the Scotia shortly; Miss Lilian Stanley opens at Burnley in the title-role of 'Little Christopher Columbus', and will be at the Royalty on April 13; Mr. Shand, I believe, goes off on tour with Little Tich; and the Little Billee of the 'Trilby' sketch (Mr. Ross) joins Mr. J. J. Dallas's company. Those who have not booked engagements return as a rule post haste to 'town', and what a place for theatrical people London is at the close of pantomime. There must be thousands of them there waiting for engagements in the spring tours. Nearly every third man you meet in the Strand is an actor, and the agents are thronged with clean-shaven men and golden-haired women seeking places as heavies, low comedians, soubrettes, singing chambermaids, and the like.[12]

In conclusion, several possible models of Glasgow's music-hall community suggest themselves. The first is that, following the implication of the figures suggested by the letter to the *North British Daily Mail*, there could well have been a large resident pool of Scottish or local Glasgow-based performers in the city that is simply not detectable for several reasons. One would be the itinerant nature of theatrical life, which has proved one of the main difficulties in tracing performers. The demands of touring were conducive to regular changes of address, and music hall performers often – in fact mostly – worked under stage names, and had a tendency to freely adapt their occupation when confronted with surveys or officialdom. The semi-professionals or occasional performers discussed in the previous chapter also prove difficult to trace, not least because they usually appeared under their trade or day job in official statistics.

A second possibility might be that the 'resident' body of full-time performers was as small as the valuation roll statistics suggest, and that the great majority of music-hall artists present in the city at any one time were simply passing through to fulfil engagements. In this case the permanent music-hall community would have consisted of a small number of locally based performers, together with impresarios, stage managers and backstage workers employed at the city's halls, and those in related areas such as theatrical landladies and baggage men. This certainly chimes with the constantly shifting nature of the profession, and with the author's view that music-hall performers in the city could be broken down into three distinct groups: visiting artists from the south, including national stars, who generally topped the bills; established Scottish performers, who were full-time and Glasgow-based, and who played an important part in balancing the bill, representing the quality end of the Scottish profession; and lastly, local semi-professionals who appeared as trial turns and on the lower half of music-hall bills but rarely progressed further.

But if the second theory might seem to call into question whether such a thing as a music hall 'community' (in the established, permanent sense) really existed in Glasgow, other factors provide ample evidence of its functioning, at least on the basis of a network or fraternity. Apart from 'pro's associations and charitable and social functions (which will be explored in the next chapter), the sense of a professional community is perhaps most evident in times of loss. The unexpected death of Robert McKean, co-proprietor of the Britannia Music Hall in May 1885, caused 'a great commotion in professional circles'. The progress of the cortège from McKean's house to the Southern Necropolis, where police constables eventually had to close the gates, attracted a large following as well as most of Glasgow's music-hall establishment. Amongst those identified in the press were managers and proprietors of the Gaiety, Scotia, Folly, Whitebait, Alexandria and Britannia music halls, an advertising agent, several musical conductors, the stage manager of the 'Brit' and half a dozen well-known performers. While this sort of turnout could be ascribed to professional respect, the range of those present and general tone of the black-lined report in the *Professional* leave a strong impression of something more personal and of a rare coming together of the local music-hall community.[13]

But perhaps the most persuasive indication of an active and identifiable community lies in the involvement of those performers and musicians who were indisputably locally based in a wide range of different sorts of professional activity. An important theme to emerge from research into performers' lives in the period between the 1890s and the First World War is how small a pond Glasgow was, theatrically and musically speaking, and how interdependent the various performing milieux were, no matter how different their social connotations with the public. A case in point would be that of Matthew Young Kay (b. 1876), who came from a family of musicians based in Hyndland in the West End of Glasgow. Together with his father and brothers, Kay appeared in the Kay family string and wind ensemble in the 1890s, playing arrangements of overtures and light classical repertoire at formal functions and dinners. One such was a Glasgow Corporation Tramways Department Social Gathering at City Hall in 1900, where, with a Provost and two Bailies present, they formed part of a programme that also included concert recitalists and the music-hall stars W. F. Frame and J. B. Preston (who sang 'She couldna Eat a Tairt'). Walter Freer, the manager of the Glasgow Corporation concerts, was a friend of the family, which also played at Good Templars' events, and Matthew Kay later went on to play in concerts at the St Andrews Hall. By the 1920s the Kay family orchestra, now offering either a string orchestra or dance band, had become popular for dances and hunt balls at venues throughout Scotland, regularly including Balmoral. But the family's wider contacts reveal the web of inter-relations, professional and social, that characterised Glasgow's entertainment sub-culture. Matthew Young Kay's wife was a granddaughter of Mrs Baylis of the Scotia Music Hall, and was born over the theatre, in a room overlooking Goosedubs. The couple may well have met whilst Kay was playing in the pit band at the Scotia, and he himself subsequently became music director at the Olympia, Bridgeton Cross, for a period in 1914. Moreover, when Kay took his family on their annual summer holiday to Largs he would renew his acquaintance with his friend Alvin Sawyer, who ran the summer entertainers party at Broomfields. And while his brother-in-law was Thomas Colquhoun, Mrs Baylis's nephew who managed several music halls before going bankrupt in the mid-1900s, the Kays also had other cousins who married into the Hunter family, longstanding employees of Hengler's Circus in Sauchiehall Street. The impression that emerges is of a jobbing musician working at all levels; on the concert platform or at dances or functions, as well as playing in pit bands and conducting at music halls when opportunities arose whilst also retaining contacts with most other types of professional musical activity. The other element that makes Matthew Young Kay's case representative is that, like many musicians, his playing often only supported him on a part-time basis, and at various periods he worked in a piano salesroom.[14]

While Kay's example was that of a local freelance musician, music-hall performers and backstage workers demonstrated similar interdependence and versatility when it came to seizing whatever employment opportunities were going when times were hard. So just as Mrs McKean, widow of the Britannia proprietor, took to advertising for theatrical lodgers to make ends meet after her husband's death in 1885, so Arthur Lloyd's father, H. K. Lloyd, a famous Glasgow actor and comedian in his day, worked as his son's stage manager in his old age in the early 1880s. And local baggage men, whose normal job was to haul 'pro's' theatrical trunks between the railway stations and the music hall they were playing, could find themselves called on to carry a spear, if the gleeful sighting of two of them in an 'Indian Ballet' at the Scotia in 1887 (as 'a pair of "Capital Kaffirs"') was anything to go by.[15] All were, like Kay, part of an informal network of contacts and acquaintances that would also have embraced most visiting performers. While this network was not exclusive to music hall or variety, it did form part of a localised professional theatre sub-culture, in which music hall was one of the largest sources of employment and into which visiting music-hall artists fitted as if by right.

Perhaps in this light the question of a Glasgow community should not be taken literally as denoting permanence (music hall 'pro's after all spent their life on the move) but interpreted more flexibly as embracing the shifting but usually sizeable pool of performers to be found in the city at most times of the year. In this sense, whatever its numerical size, the 'community' resided in music hall's professional culture and institutions, aspects to be explored in the next chapter.

## Notes

1  W. Macqueen-Pope, *Marie Lloyd, Queen of the Music Halls* (London, Oldbourne, 1954), p. 17.

2  George Mozart, *Limelight* (London, Hurst & Blackett, 1938), pp. 79–80.

3  Davis, *Actresses as Working Women.*

4  See Frame, *Tells His Own Story*, and James Houston, *Autobiography of Mr. James Houston, Scotch Comedian* (Glasgow and Edinburgh, Menzies and Lowe, 1889).

5  See Appendix, Table A1 for full figures; but generally the number of Glasgow music halls fluctuated between 4 and 5 in the 1870s, rising to 8 in 1876, but declined to 3 in the early 1890s, before sharply rising in the early 1900s to 5 in 1903, 8 in 1904, 11 in 1910, and 18 by 1914.

6  Letter from Harry Harcourt to Capt. McCall, 3 March 1875; GCA SR22/62/1.

7  Davis, *Actresses as Working Women*, p. 45.

8  *North British Daily Mail*, 13 March 1875.

9  See *Era Almanack* 1874; See also Rutherford, '"Managers in a small way"', p. 100, where she quotes the 1872 *Almanack* total as 1,416, very close to the *North British Daily Mail* total of 1,459.

10  'Music Hall Gossip', *The Professional and Authors' Journal*, No. 156 (July 1888), p. 8.

11  Compton Mackenzie, *Carnival* (London, Macdonald, 1951 [1912]), pp. 94–101.

12  'Theatrical and Musical Notes of the Month', *The Amateur and Singer's Journal*, 322:28 (March 1896), p. 8.

13  'Death and Funeral of Mr R. McKean', *The Professional and Authors' Journal*, No. 19 (16 May 1885), p. 4.

14  Information kindly supplied by Mrs Greta Eves, daughter of Matthew Young Kay and great-grandaughter of Mrs Baylis.

15  For Mrs McKean see 'Professional Apartments', *Professional*, May 1885 onwards; for H. K. Lloyd see Arthur Lloyd's Shakespeare Music Hall programme, undated (c.1881), MLGC; for baggage men see 'Notes by Roving Jack', *Professional*, 12 February 1887, MLGC.

# 6

# Performers III: 'Deceitful Minnie Reeve' – respectability and the profession

This chapter will examine Scottish performers' working culture, and in particular the notion of a music-hall 'profession' that emerged in the 1880s and 1890s, assessing whether it contributed to an improvement in the social acceptance of music hall as an entertainment form.

The chapter will first examine popular perceptions of music hall, with reference to public attitudes towards the artists themselves, before going on to examine performers' own self-identity and aspirations as embodied in the new culture.

Whether the new emphasis put on the respectability of the profession from the 1880s onwards succeeded in improving the public perceptions of music hall is difficult to judge. Certainly a marked improvement in attitudes did occur between the 1850s and the 1880s, but this seems more likely to have resulted from the general increase in popular entertainment that took place over the same period, which brought with it a softening of certain moral attitudes towards leisure and enjoyment. In his autobiography (published in 1889) veteran James Houston wrote of his upbringing in New Cumnock in the 1840s that

> When the name of theatre was mentioned in our house, you would really believe you smelt brimstone; there was such a strong prejudice at that time against play-acting, as it was called then. Not many years ago – it was considered suspicious, to say the least of it – for a young lady or gentleman to assist at a concert, and as for the theatre, that was hopeless. But all that is changed now, as I have occasion to say in the character of Dumbiedykes; 'I hate playhouses, for I was never in one in a' my life;' my father never was in a theatre in his life, hence, like many others, his bias against such places. But now, on my concert tours, we have the minister in the chair, his daughter accompanying the singers on the pianoforte, the doctor's daughter playing a solo on the violin, and three of the choir dressed in character singing, 'Willie brew'd a peck o' maut,' and not a creature can see any harm in it.[1]

As Houston suggests in discussing his father, not the least part of this transformation in social attitudes was the increase in opportunities to see and judge for oneself. This explanation, that as theatre and entertainment became more widely acceptable socially so did its practitioners, seems credible in the broad sense. Perhaps as significant was the fact that disapproving commentators were, by the 1880s, prepared to meet the profession half way by admitting that shortcomings in music hall as an entertainment were as much the fault of the public as the performers. As early as 1873 a 'Men You Know' profile of David Brown, one of the fathers of music hall in Glasgow, justified his elevation to its pages by explaining away the past excesses of his establishment in the following terms: 'It is not his fault that music of a higher class than the ordinary standard is not given at his house, but the fault of the public, who will not come to listen to anything better than he is compelled to by their want of appreciation.'[2] The profile went on to suggest that Brown's efforts to provide a better quality of entertainment caused him to go bankrupt when the public failed to support his initiative. Whether or not this was strictly true, Brown was at least given credit for trying to improve the tone of the entertainment. Not everyone went that far. A variation on the same case was put, less charitably, in an *Evening News* article of April 1887, which, estimating the weekly audience at Glasgow music halls at 40,000 people, no doubt summarised a popular view in stating that

> The music hall has too great an influence with a large portion of the public to be ignored. The best thing to do, then, is to recognise it, and to endeavour to elevate the moral tone of its patrons. When the morality of those who frequent the music halls is raised to a higher standard, rest assured the management and artistes will follow. It is bread and butter with them to keep pace with their audiences.[3]

Most damning here was the presumption that artists' moral degeneracy could be taken as read, and that the music-hall fraternity consequently would have no interest in improving the quality of the entertainment beyond pursuit of profits.

In this it was echoing the demonising tendencies of crusaders against music halls of the 1870s, one of whom had written that 'one's blood runs cold to think that there are men and women in our midst who can pander to the vile tastes of those who frequent such places'.[4] The 1887 article, which had earlier acknowledged that some improvement, in the form of 'a refinement of the entertainment' had taken place, then went on to attack standards of performance, the vulgarity and suggestiveness of much of the material, and the complete banality of the entertainment as a whole, concluding that 'to the majority of music-hall artistes wit is a sort of undiscovered country'.[5] Although its charges were bitterly refuted, particularly in respect to both audience and performers' tolerance of double entendres, this critique was to retain its potency until well after the First World War. Most galling of all, given performers' striving to be considered members of a legitimate profession, was its condescension in abnegating them from their social responsibilities as citizens by dint of their being morally corrupted due to their occupation.

Social attitudes towards performers seem to have remained polarised in this way between the 1880s and the 1900s. As variety became increasingly popular around the turn of the century so performers had, as a matter of convention, to be accorded recognition as a trade of sorts. But there remained clear limits to this social acceptance, and a diminishing but vocal minority of Scottish opinion, heavily influenced by Presbyterian teachings, continued to insist that music-hall performers, if not now accepted as the cause of the audience's moral 'fall', nevertheless remained a symptom of it. As late as 1909 a correspondent to the *Glasgow Herald* was berating music hall, and by inference its practitioners, for ridiculing the ministry and being places where 'young men and girls … come into contact with drinking and smoking, and also with members of the "demi-monde"'.[6]

Part of the problem was that artists' appearances and lifestyles tended to reinforce public stereotypes of performers as 'fast'. Offstage, music-hall artists of the 1880s and 1890s dressed in an exuberant, extrovert style that made them instantly recognisable. A sketch evoking the panoply of street life in Glasgow's Sauchiehall Street in the early 1890s described how

> The daytime is when the actor-folk come out for an airing, and many are the heads that are turned to look after Lily Pompom, the well-known burlesque actress, who passes dressed in the very height of fashion – high heels, high sleeves, and high hat – arm in arm with Paul Patterer, the funny comedian.[7]

Fashions spread by touring professionals included hats 'with the dinge-in down the centre of them', after the American fashion of the time, and in particular fur, which was so popular with performers at one point that 'many of them considered they could not be artistes without wearing fur on their collars and cuff'.[8] Harry Lauder, when starting out on his career, was so impressed by a visiting English professional's Astrakhan coat that the next day he bought a strip of fur and had it sewn on to his own collar.

The voluptuary associations of such extravagance were not lost on wider society. The point that performers went promenading in their finery during the daytime because they worked at night might have counted for more with the 'Unco'guid' had their dress been more restrained or less ostentatious. As it was, performers' flamboyant appearance – which in the case of touring 'pro's could be decidedly metropolitan and foppish – offended on several counts. In a society that promulgated the importance of the work ethic, and espoused the virtues of understatement and personal modesty (especially in the social context of not 'getting above' oneself, or of 'knowing one's place'), such conspicuous display by people who seemed to have nothing to do all day but stroll around and meet friends in bars inevitably registered as dissolute. Moreover, it was seen as setting a bad example to the clerks and shop workers who reflected performers' celebrity by copying their fashions and affectations. The sort of corrupting influence middle-class moralists had in mind was described by the Paisley-born poet John Davidson (1857–1909) in his poem 'In a Music-Hall' (1891). Drawing on Davidson's own experience of giving up his teaching position for a clerical job in a thread mill, it opens

> In Glasgow in 'Eighty-four,
> I worked as a junior clerk;
> My Masters I never could please,
> But they tried me a while at the desk.

When disaffection sets in ('Nothing could please me at night / No novels, no poems, no plays') the young man's resort is predictable:

> I did as my desk-fellows did;
> With a pipe and a tankard of beer,
> In a music-hall, rancid and hot,
> I lost my soul night after night.[9]

When the poem describes the six 'artists' the author gets to know in the bar, they include a former governess turned singer, an ageing chorine who is clearly available for casual prostitution, and an erotic dancer, confirming the impression of music hall as an irredeemably dissolute form.

If performers' public dress and behaviour hinted at degeneracy, their social and private lives were also the subject of intense public speculation, the most harmful of which concerned drinking and loose morality. In the case of alcohol, by the 1890s, despite the reform of music hall presentation, and the presence of performers with Temperance affiliations (such as W. F. Frame), drinking continued to play a prominent role in backstage culture. 'Pro's were a gregarious and sociable group for whom bars were a natural rendezvous or 'office' for meeting and gossiping with colleagues. Doubtless as a result, a number bought into licensed premises on their retirement, W. H. Lannagan becoming landlord of the Rising Sun at Bridge-of-Allan, while in Glasgow the former Acting

Manager of the Scotia Music Hall, Ritchie Thom, ran a popular theatrical bar in the late 1890s, as did the comic Jock Mills between the wars.[10] Not surprisingly, the pressures of performing, combined with the disruptive effects of touring life, which left large expanses of free time in the middle of the day, seem likely to have resulted in considerable alcoholism amongst Scottish performers. There is little direct evidence to support this, as professional journals' obituaries generally cite only primary causes of death, and in any case would not have been able to discuss drinking in a public forum. However, the few examples that we do have of well-known individuals with drink problems, together with what seems, in the mid-1880s, to have been a very high incidence of deaths of leading artists in their late thirties or early forties, suggests that this may have been a major problem affecting performers. Of those artists mentioned in chapter 4, W. H. Lannagan died at 39, Tom McAusland in his 40s, J. C. Macdonald at 42, the songwriter William Preston at 34, and Tommy Lorne at 45; all died of unattributed natural causes, with the exception of Macdonald, who death was stated as being caused by 'an affliction of the heart'. Lorne was known to have had a problem with alcoholism. The Scotch comic Jack Lorimer, the father of Max Wall, who billed himself as 'The Heilan' Laddie', died of TB at the age of 37, weakened by years of excessive drinking.[11] In parenthesis, it should be pointed out that a number of leading stars, including probably the two greatest, Marie Lloyd and Dan Leno, also died early deaths due to stress brought on by years of overwork; Marie Lloyd, prematurely aged at 52, and Leno at 44 following a mental breakdown.

In the end it did not make much difference whether artists actually drank or not; from the public's point of view their social milieu was so steeped in the principle of hearty conviviality, and so suffused with the culture of drinks and spirits, as to make refutation of the charge not only impossible but pointless.

The same might have been said of the assumption that performers enjoyed libidinous sexual existences beyond the bounds of normal experience. To the music hall public the proof of this was all around them, no matter what performers themselves claimed. Almost alone at the time, music hall offered a representation of female sexuality as 'active', in the form of women stars knowingly discoursing with the audience on two levels (by use of innuendo and double entendres) whilst retaining an outwardly demure exterior. One result of women initiating a sexual dialogue in this way seems to have been the liberating effect it had on the women in the audience. J. B. Priestley, who went to music halls in the north of England as a young man, commented of the songs used in these 'naughty but nice' acts that 'Freud could have revealed their symbolism and significance in under two minutes. The women in the audience were quicker than that: they always laughed first – and louder.'[12] Moreover, the appearance of female acrobats and dancers in what were considered states of semi-nudity carried an enormous erotic charge for male members of the audience. The introduction of further twists in the form of gender-swapping and cross-dressing, also much practised by female artists, evidently added to the sexual turbulence. The rather breathless tone of a Glasgow police Superintendent's report from 1875 describing 'The Two Sisters Ridgeway', observed on stage at the Whitebait music hall, gives a vivid impression of the frisson created by such performances. The sisters' act consisted of

> going through a variation of tomfoolery, by taking hold of each other, throwing up their legs towards the roof of the Hall and dancing something in the 'Can-Can' style. The one represents a male and the other a female. The male named Rose & the female Helen both residing in lodgings with their mother at 7 Park Place, Stockwell Street.

Their costumes, described in detail, gave further grounds for concern;

> Rose wears a dress which consists of a flashy blue silk body with light trimmings & akin tights disclosing the form of her legs and thighs up to her hips, in fact, the skirt scarcely comes down to the private parts but is quite modest so far as the upper part of the body is concerned. She appears to be a model in figure & in her performance she throws up her legs in such a manner as to cause an impression on the minds of her audience that it is done for the purpose of showing off her figure to the best possible advantage, & gains great applause. In my opinion her conduct is very unbecoming to her sex.[13]

This account is valuable not only for its detail and generally objective tone, but also for setting out clearly the grounds on which elements of the performance were found offensive. Immediately striking is that the initial mention of male and female roleplaying is followed by a note of the sisters' joint address, suggesting either that the women seemed rather young to be performing (in which case one would have expected a more explicit reference), or sought-for confirmation that, given the sexual overtones of the act, their relationship was what it seemed. More significantly, the Superintendent's conclusion in finding the performance offensive was not based solely on its content, but also on his assessment that its intention – embodied in both the costumes and choreography – had been to shock or gratify the audience. In other words, the act deliberately set out to provoke. This objection, far from the knee-jerk response of religious critics, comes very close to the criteria regarding stage indecency applied today, which are closely related to issues of artistic integrity and intentions.

This allegation – that performers (and especially women ones) knew exactly where the line of public decency was drawn at any given time, and continually flouted it for commercial gain – lay at the root of longstanding disparagement of artistes' morality. After all, music-hall performers were not actors; although they often delivered songs in character, both the characterisation and material were unique to and emanated from the performer, who appeared as his or herself. It was therefore perfectly understandable that the public should assume that any risqué or licentious material featured reflected performers' own sexual permissiveness. The implication of this was disastrous for performers' aspirations to acquire a greater degree of acceptance by sections of society that had previously remained closed to them. The attitude of the public, who enjoyed such material hugely, seems nevertheless to have hovered between condemnation and fascination.

The principal victims of this sort of stereotyping were female performers. Ironically music hall songs themselves often promoted the image of women the-atricals as oversexed and duplicitous. One such song, 'The Serio Comic-Singer', which appears in a Glasgow-published songsheet that probably dates from the 1880s, describes how a young man meets a girl 'while dancing at a ball'. She demurely gives her name as Mary Jane and says that she is a milliner, but when she proves to be unknown at her address, the young man wanders into a nearby concert hall:

> When I saw my love upon the stage,
> My eyes would scarce believe,
> I read the bills and there I found
> Her name was Minnie Reeve!

The story's reaches its denouement in the final verse;

> I felt so much enraged,
> To think I'd been a fool
> So I rushed behind, and asked her
> How could she be so cruel.
> She only laughed and said to me,
> Please make no fuss at all,
> For I'm married to a fiddler
> Of a Popular Concert Hall.[14]

This image of the crystalline stage beauty as hard-hearted and adulterous proved remarkably resilient. Chorines or dancers were popularly characterised as being at best more worldly than was proper, and at worst sexually available. A long-running series of humorous pen-and-ink sketches published in the Glasgow-published *Quiz* of the late 1890s depicts backstage encounters

## QUIZ

A DISAPPOINTMENT.

CALL BOY.—" Gent. wishes to see you, Miss."
EXTRA GIRL.—Ask him to come straight up here."
CALL BOY.—" I think it's your husband, Miss."
EXTRA GIRL.—" Tell him I'll see him in the bar after the show."

**19**    *Quiz,* 3 February 1898

between chorus girls and 'stage door Johnnies'. Although the dinner-jacketed roués, nearly always older men, are often the butt of the joke, the girls, usually scantily clad 'dumb blondes', are always shown as promiscuous and venal. The following dialogue caption from 1898 is typical of the series. A showgirl powdering herself at her mirror in her dressing room: a knock on the door;

> CALL BOY.—"Gent. wishes to see you, Miss."
> EXTRA GIRL.—Ask him to come straight up here."
> CALL BOY.—"I think it's your husband, Miss."
> EXTRA GIRL.—"Tell him I'll see him in the bar after the show."[15]

Innocuous enough on their own terms, these caricatures convey the received view of variety performers 'at it' in the dressing room.

It is important to qualify some of the generalisations made with respect to part-time performers. Regarding suggestions in chapter 4 that a sizeable proportion of Glasgow's resident performers may have been part-time or semi-professional, it seem likely that this group were exempted from the generalised prejudices that applied to touring 'pro's. After all, the part-timers dressed conventionally after the fashion of their daytime trade, conformed to established social mores, and as known personalities in the community were presumably considered perfectly ordinary citizens. Semi-'pro's such as Norman McLeod were members of the Orange Order, and other resident music-hall performers and backstage workers were active in Masonic orders in Glasgow, albeit as members of separate theatrical lodges.[16]

Having discussed those aspects of music-hall culture that most lent themselves to misrepresentation by moral arbiters – namely performers' dress, drinking and perceived loose morality – we shall now move on to examine the means by which, from the 1880s onwards, the profession attempted to improve its public image.

As has been indicated in chapter 5, by the mid-1880s the music-hall community in Glasgow had developed a strong collective sense of professional identity. This was reflected in the use of the terms 'artiste' and 'professional' (shortened to 'pro'), and by a new assertiveness on the part of performers over issues of professional stature and rights. This new consciousness was most evident in columns such as the *Professional*'s Roving Jack, which combined trade gossip with what seems to have constituted editorial comment, and manifested itself in various ways. Performers' professional status was fiercely upheld, not only in matters of form, such as decrying the practice of 'pro's having to share dressing rooms with amateurs ('a very bad arrangement [that] exists during the festive season at several of the Glasgow Music Halls'[17]), but also by stressing performers' own obligation to conduct themselves in a fitting manner. The following censure of W. H. Vane, 'The Banjo King', was no less effective for its moderate tone. Vane having been

the means of upsetting the programme on Monday, he made a speech in which he referred to his small position on the Bill, and threw out some nasty hints regarding other parties engaged at the establishment; now this is entirely out of place, for if performers have any difference with one-another privately, they should not *cry* before an audience in order to gain sympathy. The Public have nothing at all to do with these matters.[18]

The deeper message here, nothing to do with sparing the audience's embarrassment, was that if performers wanted to be taken seriously as a professional group, then they had to learn to act like one by behaving responsibly. As with other professions, the rule was never to act in such a way as to compromise one's colleagues or the reputation of the professional body as a whole in the eyes of the public. The artiste in this case probably knew this but let his pique get the better of him, providing grounds for a ticking off for himself and the pretext for a warning to others.

Also singled out for disapprobation were performers who sought to undercut their rivals, such as 'a certain Scotch Comic located in Glasgow' who had been 'offering the services of himself and those that he is in league with at ridiculously low terms for concerts', which was objected to as 'very unfair, as it don't give other artistes a chance to get a decent price'.[19]

If the above were examples of misconduct or sharp practice, trade papers were equally quick to expose more serious offences, such as instances of performers fraudulently working under stage names made popular by other artists, usually while the original parties were operating in another part of the country, to the detriment of the originals' good name and reputation. Injured parties in such cases sometimes had recourse to law, as was demonstrated by a report from 1887, in which it was found that the accused artists,

> known as the 'Merry Macs' (Maccabe and Macnally) had made an infringement by using the names of the 'Two Macs' (Mike and Joe). The presiding judge put in an injunction against the first named two copying the other parties names.[20]

Most seriously regarded of all seems to have been the stealing of other performers' songs, particularly where their authorship was falsely claimed. Many artistes' livelihoods rested to a large extent on the effectiveness of their material, particularly their comic songs and monologues, much of which was often unique to them, having been either written by themselves or commissioned from a professional songwriter. The cribbing of bits and pieces of patter from other acts had long been a contested feature of stage life, and there already existed a process of sorts whereby successful songs and monologues soon entered the public domain through publication in trade journals or songbooks. But falsely claiming authorship of songs by fellow professionals was regarded in music-hall circles as a particularly heinous offence, and one which exercised the aggrieved songwriters even more than the performers concerned. By the 1880s these cases, where found, were being given considerable coverage by trade papers, in an effort to maximise exposure of the perpetrators of such frauds.

One such case involved the appearance at Moss's Varieties, Edinburgh in June 1891 of one Arthur Hillcoat, billed as 'the famous Scotch comedian and author of all Bessie Arthur's songs'. Bessie Arthur being a successful male impersonator with a large repertoire of popular songs, this blanket claim to their authorship, apparently untrue, was hugely provocative. The *Professional*, owned by the Glasgow music publishers Barrs, immediately denounced Hillcoat as a char-latan, stating in reply to an indignant correspondent that 'This adventurer's name is Adam McDade, a tinsmith or Tinker by trade. He went under the alias of Adam Arthur for a long time, but has changed his alias to Arthur Hillcoat.'[21] Completely refuting his claims to authorship, it went on to supply the real provenance of sixteen or so of the songs in question, many of which, by Glasgow authors such as McAusland, Melville and the deceased Pettigrew, had been published in its own pages. Following an 'unrehearsed scene' in the hall on the first night of Hillcoat/Arthur/McDade's appearance, the management moved his act to last, no doubt in an attempt at damage limitation. The letters pages of subsequent issues were given over to condemnatory outpourings from the offended parties, several of which expressed views similar to an anonymous writer who stated that 'I hope there won't be a singer of the name of Hillcoat appear at Moss' for a long time, as it might be dangerous for his person, and it would be a pity to see another man suffer for what he knew nothing about'.[22] A copy of the notorious Bill was framed and put on display in the *Professional*'s offices. What impresses about the episode was both the depth of feeling it aroused (amongst the lowest-paid sector of the music-hall business) and the fact that the management, recognising their error, immediately backed down in the face of overwhelming pressure from the professional community.

As the above incident suggests, this emphasis on professional standards and rights was not restricted to performers. Managers suspected of shortchanging performers or (even worse) the public by misrepresentation or low professional standards could equally find themselves the subject of acerbic comment. D. S. McKay, manager of the Gaiety and Star Music Hall in the mid-1880s, was the butt of a long-running campaign in the *Professional*, apparently on the basis of what were perceived as his shoddy work practices. Some of their specific com-plaints surface in the following piece of invective provoked by McKay's announcement of a benefit performance, the proceeds of which were to go to himself. With heavy irony the *Professional* enquired

What in the name of common sense does he want with a Benefit? Has not every-thing been done for his Benefit? Workmen have been cut down in their wages. Artistes have been engaged at the cheapest terms procurable, and even subjected to all sorts of fines for his Benefit. Has not his halls been closed at the holidays for his Benefit, and to the disadvantage of his staff. Has he not added a rule that Pro's pay their own cab fare, for his Benefit, and now he wants to crown it with a special night at both Halls, for his Benefit! Oh, self! self! When will it end?[23]

If such withering public criticism of managers reflected performers' new awareness that, as professionals, they were entitled to fair treatment, we should not confuse their assertiveness for militancy. Despite the suggestion of exploitative practices contained in the grievances listed above, these criticisms were offered strictly on the grounds of preventing debasement of professional standards. As such they were simply an extension of plain speaking, in which natural justice demanded that individual managers should be called to account for their conduct, just as performers were, for the greater good of the profession as a whole. The only hints of an emergent political consciousness are to be found in odd snippets and asides contained in trade columns, generally on the subject of managers' love of profit. Typical was Roving Jack's wry observation that although pro's engaged at Glasgow Music Halls for the holiday period (Christmas) would not be sorry to see the end of it, 'proprietors could stand holidays to last the whole year round, *if the money kept coming in all along the same*'.[24] Even by the 1900s there is no evidence that Glasgow artists possessed the will to organise or take collective action demonstrated by London 'pro's in the London Music Hall strike of 1907, although the causes of that dispute admittedly involved working conditions unique to the capital.

In upholding professional standards so assiduously the trade press was merely reflecting performers' desire to improve the social status of their occupation. This was partly born out of a recognition of the growing commercial success of variety, perceived as resulting from its improved public image. Just as managers regarded their presentations as worthy of respectable attention, so performers claimed the right to be recognised as members of a legitimate profession.

As part of this process social occasions acquired a new formality and structure. Mirroring the practices of other trades and professions, commemorative ceremonies and presentations, involving speeches followed by votes of thanks, became regular features of back-stage life and were much reported. Typical was the presentation made to Charles McConnell at the Scotia Music Hall on 3 August 1889:

> on the conclusion of the McConnell family entertainment, Mrs J. S. Baylis, the popular proprietrix, presented Mr Charles McConnell jun., with a gold-mounted umbrella, in recognition of his abilities as an artiste, and also on his coming of age that day.[25]

On other occasions well-known performers and music-hall managers were honoured by businessmen in related trades, such as 'Bob' Stoddart, manager of the Era Vaults, and 'the pro's well-known friend', who

> presented Mr W. H. Howard (manager Gaiety Theatre) with a splendid cigarette case and travellers companion; also J. C. McDonald, the Scottish Chevalier, with a traveller's companion. The following gentlemen were also recipients of suitable presents:– 'Bob' Singleton (musical director, Scotia), 'Tom' Bears (stage manager, Scotia), Edgar Thorpe (musical director, Gaiety). Marcus Boyle (comedian), Mr. Watson (of Tableaux Vivants fame).[26]

If occasions like that above seem almost Rotarian in character, merely pretexts for mutual admiration, it is important to realise that such tokens of esteem by their peers were taken very seriously by performers, whose autobiographies are littered with references to presentations of citations and trophies. The formal correctness of the reporting of these events was also significant, inviting as it did comparison with similar proceedings held by more established bodies, although in truth the tone was petty bourgeois, more that of a guild or skilled trade than a profession. By 1914 the Glasgow Panopticon proprietor A. E. Pickard was investing his birthday party with as much pomp and aggrandisement as the occasion could take:

> On Sunday Evening last Mr A. E. Pickard, the well known City Entertainer, held a big birthday celebration at his popular theatre in the Trongate, when the staffs of his various music-halls along with a number of the leading managers and members of the profession met to do honour to mine host. Prince Bendon, ventriloquist, an old friend of Mr. Pickard's, presided, and a capital chairman he made, keeping the audience in good humour all evening. Among many tokens of esteem special mention should be made of the handsome dressing case from the managers of the halls of the circuit, and a fine inlaid writing bureau from the associated staffs.[27]

Organised social activities involving artists' and backstage workers' families, another aspect of the trappings of a profession, also became more sophisticated. The range of events held in Glasgow included dances and balls, charity functions and various sports days, although the fact that they were mostly organised on an ad hoc basis made for variable results. The Professional Ball held at the Grand National Halls, Main Street, Gorbals on 28 April 1887 (music supplied by the 'Royal' band) was not well attended by 'pro's, although 'those present made the best of it, and thoroughly enjoyed themselves'. In comparison, the Scotia Cup, run as part of the Glasgow Regatta of the same year, was a much livelier event. The *Professional*'s correspondent found 'a good sprinkling of "pro's" amongst the crowd', and later remarked 'I also noticed C. R. Armstrong the song-writer flying past on the Referee's Machine'. The starter for the race was Mr. J. Taylor, 'a successful local comic vocalist and author', and the trophy was presented by the Scotia's stage manager, Willie Kinnaird, while 'the working of the entire day's proceedings reflect great credit on the working committee'.[28]

Charitable events similarly allowed music-hall stars to lend their celebrity to good causes. As with many aspects of professional culture covered in this chapter, the nature and character of artists' involvement in such events, once established in the 1870s and 1880s, remained virtually unchanged up to the First World War. A 1917 report in the *Glasgow Programme* entitled 'Theatrical Profession assist Red Cross', stated that

> Members of the theatrical profession lent assistance for the Glasgow Wholesale Meat Trades' Flag Day and Pageant last week. Mr Wilkie Bard, Mr Seymour Hicks and Private Christian Grant (Mr. Grant was formerly manager at the Grand Theatre) were judges for the tableaux, which were provided by the Empire, Coliseum, Princess's, Pavilion, Royal and Alhambra and Royal Theatres, Hengler's and Empress Playhouse. Miss Marie Loftus acted as judge of costumes, and gave the kick off in the football tournament at Ibrox. The Misses Elliott Savonas took a collection on the stand at Ibrox.[29]

If such events were part of the public relations 'face' of variety, the profession's involvement in charitable subscriptions for sick or elderly performers who were unable to work showed the music-hall community at its most cohesive, looking after its own. Such initiatives were usually begun by friends of the stricken individual, but attracted widespread support, including that of well-known stars. Appeals were often publicised through items in trade journals such as the following from March 1887:

> I SEE that Mr. George Ripon with his usual generosity has started a subscription on behalf of Arthur Young who is at present lying helpless in a Glasgow Hospital. This is a very deserving case, as Young has completely lost the sight of one of his eyes, and the other is nearly gone. As he has a wife and two young children dependent upon him Ripon will thankfully receive any subscriptions that may be sent in on his behalf to 116 Kennington Road, Lambeth, London.[30]

That Ripon, a rising star in great demand, should have gone to the trouble of organising help for an older Glasgow performer, presumably a colleague or mentor, and from London, says a great deal about the way stars remained an integral part of music-hall society. Such practical support for colleagues who had fallen on hard times signified a profession that knew the value of self-help. Furthermore, collective assistance of this kind was not restricted to performers but could be extended to others in the music-hall community. When Michael

Lovelle, a much-liked Glasgow baggage man, was taken ill for an extended period early in 1887 Willie Kinnaird, the aforementioned stage manager, started a subscription on his behalf, to which the *Professional* added that, in its opinion, 'a general subscription through the halls would be the proper thing for a case of this kind'.[31]

This collective willingness to contribute to colleagues' financial support is among the most compelling evidence of Glasgow music-hall performers and workers functioning as a genuine community, although no doubt part of the impetus for such participation came from individuals' dread of similar misfortune occurring to themselves. Seen in this light, every appearance at a colleague's benefit was a downpayment on one's own future support should disaster strike. Fear of illness and destitution clearly haunted many. In his autobiography, Harry Lauder revealed that he had 'seen so many "stars" in an improvident and always uncertain profession come to financial grief' that he was determined to secure his own independence: 'There were to be no "charity benefits" for Harry Lauder!'.[32] In the event, a formal organisation to help performers was established in 1895, when W. F. Frame started a Benevolent Fund in his name, with a rest home in Eaglesham, which formed the basis for the current Scottish Showbusiness Benevolent Fund. Interestingly, this initiative markedly preceded that of the English profession, whose home for retired artists, Brinsworth House in Twickenham, did not open until 1911.

The features of performers' working practices from the mid-1880s outlined so far – more disciplined conduct on stage, a more assertive approach to performers' rights over material, greater readiness to tackle managers over unjust practices, and a new general awareness of the importance of cultivating a positive image with the public – all reflected a widespread desire to improve the professional status of music-hall performers in the public eye. If some aspects were the result of intensive promotion by the editorial 'voices' of trade papers, who doubtless chose to present a selective, rather idealised model of the way artists should conduct their professional lives, rather than reflect older mores or attitudes that they considered unhelpful, then there is no reason to suppose that these journals did not reflect the progressive aspirations of the majority. What is impressive is that these journals correctly identified the importance of building the new professional culture from the inside out, by encouraging performers' self-esteem and sense of professional worth, and convincing them that the scrupulousness of their conduct towards one another and in respect of managements was, in the long term, just as important as the more obvious attention given to issues of public propriety.

In conclusion, if performers did not succeed to any marked degree in convincing a sceptical public of the reformed nature of the profession, it is probably because the artists equated respectability with the trappings of a professional body or trade association, with all its decorum and institutions, while the public's misgivings about artists involved basic issues of morality. (The fact that the audience's own double standard was a crucial factor in the continued success of variety, where propriety was all but titillation was never far from the surface, is another part of the equation.)

A second observation is that attempts made in the 1890s to develop institutions and activities that reflected the profession's new maturity – charitable work, benevolent funds, balls and social activities – only served to further emphasise that part of the professional body served a different constituency, one that enjoyed alcohol and a more robust brand of music-hall entertainment. Charles Coburn, famous as The Man Who Broke the Bank at Monte Carlo, may have been a leading figure in professional organisations like the Music Hall Artists Association, but that didn't prevent him being given the bird at the notoriously rough Paisley Empire, where 'it was quite common to see the stars throwing up their engagements at the end of the first house on a Monday night', and where Coburn 'couldn't be heard at all'.[33] These cheaper halls may have only been a rump, but they were also the lowest common denominator, and gave the lie to the wider profession's protestations of moral unimpeachibility. Moreover, links between alcohol and the mainstream profession were still very evident through endorsements and association. In 1900 advertisements for the Comedy Bar, owned by Richie Thom, the popular former Acting Manager of the Scotia, also proclaimed him as the Glasgow agent of the MHARA (the Music Hall Artists Railway Association). Similarly, programme advertisements for Hillcoat & Sons Britannia Vaults ('The Resort of Professionals'), situated directly next door to the hall's entrance in the same building, and Hugh Cowan's Favourite Bar on Main Street, Anderston ('"Era" and all Professional Papers Taken'), made it clear that performers were valued customers.[34] The latter bar even boasted an endorsement in verse from the veteran Scotch comic N. C. Bostock:

> When tae the 'Tivoli' ye gang, dinna forget tae ca'
> On Hughie Cowan, wha sells a dram tae suit baith great an' sma';
> His whisky's guid, his yill's guid, his brandy'sa' three staur
> There's nae hoose in Glesca can bate the favourite baur.

In assessing the broad public view of music-hall/variety performers over the period of this study, it is important to realise that the sort of blanket prejudices that have been detailed, which reflected attitudes regularly expressed in editorials and letters in the press, were tempered by the everyday experience of most people who came into contact with performers, even the most visible of touring professionals. Then as now the public enjoyed interacting with celebrities, and it was a paradox of the double standard then in operation that reservations which, taken as a whole, should have guaranteed ostracism of the professional group concerned, in fact amounted to no such thing. As variety became increasingly popular between the turn of the century and the First World War, performers were if anything even more fêted. But if the general public's attitude towards music-hall performers as a group remained affectionate, never approaching anything like the hostility or censoriousness of the minority who attacked them, neither did it ever overcome reservations as to their moral character. It is probably unjust to accuse the public who enjoyed attending music halls, but would rather not have their son or daughter marry a performer, of hypocrisy. In a society in which interaction between classes was both complex and subtle, the relationship of performers to what could be termed more mainstream conventional society was perhaps better compared to the workings of a caste system, in which theatricals played an important and appreciated role, but were, in the final analysis, set apart.

Perhaps for this reason the more profound explanation as to why performers remained marginalised by sections of society, of which the causes already mentioned were merely symptoms, lay in the cosmopolitan nature of music-hall culture, one of the subjects of the next chapter.

## Notes

1 Houston, *Autobiography of Mr. James Houston*, pp. 7, 8; MLGC.
2 'Men You Know', No. 39, *The Bailie*, 16 July 1873, p. 1; MLGC.
3 'The Modern Variety Theatre', *Evening News and Star* (*Glasgow Evening News*), 29 April 1887, p. 4.
4 'A Night in a Glasgow Music Hall' letter, *North British Daily Mail*, 24 February 1875, p. 4.
5 'The Modern Variety Theatre', Evening News, 29 April 1887.
6 *Glasgow Herald*, 5 April 1909, p. 5, letter titled 'Music Hall and Public Morals', and signed Halifax NS, March 20.
7 Hammerton, *Sketches From Glasgow*, p. 120.
8 'Notes by Roving Jack', *Professional*, 6 February 1886.
9 John Davidson, 'Prologue', *In A Music-Hall and Other Poems* (London, Ward & Downey, 1891), pp. 1–13 (pp. 1–2).
10 'Death of W. H. Lannagan', *Professional*, no. 172 (6 April 1889); MLGC.

11  Wall, *The Fool on the Hill*, pp. 42–45, 52; Wall also tells how, on his fourth and last tour to South Africa, Lorimer's DTs had got so bad that 'he had had to be put into a taxi to be taken to the ship home'.

12  J. B. Priestley, *The Edwardians* (London, Heinemann, 1970), p. 173; for a vivid impression of the power of female physicality as featured in variety see the description of 'Nonie' at the beginning of Chapter 3 of Priestley's novel *Lost Empires* (London, Heinemann, 1965).

13  *Report of Visits to Music Halls on 27th of February 1875*, dated 1 March 1875 by Superintendent Brown, to Captain McCall, Chief Constable; Glasgow City Archive. For sexual politics see also J. S. Bratton, 'Beating the bounds: gender play and role reversal in the Edwardian Music Hall', in Michael R. Booth and Joel Kaplan (eds.), *The Edwardian Theatre: Essays on Performance and the Stage* (Cambridge, Cambridge University Press, 1996).

14  The song's chorus is; 'Her hair was light, / Her eyes were bright, / Her waist was neat and small, / She's a serio-comic singer at / A popular Concert Hall'; sung by Mr Alfred Arthur; from *Scotia's Music-Hall Songbook*, No. 8 (undated); STA.

15  *Quiz*, 3 February 1898, p. 201; See also *Quiz*, 30 December 1897, a variation of the earlier theme, which depicts the showgirl as dense as well as avaricious; dinner-jacketed 'mature' admirer to chorine; He: 'I thought you were engaged to be married to a toff?' She: 'Yes, so I was, but he told me he was a lord, and I have since found out that he is only a duke!'

16  See Houston, *Autobiography of Mr. James Houston*, pp. 105, 106 for references to the Lodges Dramatic 571 and 511 in the mid-1870s.

17  'Notes By Roving Jack', *The Professional and Authors' Journal*, No. 54 (16 January 1886), p. 4; MLGC.

18  'Glasgow Music Halls; Britannia Music Hall', *The Professional and Authors' Journal*, No. 32 (15 August 1885), p. 4; MLGC.

19  'Notes By Roving Jack', *The Professional and Authors' Journal*, No. 55 (23 January 1886), p. 4.

20  'Notes By Roving Jack', *The Professional and Authors' Journal*, No. 143 (1 October 1887), p. 4.

21  Correspondence, *Barr's Professional Gazette and Advertiser*, 11 July 1891, p. 5.

22  Letter of 29 July, *Barr's Professional Gazette and Advertiser*, 2 August 1891, p. 5.

23  'The Boss of the Gaiety and Star, and Complimentary Benefits', *The Professional and Authors' Journal*, No. 141 (17 September 1887), p. 4.

24  'Notes by Roving Jack', *The Professional and Authors' Journal*, No. 54 (16 January 1886), p. 4.

25  'Presentation to Mr Charles McConnell', *Professional*, 10 August 1887; MLGC.

26  'Theatrical and Musical Notes of the Month', *The Amateur and Singer's Journal*, August 1894; MLGC.

27  *The Entertainer*, 28 February 1914, p. 8.

28  'A Peep at the Professional Ball', *The Professional and Authors' Journal*, No. 122 (7 May 1887); for the Regatta, see 'Notes by Roving Jack', *The Professional and Authors' Journal*, No. 140 (10 September 1887), p. 4.

29  *Glasgow Programme*, 30 July 1917; MLGC.

30  'Notes by Roving Jack', *Professional*, 5 March 1887.

31  'Notes by Roving Jack', *Professional*, 28 January 1887.

32  Sir Harry Lauder, *Roamin'in the Gloamin'* (Philadelphia and London, Lipincott, 1928), p. 152.

33  Rutherford, 'Managers in a Small Way', pp. 103, 107; for Paisley see Neil McFadyen, 'My Nichts o' Fun with Famous Scots Comedians', *Weekly News*, 17 September 1932, p. 5.

34  See Britannia and Tivoli programmes in 'Music and Music Halls, 1900–1901' volume (bound collection of music-hall programmes), MLGC.

# 7

# Patriotism, empire and the Glasgow music hall

One of the problems of trying to assess the political or social complexion of music hall through performing material is that the material itself encompassed a wide range of ideas and attitudes, which often seem contradictory. The difficulty is largely one of interpretation; faced with songs that express different views, how do we determine which best reflected contemporary opinion, and to what degree? The case is particularly complex with regard to issues of empire, or matters where the Scottish audience's loyalty and patriotism were invoked in the face of foreign threat. Visiting English stars of the 1880s and 1890s treated Glasgow audiences as citizens of empire, introducing the word 'Scottish' into song lyrics wherever possible, but often regarding 'British' and 'English' as interchangeable. Imported English jingoism proudly invoked the examples of the dominions – Australia, Canada, South Africa, India – in coming to the aid of the Mother Country in her hour of crisis, but took Scottish loyalty as read. In contrast home-produced Scottish songs on similar themes, whilst equally resolute in defence of empire, possessed a distinct cultural agenda of their own, usually involving a strong emphasis on Scottish military prowess and separate national identity. The Scottish music-hall establishment, like other institutions culturally attuned to the postal residency of N.B. or North Britain, saw itself as part of a national industry centred on London. But as a popular entertainment medium, it was also acutely aware of the different cultural outlook and aspirations of its audience, and of its need to accommodate them. The contradictory signals given off by this material lead us to question quite what, in cultural terms, was going on. Were the Glasgow audiences cheering these songs (when they did so) because they saw themselves as British, or out of economic self-interest? Or did they support empire because it seemed to offer a prominent role for Scots as a distinct national grouping within the family of empire? Quite where loyalism stopped and overt nationalism began is open to debate.

Perhaps the key lies in defining the notion of Scottish identity conveyed in music hall. It seems reasonable to suppose that the Glasgow audience's attitudes to the wider world were at least partly conditioned by their own cultural self-image, in the form of the national stereotypes projected back at them from the music-hall stage. We will therefore examine these first, before moving on to look at attitudes to empire revealed in Glasgow music-hall songs and material.

Recent writers on popular culture have argued for a reappraisal of the Scotch comic, suggesting that, far from debasing Scottish culture, it represented an attempt to provide a composite image of Scottish identity where none had previously existed. Bill Findlay traces the contradictions inherent in the figure back to the Highland/Lowland divide and the National Drama itself, writing that 'Given … the migration of Highlanders into the developing urbanised centres of Central Scotland, it is perhaps little surprising that there arose out of this repertoire of Scottish types a hybrid Highland-Lowlander who wore Highland garb but spoke Scots and was pawkyness incarnate'.[1] Glasgow music-hall songs certainly reflected the cultural tensions within Scottish society, born out of changing demographic patterns and the shift from rural to urban living. Performing material from the 1880s to 1900s offered a sentimentalised view of the past, tempered by the day–to-day realities of modern urban life. Much of the humour of these songs and sketches came from pointing up the incongruity of cultural exchange, and in the process they threw up a new set of stereotypical urban figures.

Prominent amongst these was the 'slow' Highlander down to see the sights of the great city, as in the story of 'Tonald and Angus from the Highlands, who [confronted by the teeming throng in Argyle Street] waited all day in an entry "until all this procession went by, whateffer."'[2] Although such country cousins are ridiculed as unsophisticated, they usually emerge as canny victors over city folks' attempts to dupe them, as in 'Don't Come Your Auld Fashioned Tricks On Wi' Me' (c.1889), where a 'hamely bit chiel' from Linlithgow called Tam sings:

> I gaed off to Glasgow ae day by the train,
> For the Great exhibition to see I was fain,
> There I met wi' some fellows wha thocht themselves smart
> But I sune let them see I could tak my ain part.

The spoken patter accompanying the song describes how, while watching a busker playing the concertina in the street,

A fellow quately slipped his hand into my pouch at the same time saying, 'What o'clock is't.' I gied him a dig in the lug that sent him half across the street. Says I, 'It's only struck one.' 'For guid sake,' says he, 'don't make it strike twelve.' 'A'richt' says I, as I began to sing

CHORUS

Ye may turn the auld jail to a gunpouther mill,
Ye may shift Tennant's Stalk oot to Vinegar Hill,
Ye may swear that the Clyde frae pollution is free,
But don't come your auld fashioned tricks on wi' me.[3]

The clever reversal of the chorus, where the topical references reveal the countryman to be well up on city affairs, in contrast to the 'old fashioned' tactics of the town sharks, completes the joke.

While country visitors remained popular subjects, Highland immigrants to the city were also themselves prominent in songs, particularly in the person of the Hielan' policeman. These occupied much the same position (worthy but 'thick') in Glasgow's popular mythology as Irish precinct cops in that of New York and Chicago, their teuchter speech and reputation for density being satirised in verses such as the following from 1905:

You'll see I'm a country loon,
And I just come into this big toon,
To be a polisman, you see,
But the folk I meet a' roar at me –

CHORUS

Cummer-ee, cummer-oo, cummer achum-chu
How dae you dae, and how dae you do?
Did she'll come frae the Hielans where they yell hurroo?
Cummer-ee, cummer-oo, cummer achum-chu.[4]

Such songs may have served to soften the impersonal face of the great city by presenting the immigrant Highland community as an extension of familiar rural society, where one could often come across someone one knew. This was certainly the case in 'Hooch, Maggie ... frae the Isle of Skye' who sings:

I cam'in at the 'buchts' tae Glesca toon,
An I wanted the sichts tae see,
An' wha dae ye think I met at the Cross,
But sonsy big Sanny McPhee.[5]

(who also turns out to be a policeman). The motive for focusing on these popular stereotypes is to demonstrate the extent to which such songs reflected the ethnic and cultural diversity of society. By helping establish such figures, music hall was contributing to new urban folklore, bridging the gap between old and new cultures in a process that represented a continuation rather than an interruption of oral traditions.

Moreover, songs could also be found on almost every aspect of working peoples' lives; from housing conditions ('The Model Lodgin' Hoose'), the perils of eviction ('They're Comin' Wi a Barrow at Half Past Twa'), street violence and drunkenness ('Down the Trongate') and the fighting Irishman ('The Terror of the Briggate'), to rent and debt collectors ('The Process Server' and 'It's a very warm Locality'), the tyranny of foremen ('The Gaffers of the Gang'), the unfair treatment of the unemployed by council leaders ('The Unemployed') and the public's love of a good argument ('The Debater on the Green'). In each case the treatment of the subject was either comic or unremittingly upbeat, adversity being met with cheery resignation rather than outrage.

Although it is difficult to know how prominent or successful these songs were in the context of the whole bill, their presence is nevertheless highly significant. However outrageous the appearance of Scotch comics (and I would agree with Cameron and Scullion that the function of tartan as worn on stage was as a short-hand indication of shared identity), it seems likely that much of their material, and certainly the characterisations they assumed, drew directly on shared experience of urban society and living. As Cameron and Scullion write, 'the totemic images of the Scotch comic ... were approved and even celebrated as symbols of a nationality which, under normal circumstances, audiences were never allowed to express'.[6] In this respect the Scotch comic could be seen as having had an influence on modern Scottish identity that went far beyond the biscuit-tin tartanry alleged by Lauder's accusers.

We should also recognise that, given music hall's influence, other genres of Scottish performer may also have contributed to framing perceptions of national identity. While Scotch comics in the Frame and Lauder mould were pre-eminent, other types of comic vocalists generally eschewed the kilt, delivering songs and character-based sketches in a range of different personae that could incorporate real pathos. In this context J. C. Macdonald's gallery of characters, which, as with Lauder and others, included drag impersonations of older Highland women, represented a wider take on contemporary society. Macdonald's songs about the lives of working men included 'Humphin' Hielan' Mary's at the Quay', about a porter at the Broomielaw unloading bags of flour, and his most famous impersonation, the 'Cairter', a figure which for

QUIZ SUPPLEMENT, SEPT. 15, 1892.

J. C. MACDONALD AT THE CITY HALL.

**20** 'J. C. Macdonald at the City Hall', *Quiz*, 15 September 1892

detail and authenticity seems to have resembled the characterisations of the great north-eastern English comic Ned Corven.[7] (In fairness the pre-eminence of Lauder's kilted image has often obscured the fact that he and other Scotch comics like him also usually performed in a number of different characters, including in Lauder's case that of the simpleton featured in 'The saftest o' the family', by all accounts his most touching portrayal.)

Moreover, music-hall bills also incorporated established Scottish folk idioms, such as traditional songs, clog and Highland dancing, which remained a popular (and officially approved of) choreographic influence well into the twentieth century. The inclusion of these elements meant that music hall in Scotland offered a more rounded and varied representation of Scottish culture than the predominance of the Scotch comic caricature has led us to expect. Not surprisingly, stage depictions of Scottish identity were to have an important influence on broader issues of nationality, in particular on attitudes towards the English and Empire. As we shall see, two key elements of the Scotch comic persona – the use of tartan and the perception of the Highlander as the archetype of Scottish identity – were to feature extensively in Scottish songs promoting the cause of empire in the 1890s.

In moving on to examine issues of empire, an initial question to arise is how Glasgow music hall's espousal of queen and country in patriotic anthems was reconciled with the simultaneous popularity of what could be termed Scottish national songs – generally stirring ballads celebrating heroes and events from Scottish history. Although such songs were usually positive and forward-looking, rather than bitter over past injustices, and avoided mentioning the English by name, their general tenor was Jacobite and left little doubt as to the identity of the old enemy. *The Scotia Music-Hall Songbook*, which probably dates from the 1880s, provides a typical mix of both genres, with rousing imperialist paeans such as 'Hurrah for the Life of a Sailor!' and 'Cheer Boys Cheer (for Mother England!)' printed alongside similarly inspirational nationalist hymns such as 'Draw the Sword, Scotland!', 'Hurrah for the Bonnets of Blue', and 'Where Hath Scotland Found Her Fame'. The latter draws on a popular romantic device by citing landscape, culture, and historical achievement to answer its own rhetorical premise. Thus 'By her mountains wild and grand, / By her lakes so calmly flowing, / By the peace that rules the land', etc., finally resolves into the affirmative present day with

Arts and science crown her name
Genius and romantic story
There has Scotia found her fame
There has Scotland found her glory.[8]

'The Highlandman's Toast' by Harry Linn, printed in the *Professional* in 1900, concentrates on the heroic legacy of Wallace and Bruce, exhorting Scots to remember 'The brave ones who fell against the numberless host, / Who tried to enslave her – in slavery degrade her'. That such songs, in drawing together the various strands of national consciousness, seem to comprise a statement of Scottish nationhood is no doubt open to oversimplification. These songs after all took their place on the bill sandwiched between such banalities as 'Think of me, Willie' and 'Mother Kissed Me In My Dreams'. But even if such songs were largely conceived for theatrical effect, the fact that they were warmly received by an audience who responded to their appeal to a distinct Scottish patriotism, but who then went on to avidly participate in other songs that required them to fight for Old England's glory, seems incongruous enough to bear investigating further.

The underlying question is exactly what the Glasgow public's perception of empire embodied, and whether support for it necessarily involved a conflict of interests with Scottish patriotism. It might be that popular Scottish sentiment viewed colonial expansion as a pan-British cause, which transcended English assertions of leadership, and that Scottish enthusiasm was focused on its external benefits in terms of potential opportunities for careers and expansion overseas. Indeed, from a nationalist perspective, the idea that the cause of empire offered a fresh horizon for Scots to escape English dominance can't have been any less plausible than Rait and Dicey's view in *Thoughts on the Union* (1920), summarised by Christopher Harvie, that 'one could be both a sincere nationalist and an advocate of the Union'.[9]

This view is certainly supported by the selective approach to Empire adopted by some Scottish music-hall material. While many songs that talked of fighting side by side for queen and country were English 'hits' re-printed in Glasgow-published songsheets, others that extolled the fame of Scottish regiments, popular with the wider Victorian public, were also products of the English music hall. 'The Scotch Brigade', published in the *Professional* of June 1885, is typical of the genre:

> On the banks of the Clyde stood a lad and his lassie,
> The lad's name was Geordie, the lassie's was Jean,
> She flung her arm round him, and cried 'do not leave me'
> For Geordie was going to fight for his Queen.

The English text and unconvincing idiom, together with the rather clichéd setting ('Over the burning plains of Egypt, Under the scorching sun …') mark this out as anglicised fantasy even before we read that it is performed 'with unbounded success by Miss Marie le Blanc' and is published by Sheard's, London. In contrast many Scottish paeans to empire prove selective in their endorsement. Despite its title, 'Aye Ready Tae Fecht For Auld England' (1894) uses the imperial strife as a vehicle for national pride:

In praise o'the land wi' the bonnets o' blue
The laddies who' ne'er kent fear,
I'll noo lilt a bit song untae you,
Which I hope ye'll a'willingly hear;
For Sandy, in battle, on sea or on land,
Has showed the hale world whit tae dae,
An when thinkin' on heroes, although they're noo gone,

CHORUS

They were Scottish born, theyir lan' they did lo'e,
They showed tae the hale world whit sandy could do,
Ither nations may brag but I'll swear there are few
Better men ever fought for auld England.[10]

If Sandy does it for England, at least nominally, other songs go further in turning what are ostensibly celebrations of British might into excuses for local propagandising. 'Glasgow Forever' (1889) relates how:

Saint Mungo's sons at Waterloo,
You'll read on history's brightest page,
Those heroes in the 71st,
Who with the foeman did engage;
For when other British regiments
Like grass were being cut down,
Their commander shouted 'Clear the way
For the men from Glasgow town.'

Those gallant Glasgow warriors,
When they saw their comrades' fate,
And heard their commander shouting,
'Chase those foemen down the Gallowgate,'
With bayonets fixed they nobly charged
And cut the foemen down,
And gained the day for Britain –
Did those men from Glasgow town.[11]

In contrast to these pieces came another variant, the Anglo-Scottish heroic ballad written to celebrate a military action, which became very popular at the time of the Boer War. Like 'The Scotch Brigade', cited earlier, these were written in English, and framed Scottish exploits in a wider British context. 'The Highland Brigade', sung by W. C. McPhie in 1901, did its best to turn the disastrous defeat at Magersfontein into moral collateral.

> Sad came the news the other day of Scotia's gallant sons,
> Who fell in myriads before the fire of great Boer guns;
> They charged the foe like tigers then, and deadly was the strife,
> But, ah! Sad day for Scotland, many there gave up their lives,

The song goes on to concede the role of human error ('Some critics say a terrible and gross mistake was made') before wringing the full emotive value out of defeat;

> In many a far-off Highland home fond hearts will mourn a tale
> Of those they loved now laid to rest in dark Tugela's vale,
> The Highlanders have proved their worth in many a Hard fought field;
> Their motto has been always 'We will die before we yield!'
> But still in many a stricken home their memory is revered
> By parents, sisters, brothers too, to whom they were endeared;
> They made a gallant struggle against the crafty Boer,
> And each man died a hero's death amidst the cannon's roar.

The final verse leaves the sound of weeping clachans behind, looking forward to the prospect of victory and homecoming, to conclude on a note of stirring triumphalism:

> When Britain's flag has risen over Afric's sunny plains,
> Our gallant Scottish lads will soon be with us once again,
> They'll get a hearty welcome when they reach their native shore,
> But still as true and willing as in the days of yore.
> Brave Wauchope let the world see what Scotchmen bold can do,
> A'tho' the men who came back from that charge were very few;
> But if war bugles sound again our boys will give a shout,
> And with their bayonets fixed soon put Britannia's foes to rout.[12]

Unlike the previous songs, which were openly chauvinist in claiming military achievements as Scottish, this sets them in the 'epic' context of an imperial vision. If the tone is English, the singer was probably Scottish. In any case, although overt propaganda (and doggerel!) the piece is dramatic and emotionally engaged, aspects that would have been heightened by the topicality of the events being described. Moreover, once the audience bought into the heroism of the song, it could not fail to be flattered by the homage being paid to Scottish soldiery. The linkage between Scottish gallantry and nobility of sacrifice, and British achievement (mentioned in consecutive lines at one point) cements the unity of purpose within an ideological setting. As Murray Pittock observes in discussing 'The Seaforth Highlanders of Hindoostan', 'The Highlanders are now "Britons"'.[13]

These last three examples show empire accommodating Scottish local and national sensibilities to varying degrees. As an officially sanctioned relationship, this marked a clear difference in emphasis from English music hall. In the English context, Senelick and others have characterised the negativity and xenophobia of jingoism at its highpoint in the late 1890s, seeing this as a symptom of working-class apathy.[14] In contrast Scottish material on imperial themes, by stressing Scottish identity and achievement in a way that resonated with an audience used to seeing itself depicted as an adjunct to England, seems to have had a generally more positive outlook. And no doubt, on the popular front, the fact that such songs seemed more about celebrating Scotland than empire made support for them, in their music-hall setting, fairly obligatory. The idea that the Scottish audience may have equated beating the drum for empire with beating the drum for Scotland is an intriguing one. And if from a nationalist perspective the price to be paid was the inferred status of vassal state within the family of empire (surely the *de facto* relationship anyway), then at least it was as a recognised national entity distinct from England and not as 'N.B.'.

But setting aside the question of Scottish identity, the other factor to be considered is the appeal of empire as a focus for a wider British identity. Linda Colley has suggested that eighteenth-century notions of 'Britishness' were initially based on a shared Scottish, English and Welsh anti-Catholicism or 'common investment in protestantism', but from 1830 onwards came increasingly to revolve around support for empire.[15] The patriotic enfranchisement this offered to sections of the Glasgow audience, such as the immigrant Irish, who had previously been excluded on religious grounds, could well have been an underlying motive for late nineteenth-century enthusiasm for the cause of empire. And indeed Colley characterises the new inclusive, broad-church British patriotism it offered as forward-looking, dynamic and active rather than simply conservative.

Penny Summerfield has suggested that English music hall's treatment of imperial themes fell into two distinct phases; that prior to 1890 songs in working-class halls tended to focus on the role of the individual, and depicted territorial expansion overseas as an act of liberation for the native peoples concerned. She goes on to suggest that by the early 1890s this libertarian outlook had been replaced by a xenophobic approach, whereby the virtuous British serviceman was either a jingo shouldering the responsibilities of Empire in sketches and revues of the 1880s and 1890s, or a humorous hero in comic patriotic songs of the 1900s and the First World War. There was no anti-imperialism: criticism was muted, parodies were self-mocking.[16]

Setting the positive effects of promoting Scottish patriotism aside, other performing material used in Scottish halls largely bears out Summerfield's assertion
that working-class attitudes to empire itself were more characterised by apathy
than active enthusiasm, certainly in the later period from the 1890s. 'There
Goes Johnny in his Khaki Suit' (c.1900) was a typical piece of swagger that
began:

> I'm Jock McGraw, frae Kelvinhaugh
> A private in the Ninety-Twa,
> They dressed me up in Khaki braw,
> Tae go tae the Transvaal in the morning
>
> CHORUS
>
> Oh, John, ye're lookin' awfu' braw,
> Ye're the pride o' the regiment, the gallant Ninety' twa
> The lassies they a' cry, as I gie them the salute,
> There goes Johnny in his khaki suit.

If the tone is jaunty, the attitude makes it clear that Johnny, like thousands of
others, quite likes the uniform but can take or leave the idea of empire. The predominance of this sort of comic-heroic number only illustrates the dearth of
songs able to make a convincing moral case for the war.

However, in other respects the demise of critical or satirical material noted
by writers like Summerfield seems overstated. Although dissenting voices are
comparatively rare in the songsheets, where found they can be surprisingly outspoken. In the *Professional* of June 1900, on a page that also features 'British
Boys; or, Let them Try', and 'War in South Africa', we find Alex Melville's
'Pretoria', which seems to begin as a straightforward piece of jingoism before
developing into something quite unexpected.

> Who dares to say that Great Britain
> Never triumphant will exist?
> As long as a patriot is living,
> As long as a lad is able to enlist,
> Her soldier sons are fighting at Pretoria,
> Her sailor sons are watching o'er the sea.
> So here's to the country that we live in,
> And drink up with nine times three.
>
> CHORUS
>
> (Air – 'Rule Britannia')
> Rule Britannia, Britannia rules the sea
> Britannia rules a lot of fools as well as you and me.

We sent out a lot of our generals
To join in the general hunt,
But a lot of these generals were backward
In going away to the front.
But we sent 'Bobs' to capture Pretoria,
And he led his troops in the van,
And he captured all he could lay his hands upon
Like a soldier and a man.

CHORUS

Rule Britannia, Britannia rules the shore,
A lot of men are working now that never worked before

RECITATIVE

God save our gracious Queen,
You all know what I mean –
Save yourselves and not the Queen.[17]

The most striking feature here is the cynicism of the lyrics. While most such songs confine themselves to criticism of the English establishment, steering clear of institutions of state, this seems to be rubbishing the whole imperial edifice – monarchy, General Staff and all. The author, Alex Melville, was a well-known Glasgow songwriter. Like other professional writers for music hall, he wrote in a variety of styles. The fact that he seems to have specialised in this sort of provocative and (particularly in the context) political piece, suggests that there was a market for items that rocked the boat, even at times of national emergency. Another example of his work is 'Not in the Land called England', which starts out bemoaning the difficulties Scottish performers have getting ahead in England, but quickly moves on to target English society and morals with insinuatory verses such as:

They all go out on the Ting, ting, ting
Married Folk must have their fling,
Modesty would be the thing,
But not in the land called England.[18]

A more open, less insidious approach was that of James Curran, a Glasgow songwriter famous for his parodies. The chorus of his 'England's in Danger', captures perfectly the overblown alarmist bluster of the music-hall call to arms:

For England's in Danger, Scotland's in debt,
Ireland's in Ireland, as no one should forget;
Then why not stand together, as I have stood before,
Those were my thoughts while rambling through the keyhole of the door.[19]

To conclude, there are a number of possible inferences to be drawn regarding the relationship between music hall's depiction of Scottish identity and Scottish audience's attitudes to empire. Firstly, it is important to recognise that Scotch comics were products of an urban society. Although the image of Scottish identity they developed came to be regarded as a travesty, it nevertheless evolved in the context of a popular commercial entertainment, and as such at least partly reflected the views and desires of the audience. The idea that the Scotch comics arose purely as a response to English variety audiences' need for a handle on Scottish identity seems simplistic, given their enormous popularity in Scotland.[20] No doubt the inanity of the persona, which was clearly a caricature, contributed to the impression that it was culturally irrelevant. In fact, its significance lay precisely in the fact that it was artificial and a composite. Cameron and Scullion have suggested that in attempting to appeal to all sections of the urban audience – rural Lowland incomers, Gaelic-speaking Highlanders, urban industrial workers, etc. – the Scotch comic represented an attempt to provide a unifying personification of Scottish nationhood where none had previously existed.[21] But it is also possible to see him as a transitional figure, consistently presenting rural values and characters in a modern urban context, bridging the gap between old and new cultures and value systems. In that sense the Scotch comic, forever in limbo somewhere between Skye and Glasgow Cross, presented a comfortingly backward-looking image to an audience that still retained a strong cultural and sentimental attachment to a recent rural past.

But if well-intentioned stereotypes could encourage social cohesion, they could also quickly ossify. By the First War the Hielan' persona pioneered by W. F. Frame and Lauder had already reached its optimum exposure. A contemporary review of one of their successors, Jock Mills, from 1914 noted that 'He moves about in the stereotyped *role* of the Highlander ... and sings a sentimental song that must have appealed to the good people on the other side of the "herring pond"', observing that 'Although the clansman is a picturesque figure on the stage, he calls for new treatment these days.'[22]

National identity similarly played an important role in shaping Scottish attitudes to empire. Although the range of performing material on imperial themes was basically the same as that available in English halls, home-produced songs' use of Scottish patriotic imagery to sell the idea of empire was distinctly different in implication. In contrast to English jingoism's rather generalised appeals to English pride, anyway debased by their frequency, the invocation of Scottish national consciousness was a much more deliberate and resonant gesture, given the institutional dominance of English culture. No doubt the identification of empire with songs that celebrated Scottishness was an irresistible combination as far as audiences in the halls were concerned, but it carried a price. When songs (and audiences) applauded imperial achievement or aspirations, it was through Scottish involvement: when they criticised or satirised, it was the English establishment that was the target, again resulting in celebration of Scottish superiority. This re-emergence of a dormant Scottish consciousness, albeit in the cause of wider British support for imperial endeavours, echoed growing middle-class assertiveness on matters of national culture (such as the readoption of the kilt), and resulted in what Christopher Harvie has termed 'a fruitful schizophrenia which enabled the Scots to run with the ethnic hare and hunt with the imperial hounds' (although Harvie goes on to note the limitations of its context, observing that 'The entente between emotive nationalism and effective unionism gelded any political movement').[23]

Moreover, by dramatising and projecting Scottish involvement, music hall contributed to the Scottish public's wholehearted embrace of the imperial ethos. Given the extent to which Scottish (and particularly Glaswegian) industries relied on overseas markets, it is surprising that there are few references in songs to the economic benefits of empire. Because of this there is little indication whether economic considerations directly influenced the attitudes of the working classes to conflicts such as the Boer War, although it is hard to believe that the very visible exchange of raw materials and finished goods did not feature in public attitudes to expansion and overseas markets. Certainly the promoters of Glasgow's Great Exhibition of 1901 were anxious that its educational displays should increase general awareness of the strides being made by foreign competitors, and of the importance of 'stimulating the energies of our workmen'.[24] In any case, songs' focuses on emotive issues of heroism were not themselves devoid of economic significance. For a country of its size and population, Scotland's military establishment and involvement overseas was disproportionately large, boosted by its importance as a major employer in rural areas. Overseas expansion also offered considerable career opportunities, particularly for the middle classes, in colonial bureaucracies as well as in entrepreneurial and mercantile capacities. For these reasons Scottish investment in the ideal or dream of empire far exceeded that of the English. Much more than an abstract concept, from the Scottish public's point of view empire translated into investment, jobs, work, and a degree of emancipation from the overweening influence of England.

Music halls themselves encapsulated this dichotomy of empire as representing both British and Scottish sensibilities. In many ways it was analogous to their own position as both part of a cosmopolitan British circuit, and propagator of a separate Scottish performing tradition. The pragmatic solution adapted was all-embracing inclusiveness, halls remaining formal adherents of the credo of North Britain whilst also offering open house to stage representations of many different national groupings, all of which were equal in the reductive world of the three-minute cultural stereotype. In the context of Glasgow this meant that Irish comics remained almost as popular as the Scotch variant, while the Jewish immigrant community ensured the presence of a number of 'Hebrew' acts. The patriotic and nationalist iconography of music hall's promotional material similarly reflected the compatibility of Scottish and Imperial themes. Scotia Music Hall programmes from the 1880s and 1890s featured, variously, Boadicea, a British Lion, and a tartan-clad Highlander shown against a mythologised Scottish landscape of loch and ruined castle, while those for Rossborough's Britannia depicted either the eponymous heroine, breastplated and helmeted, or a rampant British Lion draped in the Union Flag, together with the municipal motto 'Let Glasgow Flourish'. Halls were decorated with flags and bunting on occasions of national celebration, as was the case with the Britannia on Mafeking Day. Sketches and material inevitably picked up on patriotic sentiment at times of conflict or international crisis, mirroring the large-scale open-air military spectacles mounted at the Barracks Carnival and by Henglers Circus, whose 'The War in Zululand' was a great success in 1894. The eventual emergence of the stereotypical Scotch comic figure, who was fiercely loyal to the crown but who definitely lived in Scotland, rather than a northern province of an English Britain, was representative of the cultural pragmatism that characterised music hall generally.

While Lauder's reputation was largely defined by his success abroad, the circumstances he exploited – the existence of large expatriate Scottish communities throughout the United States and British Dominions – had also been recognised by earlier performers.

The tenor David Kennedy (1825–86), a popular exponent of Scottish song and patriarch of a talented musical family, embarked with them on a world tour between 1872 and 1876, later chronicled by his daughter Marjory Kennedy-Fraser.[25] A concert singer who combined traditional Scots songs with oratorio and sacred music, Kennedy was 'always a great favourite with the Scottish clergy', a fact which stood him in good stead with expatriate communities whose social life often revolved around the church. He was also, in contrast to more opportunistic performers who came after him, a man with a cultural mission who 'believed in his vocation to carry the songs of Scotland round the world to all the Scots scattered abroad.' Setting sail from Glasgow on 6 March 1872 with a four–and-a-half-octave cut-down grand piano, the Kennedys arrived in Melbourne in June after a three-month voyage. Fêted in the city, they sang six nights a week for the next three months, and on leaving were honoured with a civic gathering, at which Kennedy was presented with an illustrated address. On the long journey from Melbourne to Sydney, the family gave their Scots concert programme, 'Twa hoors at hame', at virtually every stopping place, with Scots from outlying areas riding up to a hundred miles on horseback to attend. Their subsequent progress through Tasmania, South Australia and New Zealand seems to have embraced the full extent of the Scottish diaspora. In Hobart, Tasmania, Kennedy met the granddaughter of the fiddler Neil Gow; in Otago, New Zealand, the family stayed with a local Scots clergyman and gave a concert for the benefit of the Kirk. In 1875 the tour continued through the United States and Canada to Nova Scotia, before finishing at St John's Newfoundland in 1876, four and a half years after it had commenced. The family's subsequent overseas visits included the Cape (1879) and India (1879/80), as well as further tours to Australasia and North America.

Back in Scotland, the family found their reputation greatly enhanced by these epic foreign stints. In 1880 the Aberdeen *Bon Accord* saluted 'The celebrated Kennedy Family, returned from [their] Indian and African tour', suggesting that 'If the "Songs of Bonnie Scotland" ever received a true reading it is from this gifted Family. All Scotchmen should take advantage of "Twa Hours at Hame" to listen and admire their national lyrics.'[26] The notion of the Family as custodians of 'national' repertoire reflected David Kennedy's status as the greatest living Scottish singer, and to that extent the Family were an institution in Scottish life of their day. But it also reflected a familiar trope in Scottish cultural circles, the enhanced kudos of success achieved abroad or at least outside Scotland as the ultimate validation.

If Kennedy was a trailblazer, other Scottish performers, who also embodied the traditional Scottish repertoire, but sometimes with a foot in other entertainment camps, began to discover the same expatriate constituency. James Scott Skinner, the Banchory-born fiddler known as 'The Strathspey King', spent his boyhood touring Britain with a juvenile orchestra, Dr Mark's Little Men, before making his reputation as a composer and virtuoso exponent of the then-popular Strathspey. While his fame was built up through touring with his own concert party, his growing reputation soon brought demand for his services from further afield. Like the soprano Jessie Maclachlan, with whom he often appeared and who was also, in his own words 'much in demand in London', his iconic status as the greatest Scottish fiddler led to increasing patronage from expatriate Scots. Much of this demand came from England, reflecting the extent of Scots migration south of the border. In his less than modest memoirs, Scott Skinner conceded that audiences at his London performances 'were generally mostly composed of Scots' and described his greatest metropolitan triumph before a packed house at the Albert Hall:

> It was a Scottish gathering pure and undefiled. In the first part of the programme I appeared in the Gordon kilt. My reception was cordial in the extreme, but when I marched on in the second half, arrayed in the Macpherson tartan, to which I had changed because I was going to play 'Macpherson the Freebooter', the scene was pandemonium in the most complimentary sense of the term. The Macphersons must have been out en masse that night … for before I had started to play my solo the whole audience seemed to be on their feet cheering frantically. Clothes make the man, it is said, and I have no hesitation in saying that the Macpherson tartan made a large contribution to my gigantic success that night.[27]

In Scott Skinner's case, the emotive power of the tartan had to be learnt. His first visit to the United States and Canada in 1893, with a company organised by the Edinburgh piper Willie MacLennan, who had made ten previous visits, proved disastrous. MacLennan collapsed and died and the tour was cut short, leaving the performers reliant on wealthy Scottish benefactors to get back to Britain. On his return Scott Skinner, who had formerly usually worn evening dress, resolved to always perform in the kilt, and it is this image of him – later in life as a whiskered, rather dour figure in jabot and Highland dress – that he is immortalised in photographs.

A feature of Scott Skinner's career was his patronage by self-made Scots, who returned from success in business or commercial ventures overseas wealthy enough indulge their passion for the music of their native country. On one occasion, he was summoned by telegram to a hotel to play Strathspeys to Jake Allan, 'a North of Scotland man, who had returned home after having made his pile in New Zealand'; another benefactor was William McHardy of Drumblair, who made £100,000 in engineering in South America and returned to live in Forgue near Huntly.[28] The added emotive value of things Scottish to such men was something that Lauder would build on in his approach to expatriate communities.

By the late 1890s other Scottish performers were active in the Dominions. Jessie MacLachlan, a strikingly handsome woman who billed herself as 'The Scottish Prima Donna' and often sang in her native Gaelic, appeared in Canada and the United States, as did Durward Lely, the Perthshire-born tenor who had created several roles in the Gilbert and Sullivan operettas but who performed Scots songs and stories to audiences in British Columbia in 1898.[29]

While the Scotch comic persona was always subsequently associated with Lauder, his achievements were anticipated by Willie Frame, who preceded him to America. Frame made a triumphant debut at Carnegie Hall on 23 November 1898, where, before an audience of 3,000 American Scots, he read an opening 'peroration' which began:

BRITHER SCOTS, WHEN FREENS MEET HE'RTS WARM:
I'm here the nicht, faur frae the shore,
Faur frae the land we a' adore –
The land that gied oor faithers birth,
The dearest land on a' the earth;
Whaur bonnie grows the purple heather –
Whaur some o' us were boys together,
Whaur bonnie does the sunlicht shine,
The land o' yours, the land o' mine;
An' you revere it, weel I ken,
Scottish women, Scottish men.
Who ne'er forget, though great or sma',
The freens in Scotland far awa'.[30]

Frame's party's success was echoed in his subsequent tour, which consisted of concerts for Clan associations and Caledonian Societies, mostly in industrial towns such as Lawrence, Massachusetts ('A real Scotch city') where their hosts were the Clan Macpherson society; in Canadian centres such as Toronto and Ottawa, where they appeared before Lord Minto, Governor General of Canada; and at a huge 'Burns Anniversary' concert in Chicago ('the tinned meat city', as Frame put it), before an audience of 10,000 Scots, and where 100 Scottish children in kilts danced the Highland Fling. The sense of the diaspora was most evident in Chicago, where there were 'more Scotch societies … than in any other American city', and where Frame was delighted to come across several Glasgow Baillies and a journalist he knew from the *Glasgow News*, visiting in connection with the Glasgow Exhibition.[31] Frame finally returned to Scotland after five months, apparently flushed with success, but did not return to the United States. As with his successful stint in London, where he won plaudits but failed to return to capitalise on his success, it may have reflected a lack of drive of Frame's part: in any event his career remained based in Scotland. No such failing attached to Harry Lauder, whose energy, drive, and natural gift for self-promotion were born for the bigger stage afforded by the American market.

Lauder's own hugely successful first visit to the United States in 1907 made an enormous impact and proved the template for his future overseas campaigns. Arriving in New York on the *Lucania*, he was met at the quayside by pipers in Highland dress and several hundred enthusiastic Scottish well-wishers, and driven to his hotel in a tartan-draped car arranged, like the pipers, by American friends. His opening performance at the Time Square Theatre was a triumph, his failsafe number 'Tobermory' 'doing the trick', helped by the presence in the audience of a vociferous crowd of Scottish supporters. This initial five-week visit proved so successful that Lauder returned the following year for a fourteen-week tour that also took in Boston, Philadelphia, Pittsburgh and Chicago. While he undoubtedly appealed to a wider audience, Lauder himself was quite candid about the importance of his Scottish supporters, writing in his autobiography that

> the exiled Scots in the States had more to do with my success than many people imagined ... they turned up at my shows in all manner of Scottish costumes – in kilts, with Balmoral bonnets, wearing wearing tartan ties, and many of them bought their bagpipes with them. They imparted an enthusiastic atmosphere to my appearances everywhere; their weird shouts and 'hoochs' and skirls provided good copy for journalists and next-day talking points for the natives. In the first twenty weeks I spent in the States I must have met personally ten thousand people who claimed acquaintance with me in 'the auld days in Hamilton, Harry!' – or Glasgow, or Arbroath, or Portobello as the case might be ...[32]

The implication was that the Scots audience was not only valuable in its own right, but could be used as a marketing tool to excite the interest of the wider population to discover what all the fuss was about. Lauder put it more bluntly when he stated 'I have never been in any misapprehension as to the publicity value of my own kith and kin throughout the world'.[33]

Lauder was by no means ploughing a lone furrow in the United States. Other Scottish comics such as Frame, James Lumsden, and Jack Lorimer, 'the Hielan' laddie', who like Lauder was piped through the streets of New York by the local 'clan', also enjoyed considerable success there. So why was it Lauder who achieved the breakthrough to iconic status and world fame? In cultural terms, whatever the views of his detractors, Lauder's stage persona undoubtedly resonated for the working expatriate Scots who flocked to see him. However much he consorted with millionaires and Presidents (and he knew and played golf with Roosevelt, Taft, Harding, Coolidge and Wilson), he retained a down-to-earth demeanour, and a classless, inclusive appeal that suited the New World. On a professional level, he was by all accounts a charismatic performer, one of the very few thought by his peers to embody something close to genius. But the extent of Lauder's achievement is perhaps best expressed in the sheer persistence of his campaign. In all he made 22 tours of the United States, returning on an almost yearly basis for gruelling visits that often lasted up to six months. He employed a highly professional, organised pattern of touring, working under the guidance of his American manager William Morris, and using leading promoters in each theatre of operations – Klaw and Erlanger in North America, and subsequently E. J. Carroll and the Tait Brothers organisation in Australia, New Zealand and South Africa. On his American tours, Lauder and his company travelled in private trains known as 'Lauder specials', which included the luxurious Riva Pullman car used by President Roosevelt. Such hard work brought huge rewards. In 1908, on his second tour of the States, Lauder was earning $5,000 a week. By 1911 he was commanding $1,000 a night, and over the almost year-long tour earned a total of $120,000.

As important as astute management – effectively marketing, in the modern sense – was the fact that Lauder also mobilised the expatriate Scottish network in a more systematic way than any of his predecessors. Caledonian associations, Burns clubs and societies organised around clan associations had long been a feature of Scottish communities overseas, one that visiting performers had naturally drawn on for support – Frame's successful Carnegie Hall debut in 1898 had been at the invitation of the Caledonian Club, 'the largest society of Scotsmen in America'. To this extensive group, Lauder added an assiduous cultivation of the Scottish-American business community, often by involvement with its leading figures through charitable organisations. Given the prominence of Scots in many areas of society – commerce, industry, politics, shipping, journalism – this constituted a highly influential grouping, one in which Lauder seems to have known almost everyone of any stature. His extensive network of friends and contacts ranged from national figures such as Andrew Carnegie, Thomas Lipton and American Burns-enthusiast Colonel Walter Scott, to provincial magnates such as the Kansas press baron Frank P. MacLennan, the son of an Inverness man, who had been dressed in a kilt by his mother as a child in Ohio. MacLennan's friendship with Lauder culminated in Lauder's 1918 visit to his Rotary Club in Topeka.[34]

Although Lauder's qualities as a performer are impossible to judge for generations who never experienced him in the theatre, one valuable souvenir of his talent remains: a short extract of early sound film from 1931, used by the late Jimmy Logan in his one-man show, that captured Lauder on stage at the

Shepherd's Bush Empire performing to a live audience. It shows a bubbling, animated figure who capers exuberantly around the stage, exuding a vivacious, twinkling charm that goes some way to explaining what the fuss was all about.

While Lauder became 'the' Scotch comic, he was not the only one, or even the first in many parts of the English-speaking world where there were expatriate communities. He didn't visit Australia and New Zealand until 1914, by which time music-hall acts offering Scottish-themed entertainment were already established. The Scottish comedian Neil Kenyon, a considerable London star, preceded him to Australia in 1910, appearing under Rickards' management in vaudeville at the Melbourne Opera House, and in pantomime for the J. C. Williamson organisation. Reportedly receiving a record salary and billed as 'Undoubtedly the Finest Scottish Comedian of the Day', Kenyon's act, although similar in some respects, was probably subtler that Lauder's, consisting as it did of longer, more developed staged sketches, with the emphasis on gentle social observation, as with his 'Postie of Dunrobin':

> In his first item he appears as a village postman who exercises in soft Scottish accents a benevolent autocracy over the correspondence of the locality. In the second scene he is 'nae sae daft' as people take him to be, and dispenses humour in a steady stream while sitting in a barrow of straw.[35]

As was usually the case, Kenyon's Australian visit was part of a wider tour that also included New Zealand and South Africa and a host of other destinations, including Singapore, Penang, Java, Sumatra, Timor, New Guinea, Egypt and Algiers.[36] On the lower rungs of professional life, in the 1890s Melbourne-based promotions such as The People's Concerts, a weekend variety series active since the 1860s, and the St George's Minstrel Burlesque and Speciality Show featured local Scottish acts like Aubrey Douglas (endman, comedian whistler, 'Special Scotsman'), Millar Fraser ('Scottish tenor vocalist') and James McMillan Carrick ('Champion Highland Dancer'). By the time of the First World War, the suburban circuit of vaudeville theatres run in Sydney by Harry Clay, the third largest chain in Australia, featured a number of Scottish acts, identified simply through their professional sobriquets and given here with their dates of known activity: Gus Stratton, 'Scottish Comedian' (c.1905, 1913); Clyde Cameron, 'Scotch tenor/Songwriter' (1917); The Caley's, 'Scottish patter artists' (1916–17), who also appeared on the Fuller circuit; James Patrick Barry, 'Scottish Entertainer' (1915); Douglas Graham, 'Scotch comedian', who performed Scottish dances and played the pipes (1916); and Jessie Howard and Little Stella, 'Scottish mother and daughter song and dance act' (1916–19), Jessie Howard having been thought to have been known as Jessie Lee before 1914.[37] We don't know anything about these performers, where they came from, and whether some might have been Scottish music-hall professionals plying their trade in Australia. The suspicion is not: while the leading Australian vaudeville managers, notably Harry Rickards, himself a well-known English music-hall singer, regularly engaged English stars to appear at their venues in the principal cities, the Clay circuit and People's Concerts were both at the bottom end of the market. It was far more likely that the performers listed were local, either immigrant Scots or from first-generation Scottish stock. While the later group from the period of the First World War might well have been encouraged in the Scottish orientation of their acts by Lauder's popularity, those from the earlier period clearly would not have been, which suggests that demand for such material predated his arrival.

While the notion of a pool of home-grown Australian kilted performers is intriguing, there is evidence for it from several sources. Editions of sheet music of Lauder songs, published under licence in Australia, in several instances carry portraits of songs' Australian cover artists: the illustration on a 1910 Allan & Co edition of 'Roamin' in the Gloamin' shows Scott Gibson in kilt and sporran; the same company's issue of Lauder's 'We Parted on the Shore' (1904), sung in that year's J. C. Williamson pantomime by Victor C. Loydall, similarly depicts Loydall in a kilt. In reality, the inter-generational complexities of emigration meant that Scots acts could come from anywhere. So Miss Jennie Glover, granddaughter of Edmund Glover of Edinburgh, could appear in Canada in the late 1890s as 'New Zealand's gifted young elocutionist and Scottish vocalist'.[38]

Whether Scottish acts were local or imported from Britain was less important than their cultural authenticity, according to a 1917 article in the Australian *Theatre Magazine*. Penned by a correspondent who signed himself 'Skean Dhu', it began by condemning a Sydney newspaper that referred to the Governor General Sir Munro Ferguson as wearing 'kilts', in the plural. Decrying the error as indicative of wider ignorance of Highland culture, the writer went on to lambaste crude stage depictions of Scottish identity, and Lauder's in particular:

> The kilt is much misused by stage folk in general. There is no good reason why it should be worn by Harry Lauder, who in his stage work is a typical modern Lowlander of the towns, corresponding to the London Cockney. Lauder is not Highland in speech, bearing or thought. And few of Lauder's imitators are even Scottish in their style, let alone Highland.

Skean Dhu went on to expand on this point – that the 'cheap vulgarity' of vaudeville traduced genuine Scottish manners and culture, and that the most derogatory material was English rather than Scottish:

> A large number of the kilt jokes or songs are cockney rubbish, with a suggestion that bare knees are indecent – a suggestion surely that should not be tolerated in a land of surf-bathers. A favourite form of allusion in supposedly comic songs from London, often heard in Australia, is in what may be seen when a Highlander ascends to the top deck of a bus, a miserable and baseless form of prurience on the part of the slum-brained type of Cockney song-writer.[39]

By the late 1920s considerable changes had taken place in the Scottish diaspora. For Scots abroad, Lauder had projected a version of Scottish identity based on the kilt and a popular song repertoire steeped in sentimental attachment to a mythologised view of the homeland. In Australia records of Scottish societies dated back to the 1850s, with the Highland Society of Sydney founded in 1877, and the Caledonian Society of Melbourne (later given the prefix Royal) in 1884. Boasting the Governor General of Victoria as its first Patron, the Melbourne society established a wide range of sporting and social activities, with the daughter of a Scots immigrant from Forfar, Helen Mitchell, later world famous as singer Nellie Melba, singing Scottish songs at its concerts and dinners.[40] Such activities increased markedly around the turn of the century.

By the time Scott Skinner made his second visit to America, in 1926 at the age of 83, a year before his death, his own iconic status had become as formalised as the rituals of the expatriate Scottish communities he encountered. Invited to represent the Royal Society of Clans in America at the fiddling championship cup of the world, the welcome accorded him as he arrived in Boston harbour aboard the *RMS Caronia* amounted to a state reception: 'The quay was thronged with clansmen, all in full Highland costumes'; while the massed brass and pipe bands of the Royal Caledonian societies played, the Chiefs came aboard to greet the 'King', after which a fanfare sounded, an address of welcome was read, and Scott Skinner and his wife were escorted to a white and gold motor coach. Fêted by his hosts, Scott Skinner was nevertheless piqued to find the championship itself favoured Irish jigs, and left in a huff, but not without the sort of parting tribute that left veteran Celts misty-eyed. Piped aboard his ship, he wrote, 'The last thing I saw at Boston was a number of girls footing "Highland Laddie" on the roof of the wharf, and the last thing I heard was the blare of brass bands playing "Will ye no' Come Back Again!"'[41]

## Notes

1  Bill Findlay, 'The Case of James Houston', in Cameron and Scullion (eds.) *Scottish Popular Theatre and Entertainment*, pp. 15–38 (p. 34); see also Cameron and Scullion, 'W. F. Frame and the Scottish Popular Theatre Tradition'.
2  Muir, *Glasgow in 1901*, p. 238.
3  'Written by John Pettigrew, sung with deafening applause by R. C. McGill, Scotch comedian'; lyrics published in *Barr's Professional Gazette and Advertiser*, No. 175 (18 May 1889), p. 5; MLGC.
4  'How Dae You Dae, and How Dae You Do?', written by Joe Holland, Alexandria. Sung by A. J. Rigby, 'Comedian and Dancer'; lyrics printed in *Barr's Monthly Professional*, No. 35 (October 1905), p. 6; MLGC.
5  'J. B. Preston's latest success. Written by J. J. Rogan, Glasgow'; lyrics published in *Barr's Monthly Professional*, No. 32 (February 1905), p. 3.
6  Cameron and Scullion, *Scottish Popular Theatre*, p. 39.
7  For Corvan, see Martha Vicinus, *The Industrial Muse* (London, Croom Helm, 1974), pp. 243–244.
8  *Scotia's Music-Hall Songbook No. 7*, STA; undated, this possibly dates from the 1880s.
9  See Christopher Harvie, *Scotland and Nationalism: Scottish Society and Politics, 1707–1994* (London, Routledge, 1994), p. 13.
10  'Aye Ready Tae Fecht For Auld England, Written and sung by Alf C. Cowie. Character Vocalist', *The Amateur and Singer's Journal*, June 1894.
11  'Glasgow Forever', *Barr's Professional Gazette and Advertiser*, No. 175 (18 May 1889).
12  'The Highland Brigade; Or, The Death of General Wauchope', sung by William C. McPhie; printed in Good Templars' Harmonic Association programme for Saturday 9 November 1901; PP.
13  Murray G. H. Pittock, 'Kitsch in Culture', in *The Myth of the Jacobite Clans* (Edinburgh, Edinburgh University Press, 1995), pp. 111–122 (p. 120).
14  Senelick, 'Politics as Entertainment'.
15  Linda Colley, *Britons: Forging the Nation 1707–1837* (New Haven and London, Yale University Press, 1992).
16  Summerfield, 'Patriotism and Empire', p. 42.
17  Alex Melville, 'Pretoria', *Barr's Professional Gazette and Advertiser*, 16 June 1900.
18  Alex Melville, 'Not in the Land called England', *The Professional and Authors' Journal*, No. 154 (May 1888).
19  James Curran, 'England's in Danger', *Barr's Monthly Professional Songwriters' and Singers' Journal*, No. 13 (July 1903).
20  Dave Russell falls into this trap by inference in 'Varieties of Life: The Making of the Edwardian Music Hall', in Booth and Kaplan (eds.), *The Edwardian Theatre* (Cambridge, Cambridge University Press, 1996), pp. 61–85 (p. 77).
21  Cameron and Scullion, *Scottish Popular Theatre*, p. 45.
22  *The Entertainer*, 2 May 1914, p. 6; MLGC.

23  Harvie, *Scotland and Nationalism*, p. 22.

24  John Shearer, *Exhibition Illustrated*, 1 (4 May) p. 15; quoted in Perilla Kinchin and Juliet Kinchin, *Glasgow's Great Exhibitions* (Wendlebury, White Cockade Press, 1998), p. 79.

25  Marjory Kennedy-Fraser, *A Life of Song* (London, Humphrey Milford, 1929).

26  'Amusements', *Bon Accord*, 18 September 1880, p. 5.

27  Skinner, *My Life and Adventures*, pp. 74–75.

28  Skinner, *My Life and Adventures*, pp. 36–7, 92.

29  For MacLachlan, see Horace Fellowes, *Music in my Heart* (Edinburgh, Oliver and Boyd, 1958), p. 14; for Lely, see Chad Evans, *Frontier Theatre, A History of Nineteenth-Century Theatrical Entertainment in the Canadian Far West and Alaska* (Victoria BC, Sono Nis Press, 1983), p. 184.

30  Frame, *Tells His Own Story*, p. 92.

31  Frame, *Tells His Own Story*, pp. 95, 103, 104.

32  Lauder, *Roamin' in the Gloamin'*, p. 169.

33  Lauder, *Roamin' in the Gloamin'*, p. 187.

34  Jim Hewitson, *Tam Blake & Co. The Story of the Scots in America* (Edinburgh, Canongate Press, 1993), pp. 200–201.

35  Melbourne Opera House advertisement in *The Argus* (Melbourne), 12 November 1910, and review, *The Argus*, 14 November 1910, p. 9. I am grateful to Frank Van Straten for this material.

36  'Neil Kenyon's Trip to Australia', in *The Era*, 30 September 1911, p. 29.

37  I am grateful to Clay Djubal for making available this research material on performers appearing in the Clay circuit theatres.

38  Evans, *Frontier Theatre*, pp. 183–184.

39  Skean Dhu, 'The Scot on the Stage', from *Theatre Magazine* (Sydney), 1 February 1916, p. 33. I am grateful to Clay Djubal, for this reference.

40  *That Land of Exiles: Scots in Australia* (Edinburgh, HMSO, 1988), pp. 114–116.

41  *People's Journal*, 29 May 1926; quoted in Skinner, *My Life and Adventures*, pp. 111–113.

# 8

# The Scottish music hall and the public

The social profile of music hall, and certainly that of variety between the 1890s and 1914, is usually largely defined in terms of the social composition of the audience. However, by the last quarter of the nineteenth century music hall's influence had permeated outwards, its songs and performing techniques having been adopted by a number of other popular entertainment genres. It was no longer necessary to go to a music hall to enjoy music-hall entertainment, which was now available in a much wider range of social contexts. This new accessibility had important consequences for the development of mainstream commercial music hall.

This chapter will look at the audience that went to music hall in Glasgow, weighing the evidence of its social composition against the claims made by managers in advertising and public relations material. It will then go on to examine music hall's wider influence on Scottish popular culture, and the ways that other social groups were exposed to generic music-hall entertainment by other means; through popular concerts promoted by improving organisations or by the City Corporation, pantomime, seaside entertainments, or through home music-making, which encompassed everything from middle-class musical soirées, where comic songs were performed from sheet music, to community singing on works outings, or at tenement parties where people sang their favourites and everyone joined in the choruses. The final section will focus on music hall's special resonance for working-class audiences, examining how the popular music-hall song tradition helped enrich and, to an extent, define Glasgow's tenement culture.

Audiences at Glasgow's music halls between the 1850s and 1870s included all sections of working-class society. If the presence of what could be termed labour aristocracy was confined to better types of establishment, the majority of the audience seems in all cases to have consisted largely of young men and boys.

Thus accounts of free and easies in the 1850s speak of audiences of '130 well dressed lads belonging to various handcrafts in the city' or, for the Jupiter Temperance Hall in the Saltmarket in the same period, as 'consisting chiefly of working lads from 12–20, with a slight sprinkling of another class of both sexes, but not so respectable'.[1] At the same time one of the larger singing saloons on the Saltmarket itself, 'beautifully fitted up, finely painted and brilliantly illuminated ... [is] frequented by the mechanic, clerk, or shop-keeper', no doubt partly because 'the singing, music and dancing in these establishments are esteemed respectable'.[2] This latter group, which could be envisaged as including skilled and semi-skilled men and artisans, as well as white-collar workers and self-employed small businessmen, may also have largely consisted of single men with disposable income or younger married men. Those who, like the teacher-turned-clerk John Davidson, could afford to indulge in 'a pipe and a tankard of beer, / In a music-hall, rancid and hot'.[3]

Much the same social hierarchy of establishments seems to have applied in the 1870s, with the difference that older pub-based venues had been superseded by music halls proper. The clientele at the cheaper of these were strikingly similar to that of the free and easies. At the Royal Alhambra music hall in 1875 the audience of around 250 was described in a police report as comprising 'chiefly lads of 12–18 years of age, and 10 females, mostly young', while the 200 or so people attending the Oxford on the same night were 'mostly young men and boys and a few females, of respectable appearance'. In contrast, the police report describes the more upmarket Royal Music Hall as being nearly half-filled by 'a respectable audience', a term denoting clear social distinction to the audiences of the Alhambra and Oxford.[4]

If the audience's working-class complexion is predictable, the question of middle-class attendance remains problematic. In her work on audiences nationally Dagmar Kift has concluded that, although by the late nineteenth century 'the lower middle class as a whole had already become an integral part of the music hall audience',[5] the middle classes themselves never became regular attenders, despite the efforts of the music-hall syndicates. In the case of Glasgow, evidence seems contradictory. One example concerns the protest by several hundred Glasgow businessmen to the city magistrates in February 1875 complaining about the lewd acts appearing at the Whitebait music hall in St Enoch's Wynd, and calling for the magistrates to exercise their powers to greater effect. This protest, which Kift has analysed with great perceptiveness, and which has been referred to in chapters 2 and 3, was based on the assumption that the halls were exerting an unwholesome and corrupting influence on the young men and children of the working classes who could be found attending them. What is intriguing is that newspaper correspondence generated by public airing of the issue suggests the audience may have been more socially diverse than the original focus has led us to believe. One correspondent, writing to correct previous letters' contradictory assertions as to the social composition of the audience, suggests that:

> 'Both are right and both are wrong'. The lower class halls are patronised by the working classes – thieves and prostitutes included; the better furnished halls inviting the more respectably dressed community. Speaking from personal observation, the latter is not unfrequently composed of not a few of excellent social standing both in the mercantile and educational world.[6]

In this context 'respectably dressed' is a relative term, but the reference to social standing is unmistakably an allusion to persons of a 'better class'. A letter from another correspondent is more outspoken in delivering what have the air of home truths;

> In regard to the statement that the audience in the two halls licensed to sell strong drinks are composed of working men, I say distinctly and can prove that they are not, but as one of your correspondents said, they are frequented almost entirely by clerks, warehousemen, shopkeepers and members of the families of many in the west end terraces whom I could almost name as regular attenders. And unless on a Saturday night, when the audience is composed of a majority of the better class of working man, and in many cases his wife and sweetheart, said halls are almost entirely upheld by the classes I have mentioned.[7]

Although the writer signs him or herself 'A Music Hall Professional' and could be an industry lobbyist, there are points of interest here. Some of the trades mentioned, such as shopkeeper and clerk, would seem lower-middle-class occupations. But the claim that these, rather than ordinary or unskilled working men, formed the day-to-day audience at the city's two licensed halls (the Whitebait and Brown's Royal Music Hall) is intriguing. It also stands in stark contrast to other testimony that, at the bottom end of the market, primitive unlicensed halls catering largely for children, often in appallingly insanitary conditions, continued to flourish. William Mitchell, principal officer of the school board, testified to the magistrates that at one such hall

> in the lower part of the house, and to one side, there is a smell so insufferably offensive that I was surprised that people could be found to sit near it; I could scarcely bear even to pass it. It is caused by certain conveniences in constant use, without water, and in filthy conditions ... One of the cheap theatres or shows is placed over the damp, cold earth, and has not even seats for an audience, chiefly composed of

children under 3, and here poor ragged barefooted boys and girls, the lowest and most neglected class, using the most filthy language and pulling one another about in the roughest possible way, nightly congregate, at the charge of 1d, and, I am told, even 1/2d is not refused. We are furnished daily by the sanitary department at the School Board Office with notices of families where fever prevails in order that other children in the house should be kept back, and thus limit contagion as much as possible; but here we have hundreds of children nightly crowding together without the slightest restraint or hindrance.[8]

Such evidence of very small children attending halls, although not conclusive, certainly lends weight to the theory that venues in the Saltmarket/Trongate area drew their clientele from the immediate community. It also emphasises that, whatever strides music hall as a form might have made by 1875, it had not been at the expense of improving conditions at the lower end of the market.

If the social standing of leading Glasgow halls had moved up a notch in the 1870s, probably on the basis of higher admission prices and better-quality acts, then the possibility of a floating middle-class attendance (or rather more than that to judge from the allusions to west-end terraces) would seem far more plausible. Dagmar Kift goes some way to supporting this by suggesting that one motive for the 1875 protest was the realisation of middle-class employers that youth as a whole (and not just warehouse boys and clerks) was in moral danger from music-hall entertainment.[9] It might also be that the threat, from the middle-class perspective, was even more insidious, and that for youth we should read middle-class males as a whole.

If this were the case, the idea that the discussion of music-hall songs and sketches generated by the 1875 protest 'demonstrated a huge gulf between working and middle-class cultures' might be disingenuous. Glasgow music hall in the 1870s was undoubtedly a product of working-class culture, but that does not imply that as a cultural experience it represented new territory. The impression left by the letters to the *New British Daily Mail*, most of whose writers hasten to add that they speak from little personal experience, is that many middle-class men were more familiar with music hall than they were willing to acknowledge.

The problem for proprietors was that the prospects of increasing middle-class attendance were constrained by the social stigma that attached to music hall. The existing presence was exclusively male and, to all intents, invisible to polite society. J. J. Bell wrote of the Scotia in Stockwell Street in the 1880s, 'I daresay that half of the middle-class patrons were there surreptitiously. University students who went to the Gaiety at half-time (and half-price) …

were deemed 'fast'. A lady in a Music Hall was unthinkable.'[10] In social terms, music hall remained marginalised, and nothing less than a complete transformation of the entertainment would open up the possibility of a broader-based middle-class clientele.

If the middle class audience for music hall in the 1870s and 1880s consisted of men who attended surreptitiously, the question remains whether the reforms of 1890, discussed in the previous chapter, really succeeded in changing the situation. Certainly the splendid new variety houses were capable of attracting a splendid clientele. *The Bailie* of 1897 wrote of the new Empire Palace that:

> A more brilliant audience has seldom graced a premier at any theatre in Glasgow, and the fashion of bringing young ladies to a variety show has been successfully established so far as the Empire is concerned. To-night ladies in evening dress were as numerous as men in the best parts of the house, and the programme was such that everyone could have listened to. I am very glad, my Magistrate, to see this old superstition about the music hall finally dispelled. It has been far too long the custom to regard an entertainment in a variety house as a shocking affair, while on the boards of another theatre, as a musical comedy or a pantomime, it would be received with the utmost favour.[11]

If the crucial objective of attracting middle-class women, a development that, in social terms, transformed the whole tone of the proceedings, seems to have been realised, it remains doubtful whether the audience present at such galas was representative. The opening of the Glasgow Pavilion in Renfield Street in March 1904 was reported in similar terms.

> On very rare occasions only does one find a variety theatre so well filled by the elite as on Monday last at the Pavilion … The opening night was more like the attendances we are accustomed to at 'Lohengrin' or 'Carmen'. Every part of the house was crowded, and in the boxes, circle and stalls there was quite a preponderance of ladies and gentlemen of quality in evening dress. Magistrates, Town Councillors, merchants, shipowners, lawyers, and accountants, to say nothing of representatives from many other places of amusement in the city, helped to swell the gay crowd.[12]

The presence of so influential a body is impressive, as is the flattering comparison with an audience for the opera. But even so fulsome an account (in this case from the *Glasgow Programme*, a free sheet supported by entertainment industry advertising) feels compelled to acknowledge that such a turnout of the 'elite' is exceptional. And the breathless noting of persons 'of quality' in evening dress gives the lie to this as anything approaching normality for a variety performance. As so often with these sketches, we are left with a vivid but selective impression which focuses on one section of the auditorium. Taken collectively,

**Table 8.1** Scotia Music Hall admission charges

|              | 1877     | 1887    | 1891    | 1895           |
|--------------|----------|---------|---------|----------------|
| Gallery      | 4d.      | 4d.     | 3d.     | 4d.            |
| Pit          | 6d.      | 3d.     | –       | 6d.            |
| Circle       | 6d.      | 6d.     | 6d.     | 1s. (& Balcony)|
| Front Chairs | –        | –       | 2s.     | –              |
| Stalls       | 6d.      | 6d.     | 6d.     | 1s. 6d.        |
| Stage Boxes  | 2s.      | 1s. 6d. | 1s. 6d. | –              |
| Side Boxes   | 1s. 6d.  | 1s.     | 1s.     | –              |
| Boxes        | –        | –       | –       | –              |

*Source:* People's Palace and Mitchell Library collections.

these various eye-witness descriptions give an idea of the different social group-ings present at music-hall performances, but no means of verifying the 'mean' of the audience in social terms. The picture remains fragmentary.

To get a broader impression of the social basis of the audience, we shall examine two specific areas: admission charges at Glasgow music halls, and atti-tudes towards and perceptions of the audience revealed by Glasgow managers' public relations.

In dealing first with admission charges, it is important to state that, in reality, figures for different venues can rarely stand direct comparison. Admission charges often stood for considerable periods of time, sometimes decades, and were often based on the location and circumstances of the individual venue. Moreover, the results of such analyses can only indicate the potential for atten-dance by different social groups, rather than confirm the fact of it. A case in point would be admission charges for the Scotia Music Hall in Stockwell Street (see Table 8.1).

The Scotia opened in 1862, and between 1870 and 1891 was managed by a longstanding 'Proprietrix', Mrs Christina Baylis, following the early death of her husband James. Charges for 1877, when the venue was known as the New Scotia, ranged from 6d for stalls and circle, with boxes (probably seating 4) at 2s., to 4d for the cheapest seats, those in the gallery. By 1887 the seating cate-gories remained unchanged, but the price for the pit (the cheaper stalls area) had dropped to 3d, making it now the cheapest part of the house. The 1887 charges stood until 1891, when some rearrangement of the auditorium evi-dently took place, resulting in the disappearance of the pit, and the introduc-tion of 'Front Chairs' (presumably what we would call the front stalls), which became the most expensive seats at 2 shillings. Poorer patrons were displaced to the gallery, where the price was dropped a penny to 3d, no doubt to keep the lowest price of admission at the same level. These were the last charges introduced by the Baylis management. The Moss, Thornton and Kirk combination, which took over the Scotia later in 1891, initially kept prices at the same levels, but by 1895 increased charges had been introduced. The front chairs disappeared and the pit was restored. The gallery remained the cheapest section of the house, but the cost of the top- and middle-price seats – the stalls, circle and balcony – were substantially increased, with the stalls rising from 6d to 1s. 6d, and the circle from 6d to 1 shilling. Although Moss's top price of 1s. 6d was lower than Baylis's of 2s., the implication is that the majority of seats in the lower house were, by 1895, significantly more expensive than they had been under the old management. Moreover, the house's charges should not be seen in isolation, but in the context of its position in the local marketplace.

In 1895 Moss were operating the Scotia in conjunction with their initial Glasgow venue, the better-located Gaiety on Sauchiehall Street (see Appendix, Table A3). While advertising for the Moss Scotia made a feature of its 'Popular Prices', the Gaiety, which had no pit, charged 6d for admission to the gallery (as against the Scotia's 4d, making it the most expensive for a music hall in the city), and otherwise offered no seat under 1 shilling. One possible implication is that the increase in charges at the Scotia might have been even more pronounced had not syndicate strategy required that the Stockwell Street hall cater for the lower end of the market, leaving the city-centre Gaiety (which used refined legitimate theatre terminology such as 'Family Circle') free to develop a better class of clientele, although quite what that consisted of remains open to debate.

If the examples of the Scotia and Gaiety seem to confirm music hall's upmarket progress as a general trend, a wider comparison of charges for other Glasgow halls raises complicating factors (see Appendix, Tables A2, A3 and A4). Viewed as a whole, the most striking thing about the figures for the broader sample is the extent of their variation, evidently the result of the wide range of social and cultural, as well as commercial and architectural considerations affecting individual venues. Faced with these, the need for caution when forming conclusions is very evident.

However, several trends can be identified. The first is that, in line with the evidence from the Scotia, it is clear that prices for more expensive seats rose generally in the 1890s and 1900s, suggesting the presence of a wealthier audience prepared to pay such prices. However, it is also apparent that such charges did not continue rising, but reached a ceiling in the 1900s, one

incidentally that fell far short of the prices charged for similar seats at legitimate theatres. This is supported by the fact that, while Empire and Pavilion
charges for stalls and circle seats in the 1900s resolved at around the 1s. or 1s.
6d mark, Arthur Hubner's two upmarket venues, the Skating Palace of 1896,
and Hippodrome of 1902–04, which charged the exorbitant rates of 2 and 3
shillings for stalls seats, both proved to be short-lived. Although the quality of
the entertainment would obviously have been a crucial factor, the suspicion
remains that the chief reason for the failure of the two venues, neither of
which offered seats under 1s., was that they were simply over-priced. It was
also true that there had always been more expensive categories of seats to cater
for passing trade from 'swells', as evinced by the Shakespeare in the early
1880s. What was new in the 1890s, and possibly 1880s, was the great increase
in the proportion of seats offered at the new higher prices, which signalled an
altered balance within the auditoriums.

A second observation is that over the same period, from the 1890s to 1900s,
prices for cheaper seats not only stayed at much the same level as the 1870s, but
if anything dropped in price in the 1900s. While some of the halls offering
gallery admission at 2d in the 1900s were venues serving local audiences, such
as the Star Palace in Partick, or were newly opened halls engaged in undercut-
ting competitors to win market share, like the Palace on Main Street, Gorbals, it
seems significant that city centre theatres of varieties such as the Pavilion and
Empire resolutely kept gallery admission down to 3d, in contradiction of the
policy to increase prices in other areas. That the retention of the core gallery
audience remained extremely important for music hall finances is confirmed by
a comparison of prices for the Moss-owned Empire and Coliseum, which shows
the south side Coliseum offering lower 'People's prices' to complement the
Empire's higher charges in an effort to maximise market share, just as the same
company had done with the Scotia and Gaiety in the 1890s.

The two points discussed – that top-of-the-range prices were rising while
the lowest were pegged, or even dropped as a result of increased competition –
would seem to imply that managers were actively pursuing a lower-middle- or
middle-class audience. In fact the case is far from conclusive. In the first
instance, it is important to reiterate that the most expensive seats for music
hall remained far cheaper than comparable seats at legitimate theatres, where
stalls at the Royalty or Theatre Royal in the 1900s generally cost 4 or 5
shillings, considerably more than the lower figure charges at the Empire or
Pavilion. That this should have been so affirms that, despite the glittering
turnout at gala openings, variety had not attained the social cachet of

legitimate theatre. In addition, and following the logic of the first policy shift, the lower prices charged by some music halls could indicate that they were consciously opting out of the race for better-class clientele and concentrating on retaining their core audience. From this perspective it is possible to argue that the continuity of prices at the bottom end of the market is the more significant feature of the admission figures, and confirms that, despite other increases, the critical mass of the audience remained in the gallery and cheaper parts of the house. Along these lines the admission charges for the 1900s also provide evidence to suggest that by this period the broadening range of admission prices and increase in competition was resulting in the emergence of two distinct types of variety theatre whose prices overlapped; the smarter city-centre palaces of varieties, and smaller venues in inner-city or outlying areas, which relied on a localised clientele and retained much of the culture of older working-class music hall.

By the 1890s alternatives to music hall, in the form of popular concert series promoted by various temperance and improving societies, had long been available.[13] Abstainers' Union Saturday Night Concerts in the City Hall began in 1854, and by 1900 were attracting audiences of 3,500.[14] Good Templars' Harmonic Association Concerts started in 1872, with programmes playing simultaneously at Bridgeton Temperance Institute in James Street, Albion Hall in College Street, and Wellington Palace in the Gorbals, artists shuttling between the three venues in Hansom cabs just as they did between music halls. By 1900 combined attendance at these three Good Templars' Halls could sometimes approach 6,000.[15] Corporation Penny Concerts, supervised by Walter Freer, began in the late 1890s and proved hugely successful, with annual attendances at the City Hall concerts alone by 1900 being estimated at over 80,000.[16] The entertainment offered at these occasions was, like music hall, heavily biased towards vocal music, and comprised a mixture of classical and light classical items, traditional airs, popular drawing room ballads and comic songs. The majority of performers were recitalists or concert singers, usually amateurs, leavened by two or three crowd-pulling music-hall acts. A representative Good Templar's concert programme from September 1889 included an 'Eminent Scottish Soprano', another described as the principal soprano of Glasgow Cathedral, a mezzo-soprano, tenor, and two baritones, together with a 'negro comedian, vocalist and dancer', and two heavily flagged star turns: Charles Coburn, 'The Man Who Broke the Bank at Monte Carlo' (his last appearance in Scotland that season), and Professor J. F. Calverto, ventriloquist, mimic, vocal deceptionist and escapologist.[17] If the tone and content of these occasions were consciously more refined than in music hall, reflecting their improving aims, the entertainment remained populist and far from punitive. The audience joined in with choruses, and comic songs and patter were much in evidence, all material having first been approved as suitable. Quite how severe the moral climate was seems to have varied. In her memoirs opera singer – (turned music-hall artist) Emily Soldene described performing at a Total Abstainers' Saturday Night Concert in the 1860s where the 'City Fathers' of the committee seated behind her on the platform complained that, in wearing white satin without petticoats rather than a crinoline, Soldene (as she put it) 'deesplayed ma feegure ower much'.[18] But Coburn, writing of a later period (probably the late 1880s or 1890s) described how the Good Templars' committee, after exercising its veto on one of his favourite songs, which had 'boozy' connotations, on many previous occasions, eventually relented and allowed him to sing it.

The success of these concerts could be ascribed to several factors. Firstly the promoters realised the importance of star names, and paid top rates to ensure that most leading performers passing through Glasgow appeared on their platforms. Moreover, their determination to keep up with – and surpass – their commercial competitors in the city music halls led to a readiness to encompass innovation and technological developments. A Corporation Saturday Afternoon Musical Recital at the St Andrew's Hall on 12 November 1900 included selections on the gramophone, and a diorama and cinematograph ('Diorama subject – Japanese Life and Customs'), mirroring music hall's own obsession with such novelties. The entertainment had anyway long since broadened beyond that normally associated with the term concert. In 1900 the following week's programme included the Macdonald Troupe of Highland and National Dancers and John Clyde and his humorous sketch company. In March 1912 a similar Corporation even featured the Histrionic Concert Party of Liverpool and their 'Hunting Scene', which included 'costumes and dresses of the Huntsmen and ladies of the early Georgian period'.

With costumed and staged sketches, choreographic elements, and speciality acts as well as comics and singing, this was variety in all but name. But perhaps the most significant factor in the concerts' success was that they offered a secure, publicly regulated environment (with some events taking place during daylight hours), and were deemed safe for women. Corporation events, advertised as 'Promoted by the Lord Provost, Magistrates, and Town Council of Glasgow', bore the unmistakable imprimatur of respectability. A *North British Daily Mail* article on entertainment in the city in 1900 opined:

There is no doubt that the Penny concerts have encouraged the taste for popular entertainments. Why, there are hundreds go to the concerts in the city hall in the afternoon and come to that under the auspices of the Abstainers Union in the evening. The fair sex in large numbers patronise the former entertainment for the reason that they can go unprotected.[19]

This factor – that such concerts were regarded as respectable, and offered a means of seeing music-hall stars without having to go anywhere near a music hall – was probably the key to their success. They evidently found a growing audience in the 1890s. The *North British Daily Mail* article states the combined annual attendance for Glasgow Corporation Penny concerts in 1900 was 216,161, as against 42,195 for the 1890/91 season.[20] This huge, municipally organised series must have had a considerable impact on commercial music halls, both by directly competing for their audience, and by setting the standard for what aimed to be (at least in aspiration) a more refined and consciously moral brand of music-hall entertainment.

While other cities came to embrace the principle of public entertainment in their own time, there were limits. In 1897 Dundee Council appointed a committee to arrange a series of Popular Saturday Evening Concerts like those of Glasgow and Aberdeen. The following year the recreation and cemeteries committee approved plans for music in parks and public places, and funds to pay for bands. But in 1899 a request by a brass band for permission to give Sunday concerts of sacred music in parks proved highly divisive, in committee, and after several meetings was ultimately rejected.[21]

If concerts offered the flavour of variety in a refined setting, the middle-class audience's first point of contact with music-hall performers was probably through pantomime. Managers of legitimate theatres first began engaging music-hall stars for leading roles in pantomimes in the 1870s, hoping to cash in on their growing popularity. The combination proved enormously successful. By the 1880s Glasgow's leading pantomimes, including the famous productions mounted by the Royal Princess's Theatre in Main Street, Gorbals, were running from Christmas almost until Easter, and their revenue was forming an increasingly important part of theatre's annual income. Much of their popular success was due to the dynamism that music-hall performers brought to the established format, although their more spontaneous approach sometimes led to friction. The Scottish comedian W. F. Frame, 'The Man U Know', was engaged for the Royal Princess's pantomime in 1891, where during rehearsals it became apparent that he was interpolating his own jokes and business into the scripted production.

At the dress rehearsal Mr Frame was ordered to keep to copy, but this he flatly refused to do, as he had come there to please the audience and make a success for himself and the proprietor. Owing to the success of the first night of the pantomime Mr Waldon congratulated Mr Frame and ordered him to *go as he pleased* in his gags, etc., – a very wise decision, as his songs and gags have become very popular all over the country.[22]

The audience that enjoyed Frame's performance was being exposed to music hall. Under the influence of the new type of performer, pantomime came to adopt aspects of music-hall technique and convention. What had been a mid-Victorian fairy story was transformed into an interactive and sometimes satirical vehicle, where performers talked directly to the audience and cross-dressing was milked for sexual worth. Many of the pantomime elements now regarded as 'traditional' – the principals' use of badinage in talking to and 'working' the audience, the leading comic's appearance as the Dame, audience participation in the song sheet – derived from music-hall practices, and the integration of speciality acts – acrobats, jugglers and animal acts – also dated from this period.

The commercial implications of pantomime's success were enormous. One contemporary source estimated the audience for pantomime in Glasgow for the 1895–96 season at 60,000 people per week (as against 25,000 per week for other variety and theatrical performances combined).[23] Moreover, artists and sheet-music publishers were quick to appreciate that a three- or four-month run of performances offered an unparalleled opportunity to promote the most popular of the songs featured. Leading productions boasted complete original scores, such as those composed by music director E. T. De Banzie for the Theatre Royal pantomimes, into which star performers would integrate their own songs. By the early 1900s music publishers were playing an increasingly important entrepreneurial role, both in securing exposure for current hits by placing them in pantomime productions, and by taking up and promoting songs that emerged spontaneously in the course of successful panto runs. Harry Lauder's most popular hit songs – 'I Love a Lassie' (1905) and 'Roamin' in the Gloamin' (1910) were both products of pantomime seasons at the Glasgow Theatre Royal. The fact that their enormous commercial exposure – through gramophone recordings and sheet-music sales – originally derived from pantomime, rather than music hall, says a great deal about the importance of the form, which in many ways seems to have represented the perfect synergy between music hall and legitimate theatre.

The other important sub-genre of music hall to emerge in the 1890s was that provided by seaside concert parties. The rise of Clyde holiday resorts coincided with the emergence of new types of entertainers. If the pierrots were the most striking, in their *Commedia*-inspired costumes and all-white make-up, their sartorial rivals included other parties who dressed in blazers and yachting caps. At Largs, Joe Wesley's minstrels were a regular summer fixture on the foreshore from the late 1890s, where they performed on a platform before large audiences of well-turned-out holidaymakers who watched from a banked slope. Competition was evidently intense. By June 1904 rival entertainments on the foreshore included 'fiddlers, dancing bears, Scotch bagpipers, Tyrolean orchestras, German bands, banjoists [and] acrobats', as well as showmen playing portable gramophones, with 'a children's minstrel company, violin and harp combination, a strong man, and an Irish comic vocalist' joining in July.[24] Although local press opinion soon expressed concern at the sheer number of attractions, stating 'we are afraid that Largs must be fast losing its character – and principal charm to many people – of a restful summer resort', and noted with alarm recent comparisons with Blackpool, criticism was generally aimed at the Council's recent deregulation of entertainment, and at independent showmen, rather than at Wesley, who enjoyed excellent relations with the Council.[25] From 1909 Wesley's group were superseded by the Smart-Set Cadets, a dapper concert party who dressed in smart naval uniforms and gave two performances a day (3.00 p.m. and 7.15 p.m.) between June and September, with an extra 11.00 a.m. show added for Glasgow Fair fortnight, proceedings adjourning to the town hall if the weather was bad.[26] With sister troupes in Prestwick and Troon, the impeccably turned-out Cadets, run by an American, Alvin Sawyer, represented the epitome of Edwardian style.

The entertainment presented by such groups was tailored to the family audience, taking its cue from the mood of optimism and well-being that pervaded the holidaymakers. Coarse, not to say political or contentious, material was strictly excluded. Combining music-hall elements with a compressed, revue-style format, shows began with an up-beat opening chorus in which the company introduced themselves and welcomed the audience, after which the programme continued with individual spots, gags and sketches. After the interval, in which a member of the company went round 'bottling' for contributions with a bottle or collecting box, the second half continued with more of the same, the show finishing with a cheery ensemble farewell. Parties usually numbered between six and eight performers, including a piano accompanist and two or three female members. The range of artists would typically include a senior comic, who would chair proceedings, a pair of sentimental duettists, a serio-comic singer, a ventriloquist or other speciality, and a comic double-act of some sort. Such parties became extremely popular with holidaymakers, not least because the performers, seen close up in stage make-up or by the light of the tilly lamps that were lit as dusk fell, seemed glamorous and exotic figures, the handsomer men often acquiring considerable local followings. Sawyer's Smart-Set Cadets performed at Largs until 1928, and there were similar parties playing at most other Clyde resorts, notably Saltcoats, Stevenson, Ayr, Dunoon ('The Geisha Boys' and 'White Coons'), Rothesay and Millport. On the east coast summer companies played at North Berwick, Portobello, Burntisland, Kinghorn, Montrose and, most importantly, Aberdeen, where the arrival of Catlin's Royal Pierrots in 1905 coincided with the opening of the Council's Beach Pavilion, which from the 1920s, under the highly successful management of the Aberdonian comic Harry Gordon, became the focus of summer variety in the city.[27]

As with pantomime, seaside entertainers represented a point of contact for sections of the public not familiar with music hall *per se*. Although the social orientation of resorts varied, such shows seem to have been pitched at a 'superior' or middle-class audience. The family holiday atmosphere, together with the need to cultivate a scrupulous reputation with local councils, resulted in an entertainment that was quickfire and relentlessly upbeat, sometimes to the point of inanity, with a strong emphasis on getting the audience singing. The lack of social comment, and topical or political content, in performing material may have been a conscious attempt to keep such shows 'classless'. In fact it often led to an over-reliance on 'nonsense' material, perhaps contributing to the derisory modern-day connotations of 'end of the pier', although there are instances of sketches drawing on urban stereotypes for broad comic purposes.[28] The fact that such performances were given outdoors under open skies, the artists being in a wooden shell or stance while the audience sat or stood in the open air, and only needed to contribute if they felt like it, all added to the impression of a wholesome, 'clean' entertainment, something that music hall in a smoky theatre could never be. If such seaside shows represented an adaptation of music-hall skills to the evolving leisure market, their influence – both as a training ground for performers and on the wider audience – was considerable.

But in discussing the dissemination of professional music hall amongst these three areas – public concerts, pantomime and seaside entertainments – we should not overlook what was arguably the form's most profound effect on popular culture in Glasgow, the role of music-hall songs in tenement culture. In examining this, it is important to first appreciate the extent to which musical life in the late-Victorian period continued to be self-reliant and largely home made. Dave Russell writing of England, suggests that despite the massive strides made by the music hall and other branches of the entertainment industry in the late nineteenth-century, it was the community itself that generated the bulk of musical entertainment, albeit entertainment drawing largely on the compositions emanating from the various branches of the musical profession.[29]

In the case of Glasgow, the popularisation of home music-making received a considerable boost in the mid-1870s with the success of the American Evangelical revivalists Moody and Sankey. Arriving in the city in February 1874, they quickly achieved cult status, particularly with middle-class audiences who had previously stayed away from revivalist meetings. At the heart of their success was the integration of music into the service, Moody being the preacher, while Sankey played the harmonium and sang uplifting hymns of his own composition in an attractive baritone. Not the least of the effects of their visit, which attracted 7,000 people to their final meeting at the Kibble Palace in the Botanic Gardens, was the new popularity it lent to accompanied vocal music, resulting in the publication of the Moody–Sankey hymnbook, a best-seller well into the twentieth century, and the introduction of accompanied music into Church of Scotland services.[30]

While music-hall songs became an important part of the popular repertoire for home music-making, transcending the halls to become the property of the wider public, their appeal meant different things to different sections of society. While the middle classes enjoyed catchy ballads and comic songs, buying them as sheet music in piano vocal parts for singing at home around the piano, they took their place amongst a varied diet of traditional and folk songs, hymns, and light classical material, popular ballads and art songs, all of which would have featured in informal soirees and musical evenings.[31] In contrast, amongst the urban working classes the popular song culture had a special resonance, not so much for the content of its material, as for its social function. No family party or celebration was complete without a singsong, when all present were called on to deliver a turn or party piece, generational differences being marked by older people's choice of favourites from previous decades. Although the songs performed also included traditional and religious material, most emanated from music halls. Glasgow novels provide plenty of examples of such occasions. Edward Gaitens' humorous short story 'A Wee Nip', set in the Gorbals before the First World War, concerns an impromptu tenement party thrown by the drunken Macdonnell family to celebrate their son's homecoming. Proceedings get underway as the company returns from the pub:

> Aunt Kate, a tiny, dark woman of remarkable vitality, went kissing all her nephews in turn and the party got into full swing. Liquor was soon winking from tumblers, tea-cups, egg-cups – anything that could hold drink – and Aunt Kate, while directing the young men to bring chairs from the parlour, sang 'A Guid New Year Tae Ane An' A', unmindful that the year was more than half done, and Jimmy, thinking a nautical song was expected of him, sang 'A Life on the Ocean Wave'![32]

Jimmy later renders 'The Lass that Made the Bed for Me', and Mrs Macdonnell requests 'The Meeting of the Waters' because it 'recalled their honeymoon in the Vale of Tralee'. Mr Macdonnell himself stirringly delivers 'Yes! Let me like a soldier fall upon some open plain / Me breast boldly bared to meet the ball, that blots out every stain!' Later, after the arrival of fresh supplies of booze, he has everybody joining in with 'I'll knock a hole in McCann for knocking a hole in me can'. No less than fifteen songs are mentioned in the course of the story. Sometimes the format of such occasions consciously aped that of a variety entertainment, as in the more sedate soirée described in David McCulloch's gentle satire 'Bottling Night' (1917), set in fictional 'Lumpertown', where a family party is held a week before a wedding as an 'undress rehearsal'. Here the entertainment begins after the dozen guests have enjoyed supper seated around a white clothed table:

> 'Order for a song,' requested Jimmy the Jew, who, as best man, was responsible for the vocal and instrumental part of the programme. 'Miss Archbrows is going to sing the 'Queen of the Earth'. Give her a little encouragement, ladies and gentlemen.' The encouragement – lusty handclapping – brought Miss Archbrows into the limelight and under the gasolier.[33]

The company includes the stereotypical figure of the failed music-hall comic, in the person of Arthur Tickle, who 'had really been a good comedian of his class, and still could have been in vaudeville, but for a thirst', and who goes on to deliver a song about 'a mother-in-law, a poker and a beak. Who sentenced him one day, oh law, to seven days and a week.' The fact that anybody and everybody knew such songs, and regarded the singing of them as part of normal social activity, at work or in the pub, gave music hall a place in the heart of working-class life, and one that marked it out from other forms of popular theatre. If songs were common currency music hall, in the generic sense, was the bank.

If songs bound the audience to the halls, managers in the city evidently appreciated both the centrality of music hall to urban working class culture and the long-term commercial value of investing in it. The syndicated managements of the 1890s, whilst going to great lengths to promote variety as a middle-class family entertainment, were careful to ensure that the venues themselves remained focal points for the community activities of working people. Glasgow halls were often used on Sundays for political meetings, the Social Democratic Federation using the People's Palace, the Clarion the Pavilion, and the Independent Labour Party the Lyceum.[34] Elsewhere, too, theatres and halls were utilised as amenities. Moreover, Moss and Thornton's acting managers in the city seem to have been given wide discretionary powers to cultivate the local audience. Newspaper advertisements for the Scotia Variety Theatre Stockwell Street in February 1895 carried an addendum that 'our soup kitchen is now in full swing, and a liberal supply of soup and bread will be given away to the deserving poor at 1pm, on Wednesday, Thursday and Friday of this week'.[35] Such public spirited-ness attracted middle-class approbation. A *Quiz* article entitled 'Music Halls and Humanity' noted that

> The Scotia and Gaiety halls have distinguished themselves of late, taking the lead in the humane work of feeding the poor and starved unemployed, and giving a cue to the churches which, unfortunately, the churches did not see their way to follow. Day by day during the great frost these two places of entertainment were open for feeding the poor with soup and beef, and were the means of enabling many a hungry waif to tide over the trying time. The food supplied was of a good quality and was invariably served nice and hot.

The piece concluded that 'Messrs. Howard and Thom [the two acting managers concerned] are to be congratulated on the humanity of their idea, and the excellent fashion in which it was carried out.'[36]

Other charitable initiatives also reinforced links with local working communities. In February 1909 Councillor E. H. Bostock, acting under the auspices of the Theatre Royal Cinderella Fund, threw open his Scottish Zoo premises in New City Road to 500 underprivileged children from the Cowcaddens district:

> Outside in the street there were hundreds of hungry and poorly-clad children waiting in the hope that they too might share in the entertainment. When the tea was over in the Zoo, the guests were taken into the Hippodrome, and fully two hundred of those waiting outside were admitted, to each of whom a bag of pastry was presented. In addition as many others were permitted to enter as there was room for. An excellent variety of entertainment was provided by a number of artistes who kindly gave their services for the afternoon, and Councillor Bostock set his bioscope agoing to the great delight of the children. On leaving, each child received an india-rubber ball, sweets, and fruit.[37]

This charitable focus on children was evidently a common trait among managers, judging by similar benefits by the managers of London venues such as the

QUIZ SUPPLEMENT, FEBRUARY 28, 1895.

AT THE "GAIETY" AND "SCOTIA" SOUP KITCHENS.

**21**     'Gaiety & Scotia Soup Kitchens', *Quiz*, 28 February 1895

Edmonton Empire and South London Palace.[38] If such events were basically philanthropic, they also signalled a recognition on the part of managers that they shared an identity of interests with the working audience.

Moreover, cultivation of the working audience was not limited to institutional patronage. In the entertainment itself managers were also careful to retain acts that embodied aspects of working-class culture, particularly sporting events. Retired or over-the-hill sporting heroes were persuaded to cash in on their celebrity with short and lucrative music-hall tours, and figures like Billy Hall, St Mirren's famous singing goalkeeper, and Alick Lafferty, 'Scotland's Bantam Weight Champion', proved popular draws.[39] The crossover between localised music-hall culture and sporting constituencies was evidently a potent force. The 1900 opening ceremony of the Empire Theatre of Varieties in Rosebank Street, Dundee (a minor hall despite the illustrious name) was held under the patronage of 'Bailie Robertson and the Dundee Football Team', while that of the Gaiety in Victoria Road in 1903 boasted the presence 'Queen's Park F.C., Dundee F. C., the Thistle Harriers and the Athletic Club'.[40] Football itself also featured as a rich source for topical humour in songs like 'The Jossie Fitba' Club', sung by J. C. Macdonald at Moss's Varieties, Edinburgh, in 1888, and although the halls generally steered clear of sectarian issues, they evidently featured in acts like Lindsay and Harte's, who played their latest football sketches – 'Celtic vs. Rangers' and 'Feeing Day' – around Lanarkshire halls. Reflecting the fairground legacy, challenges or competitions of various sorts continued to be popular, head-to-head contests between champion clog dancers being superseded in the 1890s by challenge bouts between star wrestlers.

Sometimes such challenges were thrown open to members of the public. A scene in Patrick MacGill's Glasgow novel *Children of the Dead End* (1914) has the working-class protagonist responding to a printed announcement that a 'well-known Japanese wrestler was offering ten pounds to any man whom he could not overcome in less than five minutes in a ju-jitsu contest.' On arriving at the hall in the south side of the city, he takes a seat in the threepenny gallery, where the coarse entertainment and seedy clientele contribute to a hostile and generally dissolute atmosphere. The first few acts on are clapped or hissed, while the girl sitting by him

> kept eating oranges all the evening and giggling loudly at every indecent joke made by the actors. She was somewhat the worse for liquor, and her language was far from choice. She was very pretty and knew it. A half-dressed woman sang a song, every stanza of which ended with a lewd chorus. The girl beside me joined in the song and clapped her hands boisterously when the artiste left the stage.

When the wrestler, the star turn, appears, the sense of excitement and unruliness of the audience is well conveyed:

> The curtain rose slowly. A man in evening dress bearing a folded paper in his hand, came out to the front of the stage. One of the audience near me applauded with his hands.

'That's nae a wrestler, you fool!' someone shouted. 'You dinna ken what you're clappin' about.'

'Silence!'

The audience took up the word and all shouted silence, until the din was deafening.

'Ladies and gentlemen,' began the figure on the stage, when the noise abated. Everyone applauded again. Even the girl beside me blurted out 'Hear! hear!' through a mouthful of orange juice. Those who pay threepence for their seats love to be called ladies and gentlemen.

'Ladies and gentlemen, I have great pleasure in introducin' U—Y—, the well-known exponent of the art of ju-jitsu.'

A dark little man with very bright eyes stepped briskly on the stage, bowed to the audience, then folded his arms over his breast and gazed into vacancy with an air of boredom.

When the formal challenge is extended to anyone who can last five minutes against 'the undefeated champion of his weight in all the world' ('"I could wrestle him mysel'," said the girl of the orange-scented breath in a whisper') our hero accepts, only to succumb after forty-seven seconds, the crowd who cheered and clapped him onto the stage hissing him off.[41]

Although fictionalised, the above account bears the hallmarks of first-hand experiences on the part of the author. Certainly Yukio Tani, 'The Great Japanese Wrestler', played south-side halls, appearing at the Coliseum, Eglinton Street, in January 1909, and E. H. Bostock similarly records the popularity of wrestlers at his Zoo and Hippodrome in the same period.[42] The unruly, almost bear-pit atmosphere evoked above seems closer to that of a sporting occasion, such as a boxing match, than to the more refined ambience promoted by city-centre variety. If we accept that the account has documentary value, it suggests that while some managers were trying to promote variety as a more urbane, theatrically based entertainment, others at the lower end of the market were continuing to tap into older rural sporting traditions associated with Glasgow Fair. This older, more dangerous constituency, and music hall's place at its centre is vividly evoked in the following description of the 'other side' of Argyle Street at the turn of the century:

At night it is the Sauchiehall Street of a slightly poorer class. The lads and lasses of Gorbals and Gallowgate come daffing in crowds, chivvying one another into the streets and up the entries, conducting their love-making by means of slaps and 'dunches,' and showing the Scots' self-consciousness that makes it so pathetically unspontaneous. If the nights are rainy, the young folk have either of the two 'Wonderlands' [Bostock's and Crouch's] or the 'Brit' for their solace, and the street

is deserted save for racing touts and hot-potato men. On Saturday night Argyle
Street holds saturnalia – not the 'Continental saturnalia' we hear so much about,
but a time of squalid licence when men stagger out of shuttered public-houses as
out of a pit, and the street echoes to insane roaring and squabbles, to the nerve col-
lapse and ends a day's debauch of drink and football.[43]

While most venues needed to attract a socially mixed clientele and syndicated
managements were constrained by their commitment to a more middle-class
music hall, the independent managers responsible for halls such as those mentioned above were freer to embrace a less pretentious audience, if that was where
their commercial interest lay. The flamboyant A. E. Pickard acquired the
Britannia music hall in 1906, relaunching it as the Panopticon. The following
unpublished first-hand account captures Pickard's showmanship, and the
excitement of the Trongate in the period around the First World War:

> Saturday was a very special day, that was when mum and dad would take us into
> town, to see all the lovely shop windows, the fun outside all the theatres and pic-
> ture houses, and not forgetting the street peddlers …
>
> The famous Mr Pickard owned the Panopticon and outside a kilty was playing
> the bagpipes, while inside before the show began there was a guy playing a honky
> tonk type of piano – the noise was awful but good fun. Mr Pickard stood on the
> pavement outside the main entrance, he had his frock coat and top hat on. He
> directed the queue and made sure nobody got bored with his patter. The old time
> go-as-you-please contests were terrific in the Panopticon.[44]

Pickard's cajoling repartee with passers-by sounds more like the old-fashioned
fairground barker than the smart variety impresario of the Moss school. J. H.
Saville, owner of the Paisley Theatre, was similarly recalled as a hands-on presence outside his other venue, the Empire music hall in Moss Street, Paisley:
'Every night Mr Saville stood at the entrance shouting the names of the company, and the prices, which were 4d, 6d and 9d.'[45] Whether in a conscious effort
to project themselves as populist figures, or through showman's intuition, managers such as Pickard and Saville established themselves as figures in the local
community, their venues becoming a familiar part of the everyday life of the
area.

But if managers used charitable initiatives and the embodiment of aspects of
working cultures in the entertainment as a means of reinforcing working-class
affinities for music hall, then their other contribution lay in promoting the
iconography of star performers, based on the notion of the star being 'of' the
people. The outstanding example from the turn of the century was Glasgow-
born Marie Loftus, who allegedly made her first appearances dancing for Mrs

Baylis at the Scotia, and thereafter went on to become a national star and famous principal boy, starring in Drury Lane pantomimes and touring throughout America and the Empire. Loftus's frequent return visits to Glasgow reflected her enormous popularity, which was heavily reliant on her local background. That this translated into commercial return is clear. The *Evening News* wrote of her visit to the Britannia in November 1895 that 'from floor to ceiling there was not a spare seat, nor a foot of unoccupied room', while the *Era* reported that 'over a thousand people assembled after the performance outside the Britannia Music Hall, Glasgow, waiting for Marie's appearance. The crowd was so great that 6 extra constables were sent down to dispel them, and several names and addresses were taken'.[46] Publicity surrounding such loyal stars often added to the working-class music-hall mythology of performers being 'of the people' by citing instances of the star's humility or acts of kindness. In the case of Loftus, *The Amateur* reported that during an earlier engagement at the Brit in 1894 she 'gave an order to a local shopkeeper for boots to be distributed amongst certain of the poor children of the city.'[47]

The corollary of the representative ordinariness of stars like Loftus was that many watching felt they were talented enough to do what she did, or knew someone who was. Music hall itself was a participatory experience, the audience joining in with all the choruses, and coming away after the performance able to sing the new songs after a single hearing, as was intended. In a society dominated by song culture, work and social life provided plenty of opportunities for individuals to discover a talent to amuse friends and workmates. As an influence or as role models of sorts, performers of all levels were everywhere; from buskers and peddlers who entertained queues outside Glasgow theatres, to the semi-professionals who appeared in parks in the summer and at Saturday night variety concerts in local public halls, to touring minstrel troupes, and the pierrots and al fresco concert parties who played on the front at seaside towns like Largs and Dunoon. Sometimes it wasn't even necessary to go out. In summer the back courts of Glasgow tenements were visited by parties of street entertainers;

> The songs were things like 'Marta – Rambling Rose of the Wildwood' and 'Danny Boy' and 'Mary of Argyll'. They were often down-at-heel men in frayed black coats and cloth bonnets and the women sometimes beside them poor-looking souls, bareheaded and sad-faced. It was usually when the woman started up her second-part harmony that you could hear a dog howling in the next building. The singing was generally excruciating…
> Sometimes we got a complete song-and-dance team in our street – four or five young men who played the dulcimer, the accordion and the saxophone while

QUIZ SUPPLEMENT, AUG. 4, 1892.

'Sketches at the Britannia', *Quiz*, 4 August 1892

**22**

their pals gave us a step-dance. They wore navy-blue or plum coloured cheap suits with narrow waists and padded shoulders, pointed shoes and natty little ties with dirty shirts.

As children we felt in awe of these fancy-stepping confident men who usually got showered with pennies from the windows of the tenements. They looked so self-assured, so competent. They were the 'professionals'.[48]

In this context the opportunities afforded by music-hall amateur nights and go-as-you-please competitions, which became popular from the 1890s onwards, were highly significant. As the demand for top stars in the 1890s resulted in a considerable increase in their fees, which only the large city-centre venues could meet, so reports suggest that in cheaper halls amateur nights often proved the liveliest and most popular of the week. Clearly the occasions were of mutual benefit, managers getting cheap padding for the bill, while the public relished the alternating pleasures of applauding or deriding the efforts of their own. Amateur nights run by Arthur Hubner at the Britannia in 1898 commenced as follows:

> The programme-indicator at the side of the stage reads 'AMATEUR' (a 'turn' less for the late occupant of the boards), a bell rings, and a make-up, intended to represent an Irish labourer and his wife, comes before the spectators. 'Boys, have you heard the news?' is the title of their somewhat dissonant song, on the termination of which a vigorous breakdance is executed. The orchestra seem to be nowhere, and although the name of the song has been caught, its purport has been lost in the rapidity or ineffectualness of the artists' utterance.[49]

Such occasions could turn into a nightmare for weaker performers, especially at the hands of chauvinist audiences. The worse to happen on the night above was some derisory barracking (a man in evening dress who tried to perform imitations of farm-yard cries was shouted at to 'Away an' black yer face', and lasted less than a minute). But the Empire, Paisley, known as the 'Rat-Pit', was recalled as 'a heartbreaking place' by veteran comedian Neil McFadyen, who went on to describe it in the 1890s:

> Although it was a rough hall I always got a good reception, and was booked there on many occasions – one week on the same bill as Charlie Coburn, of the 'Man Who Broke the Bank' fame. But the Empire audience seldom took to a La-di-dah turn, and Coburn was no exception. I have seen many great stars being 'howled off' there.
>
> Every Friday night was amateur night. These trial turns were allowed on between ours. Many of them were lassoed by the neck and dragged into the wings, or a shower of old biscuit tins dropped on them from the flies. Others were handed an old stale loaf and shown off.
>
> There was a local worthy in Paisley at that time, Sandy the Sweep, who had the credit of falling from more roofs than any man living. He was very deformed. They put him on as a trial turn one night. Large cabbages and bouquets of rubbish poured on him from all parts of the hall. Ultimately even the band was forced to take refuge under the stage.[50]

If such hostility seems brutal, and on the face of it appears to discredit the event as constructively interactive with the audience, the opening paragraph at least puts the behaviour into broader context. This was a tough house, not for the faint-hearted. Those in the audience worked hard at their jobs, serving others. On their nights out they expected to be entertained, and if the artists disappointed, they relished exercising their right of veto, the main empowering aspect of music hall. Seen from this perspective the treatment meted out to amateurs was not intentionally malicious, so much as an extension of plain speaking. Success on the stage was anyway thought to lead to a 'soft' life. Respect had to be earned, and when acts were bad – and many clearly were – they deserved what they got, the audience deriving its pleasure instead from their humiliation.

These Amateur Nights proved enormously successful, and developed into an important feature of smaller and suburban halls in Glasgow well into the inter-war period and beyond. Those organised as competitions offered prizes or an opportunity on a professional variety bill. The Star Palace in Dumbarton Road, Partick, was advertising its Third Amateur Carnival, featuring 'The Cream of Scotland's Talented Amateurs', together with Handsome Prizes, an entry of 80 contestants, and scheduled finals and semi-finals, shortly before its closure as a live venue in 1920.[51] In 1915 Wishaw Pavilion, another cine-variety house, was similarly offering a 'Grand Go-As-You-Please Competition' each Friday and Saturday night, open to 'Singers, Dancers, Comedians, Strong Men etc'.[52] The most famous of the regular events were those at the Panopticon (formerly Britannia) in Trongate, where from 1906 A. E. Pickard resumed Hubner's Friday amateur nights, which became a Glasgow institution. The following account of a visit to the Panopticon, probably from the 1920s, when the venue had declined considerably, vividly conveys the ambience of the experience:

> Outside the main entrance of the hall, which was brilliantly illuminated, stood the doorman, in all his elegance. He would be wearing a Frock Coat, striped trousers, starched shirt, front collar, black tie, crowned with a Black Top Hat. He had a waxed moustache and red face. All he required was a long whip in his hand and he would have been the proverbial Ring Master. The Pay Box was occupied by a woman who was blonde with highly rouged cheeks. There was a wide staircase leading up to the balcony and the landing was covered with all sorts of distorting mirrors. The mirrors were part of the evening's entertainment. Many of the patrons who were under the influence of the 'water of life' spent the best part of the evening either admiring themselves in these mirrors or making up their minds as to whether they should sign the pledge or not.
>
> ...
>
> The balcony was 'U' shaped and those who sat at the top ends of the U used to pester not only the turns but the poor old man who was the leader of the orchestra. I have heard older men speaking about how before or during the Great War the

apprentices from the shipyards used to collect the old fruit from the Fruit Market which was off Candleriggs, this being used as ammunition for throwing at the turns, who surprisingly enough took it all in their stride. They also collected pigs bladders which when blown up like footballs and tied to a long string were used to belabour the poor orchestra leader. Eventually protection had to be provided for him by sort of boxing him in. As a form of derision the audience would throw pennies on to the stage at the turns, some of whom even in their desperation were not dismayed so they just picked them up, thanked the audience, made their bow and departed.[53]

The amateur night epitomised the shoring-up of the relationship between audience and performer, and allowed for the perpetuation of a familiar, community-based entertainment that in ethos harked back to the older music hall of the 1860s. Its presence as a weekly or occasional event was of much more than token significance in determining the tone of the venue. In fact it was to become a defining feature of what, in commercial terms, was by the early 1900s emerging as a secondary tier of music halls. This was to include smaller halls in suburban districts or unfashionable city-centre areas, as well as in urban pockets of Lanarkshire, and ranged from the Panopticon and Queen's Theatre by Glasgow Cross, the Olympia at Bridgeton Cross and Star Palace in Partick, to Pickard's other venues at Clydebank and Townhead, the Hamilton Hippodrome (which closed during the miner's strike of 1912), and the Wishaw Pavilion (where, unlike at city centre halls, children were admitted at half-price).[54] The songs and material generated by these working-class halls and the audiences and performers who patronised them made an important contribution to the development of Glasgow's urban culture, and to what S. G. Checkland in *The Upas Tree* characterises as

> a working class folk lore, centred upon the tenements, often confirmed and projected by music hall and pantomime songs and jokes. The factor (the owner's agent and rent collector) was a favourite figure of derision, collecting his rents, ignoring the bugs behind the wallpaper, and complaining that the coal bunker has been chopped up again. Games in streets and on middens, infant terrors of going in the dark to the toilet far from the safety of home, women taking turns cleaning the stairs, the 'jawbox' (the kitchen sink) with its multiple uses, visits to the pawnshop – these were the things of which much of life was composed, elements of a shared culture on which a humour of self deprecation and hidden rancour could be based.[55]

In conclusion, the evidence of this chapter seems to confirm music hall's social complexity. As an urban form originally developed to meet the demands of early industrial society, music hall continued to be regarded by its working-class audiences as something of their own, even after promoters tried to graft middle-class values onto it in the 1880s. Although a cleaned-up and relaunched music hall, in the form of city-centre variety, did manage to attract the middle classes, they experienced it on a different basis. In a highly mobile society the deeper cultural resonances of music hall may well have been uncomfortable to those in the middle and lower middle classes whose own upward social progress was too recent to be taken for granted. Patrick Joyce[56] has pointed out that, in the context of the 'popular' (as opposed to exclusively 'working-class') music-hall audience, there were many more sources of social identity than class to consider, views that will be examined more fully in the conclusion. But in a highly stratified society attitudes to institutions such as music hall could in themselves constitute important statements of an individual's class orientation, respectability and social progress.

Even in terms of format and content music hall had long since lost its exclusive rights to the entertainment it offered. By the 1890s it had been in existence for at least forty years, and as the dominant popular entertainment of the age had spawned a number of newer sub-genres that better reflected the lifestyles of their target audiences. It was a paradox that, by the time music hall finally managed to present itself in conditions in which a wider audience would appreciate it, these other media – pantomime, popular concerts and seaside entertainers – were already helping assuage the middle classes' appetite for an entertainment that they may anyway have felt ambivalent about on anything other than an occasional basis.

With regard to Glasgow audiences, conclusions need of necessity be broad. Certainly the original free and easy audience seems by the 1870s to have given way to one that, though more socially diverse, was still dominated by working people on low incomes. As we have seen earlier in the chapter, evidence of admission prices from this and later periods supports Penny Summerfield's theory that most leading halls were of necessity socially heterogeneous. However, as variety developed from the early 1890s, the gap in aspiration between the new city-centre palaces of varieties and older venues seems to have widened, as cheaper halls, unable to compete, cut their losses by concentrating on a more socially specific working-class clientele.

## Notes

1  *The Abstainer's Journal*, 1854; Shadow, 'Jupiter Temperance Hall', No. 10, Thursday Night, in *Midnight Scenes and Social Photographs*, pp. 84–85.
2  Shadow, *Midnight Scenes and Social Photographs*, p. 85.

3  Davidson, *In A Music-Hall and Other Poems*, p. 2.

4  Report of Lieutenant Andrew, 9 March 1875.

5  See Kift, then writing as Dagmar Höher, 'The Composition of Music-Hall Audiences, 1850–1900', in Bailey (ed.), *Music Hall: The Business of Pleasure*, pp. 73–92; for the crossover between theatre and music-hall audiences in London, see Davis and Emeljanow, *Reflecting the Audience*.

6  'Another Eye-Witness', *North British Daily Mail*, 8 March 1875, p. 4.

7  *North British Daily Mail*, 13 March 1875, p. 5.

8  'The Morality of the City: Important Deputation to the Magistrates', *North British Daily Mail*, 2 March 1875, p. 4. For other instances of widespread juvenile attendance at music hall and theatre see Robert Poole, *Popular Leisure and the Music Hall in 19th-Century Bolton* (Lancaster, Centre for North-West Regional Studies, University of Lancaster, 1982), pp. 63–64; Douglas A. Reid, 'Popular Theatre in Victorian Birmingham', in David Bradby, Louis James and Bernard Sharratt (eds.), *Performance and Politics in Popular Drama* (Cambridge, Cambridge University Press, 1980), pp. 70–72; and, for an overview of much existing research, Kift, *The Victorian Music Hall*.

9  Höher [Kift], 'The Composition of Music-Hall Audiences', p. 116.

10  Bell, *I Remember*, p. 131.

11  *The Bailie*, 7 April 1897, p. 5.

12  'Notes by the Way', *Glasgow Programme*, 7 March 1904; MLGC.

13  See King, 'Popular Culture in Glasgow', pp. 163–164.

14  *North British Daily Mail*, 6 January 1900, p. 2.

15  *North British Daily Mail*, 6 January 1900, p. 2.

16  *North British Daily Mail*, 6 January 1900, p. 2.

17  Programme, Good Templars' Harmonic Association Saturday Night, 21 September 1889; PP.

18  Emily Soldene, *My Theatrical and Musical Recollections* (London, Downey and Co, 1897), pp. 46–47.

19  *North British Daily Mail*, 6 January 1900, p. 2.

20  *North British Daily Mail*, 6 January 1900, p. 2. Attendance at Corporation concerts breaks down as follows: the City Hall, 80,250 persons; the St Andrew's Hall, 66,474 persons; the Grand National Hall, 44,375 persons; the Camlachie Institute, 12,808 persons; and the Bridgeton Public Hall 12,254 persons – the grand total being 216,161.

21  For Saturday Evening Concerts see Minutes, Dundee Council, 8 Nov 1897; for music in parks see 19 April 1898; for Sunday concerts see 6 July 1899: Dundee City Archives.

22  *Professional*, 7 March 1891.

23  *Glasgow Harlequin*, 1 (17 December 1895), p. 1. If the attendances cited seem highly optimistic (the short-lived journal seems to have been a promotional publication for panto managements), rough calculations suggest that they might not have been as exaggerated as first seemed likely.

24  See *Largs and Millport Weekly News*, 11 June 1904, p. 4; 25 July 1904, p. 4.

25 'The Largs Entertainers', *Largs and Millport Weekly News*, 23 July 1904; and 6 August 1904, p. 5.

26 See Andrew Miller Brown, *Largs and District in Old Picture Postcards* (Zaltbommel, Europese Bibliotheek, 1998).

27 Frank Bruce, *Scottish Showbusiness. Music Hall, Variety and Pantomime* (Edinburgh, National Museums of Scotland, 2000), p. 53.

28 See Renee Houston, *Don't Fence Me In* (London, Pan, 1974), p. 22, in which she describes (at the age of 14) playing a sketch with Charlie Kemble about 'two old women in a Glasgow tenement building, arguing' whilst with Fyfe and Fyfe's Rothesay Entertainers in 1916.

29 Dave Russell, *Popular Music in England 1840–1914: A Social History* (Manchester, Manchester University Press, 1987), p. 249.

30 See Callum G. Brown, 'Religion and the Development of an Urban Society: Glasgow 1780–1914', unpublished PhD thesis, University of Glasgow, August 1981, pp. 436–441.

31 For detailed descriptions of different song genres see Russell, *Popular Music*, and Ronald Pearsall, *Edwardian Popular Music* (Newton Abbott, David and Charles, 1975).

32 Edward Gaitens, *Growing Up And Other Stories* (London, Cape, 1942), pp. 38–53.

33 David M. McCulloch, *The Swinging Tub* (London, Hodder and Stoughton, 1917), p. 220.

34 See King, 'Popular Culture in Glasgow', p. 181. Edward Gaitens' short story 'My Wee Fifi' also mentions a socialist meeting in a music hall; see *Growing Up*, p. 105. Elsewhere too theatres and halls were utilised as amenities. When the Prime Minister H. H. Asquith visited Kirkcaldy in 1908, the civic ceremony to add his name to the Burgess Roll was held in the Hippodrome: see Sandy Elder, *History of the King's and other Kirkcaldy Cinemas* (Kirkcaldy, Kirkcaldy Civic Society, 1998), p. 29.

35 *North British Daily Mail*, 20 February 1895, p. 1.

36 'Music Halls and Humanity', *Quiz*, 28 February 1895, p. 161.

37 *The Eagle*, 18 February 1909, pp. 12–13.

38 See Andrew Horrall, *Popular Culture in London c.1890–1918, The Transformation of Entertainment* (Manchester, Manchester University Press, 2001), p. 25.

39 For reference to Hall's booking at the Tivoli, Anderston see McFadyen, 'Fire! Cry That Ended in Death-Rush for Exit'; for Lafferty see advertisement for Craigneuk New Picture and Variety Theatre, *Motherwell Times and General Advertiser*, 12 December 1913.

40 For Gaiety see *Dundee Advertiser*, 13 April 1903. For many similar examples of London music halls' interaction with sporting fraternities, particularly football, see Horrall, *Popular Culture in London* .

41 Patrick MacGill, *Children of the Dead End: The Autobiography of a Navvy* (Ascot, Caliban Books, 1980 [1914]), pp. 259–262.

42 See *The Eagle*, 14 January 1909 for Tani advertisement; E. H. Bostock, *Menageries, Circuses and Theatres* (London, Chapman and Hall, 1927), p. 288.

43  Muir, *Glasgow in 1901*, pp. 240–241.
44  William Lindorf Duff, 'Biography of an Ordinary Working Man', unpublished manuscript; reproduced by kind permission of Mrs Aileen Monaghan.
45  Neil McFadyen, 'Fire! Cry That Ended in Death-Rush for Exit'.
46  'The Britannia', *Glasgow Evening News*, 13 November 1894, p. 7; *The Era*, 17 November 1894.
47  *The Amateur*, December 1894, p. 8. A similar story – in this case that she bought eighty pairs of shoes for pupils of her former school in Hoxton – was attributed to Marie Lloyd: see W. Macqueen-Pope, *Marie Lloyd, Queen of the Halls* (Oldbourne, undated), p. 53.
48  Roderick Wilkinson, *Memories of Maryhill* (Edinburgh, Canongate, 1993), pp. 14–15.
49  'An Amateur Night at the Britannia Music Hall', *Quiz*, 3 March 1898, p. 270.
50  McFadyen, 'Fire! Cry that Ended in Death-Rush for Exit', p. 10.
51  Partick Star Palace programme, week commencing 1 March 1920; MLGC.
52  See Wishaw Pavilion advertisement, *Wishaw Press and Advertiser*, 29 January 1915.
53  Eddie Perrett, *The Magic of the Gorbals: How we Lived, Loved and Laughed 1914–60* (Glasgow, Clydeside Press, 1990), p. 63.
54  The Hamilton closure is referred to in an unpublished notebook kept by Herbert Doughty, the trombonist in the ten-strong theatre orchestra; his entry for 25 March 1912 reads '4th week of Coal Strike. Hippodrome to close Saturday 30 March until end of strike'. Evidently the hall's clientele consisted largely of miners or those dependent on the mining industry, without whose presence it ceased to be viable. Band members were paid half-salaries for the following week, but the dispute presumably ended shortly afterwards, as the entry for 8 April shows the hall open with a new bill; I would like to thank Mr and Mrs T. I. Graham for kindly making this document available to me.
55  S. G. Checkland, *The Upas Tree: Glasgow 1875–1975 … And After 1975–1980* (Glasgow, University of Glasgow Press, 1981), p. 44.
56  See Patrick Joyce, *Visions of the People: Industrial England and the question of class 1848–1914* (Cambridge, Cambridge University Press, 1991), pp. 305–328.

# 9

# Conclusion

Music hall and variety were critical developments in entertainment. They simultaneously resonated with older, pre-urban forms of sociability and community celebration and activated a lineage of modern leisure forms stretching from cinema to television. But they did not only fuse the pre-industrial and industrial; as a force for social cohesion they also helped counter – even heal – society's concerns with social and moral division. In this music hall exemplified a converging of sensibilities.

The fact that music hall was about a shared urban experience, which happened to be predominantly that of the lower classes, did not make it a working-class form in any politicised sense. Patrick Joyce's perception of the studied social neutrality of music hall, *de facto* working class in terms of audience but affecting a petit bourgeois sensibility, and, whilst self-evidently shot through with social resonances for its audience, fighting shy of a single-class viewpoint, seems highly apposite for Glasgow.[1]

Moreover it is wrong to assume that music hall necessarily lacked resonance for the middle classes. Victorian and Edwardian society was highly mobile and many who began on the lower rungs of the ladder and went on to better their economic or social position retained an affinity with music hall from their early lives. The question was whether this constituency felt comfortable acknowledging this shared experience publicly. Members of the lower middle classes in particular may have been anxious to differentiate themselves from the lower social orders they had so recently left, not only in physical terms inside the theatre, but also in the agenda of music hall's performing material which, although diluted, continued to revolve around humorous stoicism in the face of social misfortune – eviction, drunkenness, financial hardship, housing conditions – aspects of life the upwardly mobile were familiar with but would have preferred not to be reminded about. This group – shopkeepers, clerks and white-collar workers – although the closest to the lower-class sections of the audience, were probably also the most socially insecure. In a Presbyterian society where class sub-strata were closely defined and 'read' by behaviour and conspicuous propriety, public perception was extremely important. What you did and where you went (and in what company), what we would characterise as the surface of behaviour, was accepted as a main indicator of social status and moral worth. The disapproval of churchgoers and the 'Unco' guid', who would never have dreamt of venturing into a music hall, could nevertheless exert considerable social pressure on others who would have liked to.

In this light the aim of the 'new' variety of the 1890s was probably to win (or win back) the wavering lower-middle-class constituency, who felt uncomfortable going to music hall, but who might be persuaded if given a separate entrance and the social pretext that music hall was now, if not socially approved, at least no longer proscribed. Alongside this was probably an intuitive impulse on the part of managers to reflect the upward social aspirations of sections of the existing working audience. In either case the tone of promotional material and the material trappings of the new theatres, as vested in modern accoutrements and sumptuous décor, were in psychological terms an important part of the reassurance that variety was now a refined and above all 'respectable' experience. Whether wider society chose to believe it or not, variety's object was to furnish those who wished to attend with a social pretext.

For established higher-income middle-class groups such as the professional and mercantile classes, responses to music hall generally involved more straightforward issues of propriety. Yet within this social grouping attitudes varied from the outrage of the Glasgow businessmen who signed the 1875 petition protesting at the licentiousness of acts at the Whitebait, to the more worldly and permissive approach of men about town, who openly admitted they went to music halls, saw nothing wrong with them (other than that they often weren't very good), and were scathing about the moral majority who got incensed by their activities. The columns of *The Bailie*, whose correspondent reported on visits to the halls, referring to managers such as 'Davie' (Brown) and 'John' (Muir, chairman of the Whitebait) by their Christian names, were quick to poke fun at reformers and the moral hypocrisy of the age, with one sharply written satirical snippet from 1875, worthy of *Private Eye*, suggesting 'That the music hall morality letters are becoming just a *leetle* too "spicy." That next to turning up at a music hall yourself, the best (or worst) thing is the reading of a spicy moral (?) letter descriptive of its improprieties.'[2] But beyond this there is little evidence of, for instance, mainstream middle-class theatre audiences of the

1890s crossing over to attend variety on a regular basis. While Glasgow fiction is littered with references to music hall and its place within the culture of working people, it hardly gets a mention in middle-class novels. Where it does feature, generally in memoirs or autobiographies, is as a rite of passage for young men in adolescent or student days, essentially as juvenilia, as in the case of James Bridie, who as a medical student was involved in the riot against 'Dr' Walford Bodie at the Coliseum in 1909. Legitimate theatre maintained its social cachet, the distinction between family fare and something racier being neatly encapsulated in a stanza from 'The Song of the Masher':

> I'm seen on 'first nights' in the stalls,
> With artful maids and mothers
> I share a box at music halls
> With festive younger brothers.[3]

One of the most striking features of Glasgow music hall was its dual nature. Joyce has written of the English music hall's 'complex interaction of different social and geographical stages – local, regional and national – upon which the sense of belonging and solidarity were played out', and concludes that 'What is evident is something much more complex than the eclipse of the local and regional by the national'.[4] This seems to encapsulate the experience of Glasgow, which by the 1860s was both an important part of the 'national' music hall circuit, attracting all leading British stars on a regular basis, and the centre of a vibrant Scottish performing culture, which produced its own Scottish stars, many of whom went on to shine in the English firmament. The two aspects of the system functioned to mutual advantage. Although it was in the nature of music hall to be local, and that of most large cities outside London exhibited strong regional or local vernacular characteristics, Glasgow's was enriched by the possession not only of a regional but a distinct national identity and culture, which offset the potentially homogenising influence of a constant stream of English performers. In this respect Glasgow seems to have been unusually cosmopolitan, with audiences able to see national stars framed within the context of what was clearly a strongly Scottish ambience, and on bills which featured a high proportion of Scottish artists. This mixed cultural dimension came to act as a focus for a particular brand of Scottish patriotism which ran parallel to and was often directly identified with support for imperial policies from the 1880s onwards.

From the performers' perspective, Glasgow was a major centre of employment. In addition to the main city-centre palaces of varieties, it also offered a wide range of concert work, from prestigious engagements in series promoted by organisations like the Good Templars and City Corporation, to local concerts and one-off variety entertainments in public halls. There was also an extensive secondary network of smaller music halls and cine-variety venues in the suburbs and outlying rural areas of Lanarkshire, and the city served as the recruiting base for small touring variety companies and concert parties. In addition seasonal opportunities included pantomime between December and Easter, and al fresco work in city parks and with parties of seaside entertainers at Clyde resorts over the summer months.

As a result Glasgow was base (if not necessarily home) to a thriving professional community of performers, musicians, impresarios, stage managers and backstage workers, who had their own pubs, theatrical digs and local professional associations with programmes of social, sporting and charitable events. Although evidence of the numbers actually resident in the city is elusive, anecdotal evidence and case studies of individual careers, together with Glasgow-published theatrical journals detailing, for instance, the activities of W. F. Frame's Vaudeville Golf Club, or music director E. T. De Banzie's induction of fellow 'pro's into his Masonic Lodge, all support the view of an active entertainment community, albeit one whose members were highly mobile and constantly changing.

A second characteristic of Glasgow was that, for all the Presbyterian excoriation of the evils of entertainment and drink, the civic and religious establishment was generally remarkably tolerant of music hall. Certainly the eradication of free and easies was a consciously planned outcome of the slum clearance schemes carried out under the 1866 City Improvement (Glasgow) Act, and the relocation of Glasgow Fair to Vinegar Hill in 1870 similarly embodied the council's determination to remove unseemliness from the heart of the city. So, too, the fact that music halls licensed to serve alcohol seem to have disappeared by the late 1880s, while the two longstanding venues, the Scotia and Britannia, both survived as temperance houses, also suggests a *quid pro quo* on the part of managers anxious to acquiesce with the moral stance of the licensing authorities. But such policies were to be expected from city authorities espousing Presbyterian values and a hefty moral agenda. What is much more striking – and surprising – by the 1890s is how closely intertwined the worlds of entertainment and moral improvement had become. The reasons for this stemmed in the first instance from the various religious and improving organisations' promotion of their own variety concerts, as a means of rescuing audiences from the wickedness of commercial music halls, a process that brought them into contact with performers and musicians. Over time this inevitably led to a blurring of lines, as officers of such organisations, now effectively impresarios, found themselves drawn into Glasgow's music-hall milieu. Fraternisation and personal contacts followed. Alongside music-hall managers attending the funeral of Robert McKean, late co-proprietor of the Britannia, in 1885 was a Lodge Secretary of the Good Templars Harmonic Society. On an institutional level, the fact that such organisations embraced variety as part of their concert entertainments negated their ability to condemn it. It was hard to demonise someone when you were planning to book them for next week. As a result contacts between temperance and evangelical groups and the entertainment world were often surprisingly close. Performers and musicians working on what could be called the two circuits, commercial and reformist, overlapped considerably. Events such as the Grand Opening of the City Corporation's Springburn Public Hall in 1902 found the music hall comedians J. B. Preston and W. F. Frame and the accompanist and songwriter James Booth sharing the stage with a bass, soprano, violinist, and the Springburn Rechabite Reed Band. Because of this, or perhaps as a predictable result of living under a set of cast-iron moral principles that few were strong enough to adhere to in their entirety, there seems to have been a degree of latitude in some instances regarding positions on entertainment. Frame himself was a lifelong temperance supporter and member of the Good Templars, and was prominent in his kirk in Springburn, where he led the church choir. But professionally he also sang boozy numbers, and once, on spotting a temperance lay preacher he knew in the audience at one of his concerts, was recalled 'launching into a roistering song about the tipple, breaking his flow of patter to address [him] across the footlights with "Ay, it wouldna suit you, Mr Honeyman, but we had a rare night's fun."'[5] Moreover, the good-natured Honeyman and his wife, despite enjoying the theatre and going to variety events such as Frame's with their family whilst on holiday at Millport, apparently disapproved of music hall and pantomime. Quite where the line was being drawn here and why is difficult to judge. It may have been to do with striking a pragmatic balance between the absolutes of pulpit rhetoric and the accepted need to permit some kinds of mainstream popular entertainment.

It is this breadth and diversity of music hall's influence that is most striking. As we have demonstrated, music hall in Glasgow was not exclusive to any one group: by being accessible in a diverse range of different forms and offshoots – through concerts, 'bursts', pantomime and seaside entertainments, and above all through the common currency of music-hall songs, sold as sheet music and sung at home around the piano – by the 1890s it had permeated most areas of society. Although the presentation and context varied considerably, what was being performed in the rough and ready atmosphere of Paisley Empire on the one hand, and before a very different type of audience as part of Glasgow Corporation Saturday Afternoon Concerts on the other, was demonstrably the same entertainment, performed by the same artists. The fact that it could be varied (and effectively self-censored) to reflect the occasion only served to demonstrate the medium's flexibility and responsiveness to social nuance.

That its appeal should have been so widespread calls into question some strands of received opinion as to music hall's function and how we should seek to evaluate it. Patrick Joyce's post-structuralist view of the inadequacy of talking in terms of class, when the significant factor was really a unifying sense of belonging on the part of the audience, seems a much more comprehensive explanation for its wide-ranging impact. Far from being class-specific, in social terms music hall in Glasgow was fluid and inclusive, offering genres and idioms of song to reflect a wide range of experiences. While certain types of act were targeted at specific sections of the audience (Irish material being aimed at the Irish immigrant audience, just as Hebrew acts were engaged to appeal to the Jewish community centred on the Gorbals), in a socially highly mobile society the resonance of such material often cut across conventional class lines, and the bill as a whole reinforced and exploited the sense of the audience as a collective entity. At the heart of this consensual appeal was the music-hall song, in which audience participation, in the form of joining in with the choruses, provided the sort of sense of communal well-being and 'oneness' – of instant community – that at the beginning of the twenty-first century can probably only be experienced at pantomime or, more vitally, in a crowd at a football match.

This contrived balance of music hall's appeal carried over into the ground rules for the format itself. Performing material parodied ethnic or social groupings, but was never consciously offensive and above all never attacked elements present within the audience itself, contention or divisiveness being anathema to the unifying principle. For this reason imperial themes served a useful double purpose, offering both a pretext for chauvinistic Scottish patriotism under the umbrella of support for imperial causes, and a vehicle for implicit criticism of the English establishment. The most constructive aspect of music-hall patriotism was probably that of enfranchising the disparate strands of the Glasgow audience against a common external enemy. The gaucheness of teuchter incomers and guttural accents of east-European Jewish immigrants might have been lampooned in everyday material. But when it came to facing up to the Boer or the Kaiser in song all were equal citizens of empire, the audience eager to unite in a shared Scottish identity for the duration of a patriotic chorus.

In this context, that of a medium concerned with promoting a sense of collective identity, ideas of the nature of music hall possibly need to be re-evaluated. Certainly the continuities with older folk and entertainment forms, translated into an urban context but re-asserting older rural notions of community, are just as apparent as its claims to be a 'new' exclusively urban development. They also go some way to explaining why music hall, rather than being radically energised, was inherently conservative, in the sense of being backward-looking and evocative of past structures. Above all the continued primacy of the song as its chief form of expression, articulating the voice and life experience of the individual and inviting the audience's empathy, provides a direct link with song-based folk traditions. In this, and in the interactive role of the audience, Adrienne Scullion's suggestion that the original free and easy format may well have been influenced by the ceilidh tradition imported to Glasgow by Highland and Irish immigrants seems very credible.[6]

This idea of music hall representing a development of older cultural themes can be extended into the variety era. Just as elements of continuity with older forms have sometimes been overlooked in the rush to label music hall a product of industrial society, so variety itself has often been too readily identified with the onset of commercialisation. Commercialisation, in the form of the profit motive, had been integral to each stage of music hall's development, a factor well appreciated by journalists of the early 1870s in references, only half-joking, to Rossborough, proprietor of the Britannia, as 'the king in his counting house'. While variety certainly brought a range of innovations, it was arguably no more than a dynamic phase in music hall's long-term development, part of an on-going process of rationalisation and re-organisation such as might be found in any fast-expanding industry. And far from being imposed or orchestrated, examination of the introduction of variety in Glasgow halls between the early 1880s and late 1890s only serves to emphasise how piecemeal the transformation was, and how reliant on local factors and the instincts of individual managers.

The fact that music hall drew on older traditions by no means discounts its relevance as a product of the industrial age. But it does underline that in cultural terms its emergence was not a commercially sponsored aberration but rather part of the continuing evolution of a living song tradition.

Given that music hall's success was based on re-engendering what was basically a sense of pre-industrial community in the context of a modern urban entertainment, it was ironic that its sophisticated successor, variety, so adept at translating the inane needs of its audience into financial return, was to contribute to its own eclipse by losing touch with its social rationale.

Variety reached its highpoint at the outbreak of the First World War, when Glasgow had eighteen music halls. Its swift decline in the interwar years was very largely attributable to cinema and the enormous artistic and commercial potential of film. However, discussion of music hall's social function should not obscure the fact that it was also an ephemeral entertainment genre, of its period and with a limited life expectancy. Most of the improvements and innovations introduced to music hall/variety between the 1850s and 1914 concerned marketing or presentation. But the basic format of the entertainment – one act following another but with the different performers at no point appearing on stage together – had scarcely altered. It took the introduction of revue just prior to the First World War to bring about the 'produced' show, with interlinked songs and sketches leading into ensemble numbers and, eventually, a finale in which the entire company appeared on stage. For those attending variety on a weekly basis, the sheer predictability of the format must have been an important limiting factor. It was not surprising that middle-class theatre audiences did not generally find variety stimulating enough to go to on anything other than an occasional basis. The same entertainment was in any case available elsewhere in more salubrious circumstances. Newspaper reviewers similarly did not usually consider it worthy of serious critical attention: the appearance of big-name stars in the city elicited interest and some analysis, but otherwise there was little to say about an evening of four- or seven-minute acts, which were much the same week-in week-out. At the other end of the spectrum, working audiences continued to visit popular theatre as well as music hall, lured by the attractions of a compelling narrative, the key element missing from music hall that led many to believe that its leading performers did their best work in pantomime. Variety's attempt to redress the balance from the 1890s onwards amounted to opportunistic colonising of whatever theatrical idea or fashion was of the moment. So sketch companies mounted elaborate dramas on oriental subjects, incorporated the new bioscopes into music-hall bills, offered their own cut-down pantomimes at Christmas and were quick to exploit whatever musical fashion was current, as with ragtime when it arrived from America in 1912. But in the midst of this increasingly desperate and aimless range of acts, the social rationale of the entertainment was fast eroding. By broadcasting its willingness to become or take on whatever was current, anything other than re-examine its own social basis or subtext, variety was signalling a profound lack of confidence in its future as a self-sustaining entertainment.

In contrast, where music hall continued in smaller halls, as in a number of Glasgow venues such as the Queen's Theatre, Watson Street, and Panopticon, Trongate, on a local scale that allowed it to retain direct contact with the community, it often outlasted its smarter city-centre rivals. This small-scale activity – comprising amateur nights and go-as-you-please competitions, cine-variety, back-court entertainers, seaside parties of al fresco entertainers and pierrot troupes – allowed for the continuity of a strongly vibrant self-perpetuating Scottish performance tradition, with, particularly in the case of Glasgow, a distinct localised identity. It continued the direct links between community and performers who, coming from the same social circumstances as the audience, shared and reflected their social outlook and value systems. It also continued to prove the training ground for several generations of Scottish music-hall stars, fuelling the larger variety theatres, until the demise of variety in the 1960s.

In conclusion, music hall in Glasgow enjoyed what was probably a unique position at the centre of social and cultural life in the city. The intervention of religious and municipal forces in promoting concerts of their own resulted in an institutional complicity in the furtherance of the entertainment. Over a period this municipal and religious patronage conferred a legitimacy of sorts which, although directed towards the generic entertainment rather than at music hall proper, nevertheless cemented the impression of a favoured genre, one which spoke as directly to habitués of the City Chambers and temperance *conversaziones* as it did to working men in the halls of Argyle Street. This adoption of music hall as a tacitly sanctioned, quasi-official entertainment, which featured in Corporation concerts and at city events and functions, and whose leading practitioners were warmly received in municipal and religious circles, was indicative of a new cultural consensuality vested in music hall. Part of its achievement was the re-establishment of a continuum with older pre-industrial notions of community disturbed by the effects of urbanisation and the trauma of social displacement. But music hall's dominance by the 1890s, when it had come to be accepted as the defining entertainment of the age by all levels of Glasgow society, from the City Fathers down, represented an unparalleled convergence of cultures and, above all, the triumph of a popular genre over previously held ideas of aesthetic or puritan elitism. Attaining such mainstream consensual appeal inevitably involved sacrifices, namely the loss of class specific radicalism and political discourse. But the fact that music hall was socially emollient did not imply that it was merely a palliative to lower-class aspirations.

In broader terms the huge appeal of its ideas of community and social well-being, vested equally in individual experience as well as collective responses to the transition to urban industrial living, signified rather the triumphant reassertion of older social values. As such, in reinventing older notions of community-derived sociability, music hall brought about a healing convergence of sensibilities that helped counter the fragmentation and division of early industrial society.

## Notes

1 Joyce, *Visions of the People*, pp. 305–328.
2 *The Bailie*, 10 March 1875, p. 5.
3 From C. J. H. Cassels, *Rhymes of the Times* (Edinburgh, R. Grant and Sons, 1891).
4 Joyce, *Visions of the People*, p. 305.
5 Webster, *From Dali to Burrell*, pp. 12, 15.
6 Scullion and Cameron, 'W. F. Frame and the Scottish Popular Theatre Tradition', p. 40, fn. 3.

# Appendix

**Table A1**  Scottish music halls, showing numbers of Glasgow's music halls and theatres, and of music halls in Govan, Edinburgh, Leith, Dundee and Aberdeen[a].

| | Glasgow | | | | Music halls | | |
| | Theatres | Music halls | Govan | Edinburgh | Leith | Dundee | Aberdeen |
|---|---|---|---|---|---|---|---|
| 1868 | 3 | 5 | – | 3 | 3 | 2 | 1 |
| 1873 | 2 | 5 | – | 1 | 2· | 1 | 3 |
| 1875 | 4 | 7 | 1 | – | 2 | 1 | 1 |
| 1880 | 5 | 4 | 1 | 1 | 1 | 2 | 1 |
| 1887 | 4 | 5 | – | 1 | – | 1 | 1 |
| 1890 | 4 | 3 | – | 1 | – | – | 2 |
| 1900 | 7 | 3 | – | 1 | – | 1 | 1 |
| 1903 | 7 | 5 | – | 3 | – | 2 | 1 |
| 1908 | 7 | 8 | – | 3 | – | 1 | 1 |
| 1911 | 7 | 14 | – | 3 | – | 4 | 4 |
| 1913 | 6 | 16 | – | 6 | – | 7 | 2 |
| 1914 | 6 | 18 | – | 5 | 1 | 7 | 2 |

[a] These figures, taken from *Era Almanacks*, the national industry yearbooks, probably reflect numbers of larger halls, and should not be taken to indicate lower levels of activity. Leith, the port of Edinburgh, probably continued to have lower–grade halls to serve its seafaring clientele after they ceased to register on the annual lists. Similarly Govan, incorporated into Glasgow in 1912, may well have continued to offer local music-hall activity. In Glasgow, fluctuations in numbers of halls often reflected the closing and reopening of venues under new managements and different names.

*Sources*: annual *Era Almanacks/Era Annuals*.

**Table A2** Admission charges for Glasgow music halls of the 1880s

| | Shakespeare[a] 1881/2 | Folly 1883/4 | New Star[a] 1885 |
|---|---|---|---|
| Gallery | 4d. | – | 2d. |
| Pit | 3d. | 6d. | 3d. |
| Circle (and balconies*) | – | 1s.* | 6d. |
| Orchestra Stalls | 9d. | – | 6d. |
| Balcony Stalls | 1s. | – | – |
| Pit Stalls and Back Circle | 6d. | – | – |
| Private Boxes | – | 1s.6d. | – |

[a] The Shakespeare and New Star were in fact the same venue in Watson Street. Like many halls, Arthur Lloyd's Shakespeare charged a higher rate on Saturdays and holidays, the Balcony Stalls rising to 1s.6d, the Orchestra Stalls to 1s., Pit Stalls and Back Circle to 9d, the Gallery to 6d, Pit to 4d. Children were full price. By 1885, under D. S. Mackay's management, the renamed venue was offering 'Popular Prices' with 'Entertainment specially organised for the working classes during dull trade'.

*Source:* Programmes in the Mitchell Library Glasgow Collection.

**Table A3** Admission charges for Glasgow music halls, 1890s to early 1900s

| | People's Palace 1893 | Gaiety 1895 | Skating Palace 1896 | Alexandra 1898 | Britannia 1900 | Tivoli 1900 | Hippodrome c.1902 |
|---|---|---|---|---|---|---|---|
| Gallery | 2d. | 6d. | – | 4d. | 4d. | – | – |
| Pit | 3d. | – | – | 6d. | 4d. | 4d. | – |
| Body | – | – | – | – | 3d. | – | – |
| Balcony | – | – | 1s. | 1s. | 9d. | 6d. | 1s. |
| Front Chairs | – | – | – | – | 1s. | – | – |
| Stalls | 4d. | 1s. | 3s. | 1s. | – | 1s.6d. | 2s. |
| Reserved Stalls | – | – | – | 1s.6d. | – | – | 3s. |
| Orchestra Stalls | – | 2s. | – | – | 1s.* | – | – |
| Circle | 6d. | – | – | 1s. | 6d. | 1s.6d. | 1s.6d. |
| Family Circle | – | 1s.6d. | – | – | – | – | – |
| Private Boxes | – | £1.1s. | – | – | – | 1s.6d. | 15s. |
| Reserved Seats | – | – | 2s. | – | – | – | – |

The Hippodrome offered reserved stalls seats bookable in advance. The Tivoli boasted 'People's Popular Prices', while the People's Palace in Watson Street (formerly the Star) termed itself 'pre-eminently The Working Man's House'.

* Pit Stalls

*Source:* Glasgow Museums: People's Palace and Mitchell Library Glasgow Collection.

**Table A4**  Admission charges for Glasgow music halls, 1904–14

| | Pavilion 1904 | Palace 1906 | Empire 1907 | Star Palace Partick 1911[a] | Coliseum 1912 | Panopticon 1913 | Olympia 1914 | Pavilion 1914 |
|---|---|---|---|---|---|---|---|---|
| Gallery | 3d. | 2d. | 3d. | 2d. | 3d. | – | 2d. | 3d. |
| Pit | 6d. | 4d. | – | 4d. | 4d. | 4d. | 4d. | 6d. |
| Second Pit | – | – | – | – | – | 2d. | – | – |
| Circle | 9d. | 6d. | 6d. | 6d. | – | 6d. | 9d. | 1s. |
| Dress Circle | 1s. | – | 1s.6d. | – | 6d. | – | – | – |
| Upper Circle | – | – | 6d. | – | – | – | – | – |
| Grand Circle | – | – | 1s.6d. | – | – | – | – | – |
| Stalls | 1s. | 6d. | 1s. | – | 1s. | 1s. | 6d. | 1s.6d. |
| Orchestra Stalls | – | 1s. | 1s.3d. | – | 1s.6d. | 2s. | – | – |
| Private Boxes | – | 2s.[b] | 7s.6d.[c] | – | 7s.6d. | 10s.[d] | 10s.[de] | 15s. |
| Fauteuils | 1s.6d. | – | – | – | – | – | – | – |

Twice nightly performances seem to have begun in Glasgow in 1904. Venues such as the Panopticon, Olympia and Pavilion offered bookable seats at extra charge. Admission prices were generally increased for performances on Saturdays and holidays.

[a] Partick Star Palace: seating categories not specified.
[b] per seat
[c] also 5s.
[d] single seats 2s.6d.
[e] also 7s.6d; single seats 2s.6d.

*Source*: Glasgow museum: People's Palace and Mitchell Library Glasgow Collection.

# Select bibliography

## Archival sources

Aberdeen City Library, Local Studies Department
Dundee City Archives
Edinburgh City Archives
Edinburgh City Library, Edinburgh Room, George IV Bridge
Glasgow City Archive (GCA)
Glasgow Museums: People's Palace (PP)
Glasgow University Archive (GUA)
Lamb Collection, Local Studies Department, Dundee Central Library
Mitchell Library Glasgow Collection (MLGC)
National Archives of Scotland (NAS), West Register House, Edinburgh
Scottish Theatre Archive (STA), Special Collections, Glasgow University Library
Scottish Screen Archive (SSA)

Court of Session Sequestrations for Bankruptcy: NAS
Glasgow Panopticon Co Limited Prospectus, 2 June 1910: SSA
Glasgow Valuation Rolls for 1861, 1881, 1911: GCA
Letter from Harry Harcourt to Captain McCall, 3 March 1875: GCA
*Old Glasgow Club Transactions*, 2:5 (1912–13); 4:3–4 (1920–21, 1921–22); 7:4
    (1936–37) (Glasgow, Aird & Coghill)
'Report of Visit to Music Halls on 27 February 1875' by Superintendant Brown, dated
    1 March, 1875: GCA SR22/62/1
'Report of Lieut. Andrew', dated 9 March 1875: GCA SR22/62/1
Statement of Wm Kean, Sederunt Book; Statement of Bernard Armstrong, Sederunt
    Book: NAS CS318/57/3

## Newspapers and periodicals

The Abstainer's Journal
*The Amateur and Singer's Journal*
*The Bailie*

*Bon-Accord*
*The Detective*
*The Dundee Advertiser*
*The Eagle*
*Educational Film Bulletin*
*The Entertainer*
*The Era*
*Era Almanack*
*The Evening News & Star* (*Glasgow Evening News*)
The Glasgow Courier
*The Glasgow Evening News*
*The Glasgow Harlequin*
*The Glasgow Herald*
*Glasgow Programme*
*Glasgow Sentinel*
*Glasgow Theatrical Annual 1899–1901*
*Largs and Millport Weekly News*
*The Motherwell Times and General Advertiser*
*North British Daily Mail*
*The Northern Figaro*
*Partick and Maryhill Press*
*The Piper o' Dundee*
*The Playgoer*
*The Professional Gazette and Advertiser* (*Professional and Author's Journal, Barr's Professional*)
*The Quiz*
Scottish Notes and Queries
*The Scots Magazine*
*The Stage News*
*Strothers Glasgow, Lanarkshire & Renfrewshire, 1911/12*
*Strother's Lanarkshire Xmas & New Year Annual, 1910–11*
*Sunday Mail*
Victualling Trades' Review, June 1906
*The [Glasgow] Weekly News Wishaw Press and Advertiser*

## Published primary sources

Baynham, Walter, *The Glasgow Stage* (Glasgow, Robert Forrester, 1892)
Bell, J. J., *I Remember* (Edinburgh, Porpoise Press, 1932)
Bodie, Walford, *The Bodie Book* (London, Caxton Press, 1905)
Bostock, E. H., *Menageries, Circuses and Theatres* (London, Chapman and Hall, 1927)
Bremner, Rev. Robert, *The Saturday Evening Concerts, A Sin and a Snare* (Glasgow, George Gallie, 1857)

Bridie, James, *One Way of Living* (London, Constable, 1939)

Carnie, William, *Reporting Reminiscences* (Aberdeen, Aberdeen University Press, 1902)

Coburn, Charles, *The Man Who Broke the Bank* (London, Hutchinson, n.d.)

Cook, A. S., 'Aberdeen Amusements Seventy Years Ago', *Aberdeen Free Press*, April 1911

'The Dark Side of Glasgow', *North British Daily Mail*, 27 December 1870–1871: Cuttings Book, MLGC GCF 914.1435 DAR

Davidson, John, *In A Music-Hall and Other Poems* (London, Ward and Downey, 1891)

Devlin, Vivienne, *Kings, Queens and People's Palaces: An Oral History of the Scottish Variety Theatre, 1920–1970* (Edinburgh, Polygon, 1991)

Fellowes, Horace, *Music in my Heart* (Edinburgh, Oliver & Boyd, 1958)

Frame, W. F., *Tells His Own Story* (Glasgow, Wm Holmes, 1907)

—, *W. F. Frame's Songs and Stories* (Glasgow?, n.p., n.d.)

Freer, Walter, *My Life and Memories* (Glasgow, Civic Press, 1929)

Hammerton, J. A., *Sketches From Glasgow* (Glasgow and Edinburgh, John Menzies, 1893)

Houston, James, *Autobiography of Mr. James Houston, Scotch Comedian* (Glasgow, Menzies and Love, 1889)

Houston, Renee, *Don't Fence Me In* (London, Pan, 1974)

Kennedy-Fraser, Marjory, *A Life of Song* (London, Humphrey Milford, 1929)

Lauder, Sir Harry, *Harry Lauder At Home and On Tour* (London, Greening, 1907)

—, *My American Travels* (London, George Newnes, 1910)

—, *Roamin' in the Gloamin'* (London, Hutchinson, 1928)

Mackenzie, Compton, *Carnival* (London, Macdonald, 1951 [1912])

Martin, George L., *Dundee Worthies: Reminiscences, Games, Amusements* (Dundee, David Winters and Son, 1934)

McLaren, J. Wilson, *Edinburgh Memories & Some Worthies* (Edinburgh, W. & R. Chambers, 1926)

Mellor, G. J., *The Northern Music Hall* (Newcastle, Frank Graham, 1970)

Miller, David Prince, *Life as a Showman, to Which is added Managerial Struggles* (London and Leeds, 1849)

Moffat, Graham, *Join me in Remembering: The Life and Reminiscences of the Author of 'Bunty Pulls the Strings'* (Camps Bay, Winifred L. Moffat, 1979)

Muir, J. H., *Glasgow in 1901* (William Hodge, 1901).

Perrett, Eddie, *The Magic of the Gorbals: How we Lived, Loved and Laughed 1914–60* (Glasgow, Clydesdale Press, 1990)

Senelick, Laurence (ed.), *Tavern Singing in Early Victorian London. The Diaries of Charles Rice for 1840 and 1850* (London, Society for Theatre Research, 1997)

Shadow, *Midnight Scenes and Social Photographs: Being Sketches of Life in the Streets, Wynds and Dens of the City* (Glasgow, University of Glasgow Press, 1976 [1858]).

Skinner, James Scott, *My Life and Adventures* (Aberdeen, City of Aberdeen, 1994)

Soldene, Emily, *My Theatrical and Musical Recollections* (London, Downey, 1897)
Urie, John, *Reminiscences of 80 Years* (Paisley, Alexander Gardner, 1908)
Wall, Max, *The Fool on the Hill* (London, Quartet, 1975)

## Unpublished primary sources

Notebook of Herbert Doughty, by kind permission of Mr and Mrs T. I. Graham.
William Lindore Duff, 'Biography of an Ordinary Working Man', unpublished manuscript; reproduced by kind permission of his granddaughter, Mrs Aileen Monaghan.
Norman Kirk, letters of Norman McLeod, by kind permission of Mr and Mrs Robert Bain.

## Oral testimony

Transcript of interview with Mr and Mrs Robert Bain, 4 November 1995.
Transcript of recording made by Mr David Gouk of Glasgow Cinema Club on 6 November 1975, at the People's Palace Museum (PP).
Transcript of October 1974 Radio Clyde interview with George Clarkson, song and dance man (Motherwell Leisure, Museum and Heritage Service, Community Museums Service Oral History transcript).
Transcript of Judith M. Rankin interview with George Clarkson, 17 February (no year) (Motherwell Community Museums Service Oral History transcript, pp. 11–24).

## Secondary sources

Bailey, Peter, '"Will the real Bill Banks please stand up?" Towards a Role Analysis of Mid-Victorian Working-Class Respectability', *The Journal of Social History*, 12:3 (1979), 336–353
—, 'Custom, Capital and Culture in the Victorian Music Hall', in Robert Storch (ed.), *Popular Culture and Custom in Nineteenth-Century England* (New York, Croom Helm, 1982)
— (ed.), *Music Hall: The Business of Pleasure* (Milton Keynes, Open University, 1986)
—, *Leisure and Class in Victorian England. Rational Recreation and the Contest for Control, 1830–1885* (London, Methuen, 1987)
—, *Popular Culture and Performance in the Victorian City* (Cambridge, Cambridge University Press, 1998)
Baird, George, *Edinburgh Theatres, Cinemas and Circuses 1820–1963* (Edinburgh, George F. Baird, 2000)
Barker, Clive, 'The Audience of the Britannia Theatre, Hoxton', *Theatre Quarterly*, 9:34 (summer 1979), 27–41
Bell, Barbara, 'The National Drama', *Theatre Research International*, 17:2, 96–108
Booth, Michael R., *Theatre in the Victorian Age* (Cambridge, Cambridge University Press, 1991)

Bratton, J. S. (ed.), *Music Hall: Performance and Style* (Milton Keynes, Open University, 1986)

— (ed.), *Acts of Supremacy: The British Empire and the Stage, 1790–1930* (Manchester, Manchester University Press, 1991)

Brown, Callum G., 'Popular Culture and the Continuing Struggle for Rational Recreation', in T. M. Devine and R. J. Findlay (eds.), *Scotland in the 20th Century* (Edinburgh, Edinburgh University Press, 1996).

—, *Religion and Society in Scotland since 1707* (Edinburgh, Edinburgh University Press, 1997)

Bruce, Frank, *Scottish Showbusiness, Music Hall, Variety and Pantomime* (Edinburgh, NMS Publishing Ltd, 2000)

— and Foley, Archie (eds.), *Those Variety Days: Memories of Scottish Variety Theatre* (Edinburgh, Scottish Music Hall Society, 1997)

— and Foley, Archie (eds.), *More Variety Days: Fairs, Fit-ups, Music Hall, Variety Theatre, Clubs, Cruises and Cabaret* (Edinburgh, Tod Press, 2000)

— and Foley, Archie, *Harry Lauder Portobello to the Palace* (Edinburgh, Tod Press, 2000)

Busby, Roy, *British Music Hall: An Illustrated Who's Who from 1850 to the Present Day* (London, Paul Elek, 1976)

Cameron, Alasdair, *See Glasgow See Theatre: A Guide to Glasgow Theatres Past and Present* (Glasgow, The Glasgow File, 1990)

—, 'Pantomime', in Liz Arthur (ed.), *Keeping Glasgow in Stitches* (Glasgow, Mainstream, 1991), pp. 197–205

— and Scullion, Adrienne (eds.), *Scottish Popular Theatre and Entertainment: Historical and Critical Approaches to Theatre and Film in Scotland* (Glasgow, Glasgow University Library Studies, 1996)

Campbell, Donald, *Playing for Scotland: A History of the Scottish Stage 1715–1965* (Edinburgh, The Mercat Press, 1996)

Cheshire, D. F., *Music Hall in Britain* (Newton Abbot, David and Charles, 1974)

Colley, Linda, *Britons: Forging the Nation 1707–1837* (New Haven and London, Yale University Press, 1992)

Collins, Kenneth E., *Second City Jewry: The Jews of Glasgow in the Age of Expansion, 1790–1919* (Glasgow, Scottish Jewish Archives, 1990)

Crowhurst, Andrew, 'Big Men and Big Business: The Transition from "Caterers" to "Magnates" in British Music-hall Entrepreneurship, 1850–1914', *Nineteenth Century Theatre*, 25 (summer 1997), 33–59

Cunningham, Hugh, *Leisure in the Industrial Revolution c.1780–c.1880* (London, Croom Helm, 1980)

Davis, Jim, and Emeljanow, Victor, *Reflecting the Audience, London Theatregoing, 1840–1880* (Hatfield, University of Hertfordshire Press, 2001)

Davis, Tracy C., *Actresses as Working Women* (London, Routledge 1991)

—, '"Let Glasgow Flourish"', in Richard Foulkes (ed.), *Scenes from Provincial Stages: Essays in Honour of Kathleen Barker* (London, The Society for Theatre Research, 1994), pp. 98–113

—, 'Edwardian Management and the Structures of Industrial Capitalism', in Michael R. Booth and Joel H. Kaplan (eds.), *The Edwardian Theatre: Essays on Drama and the Stage* (Cambridge, Cambridge University Press, 1996), pp. 111–129

Edward, Mary, *Who Belongs to Glasgow? 200 Years of Migration* (Glasgow, Glasgow City Libraries, 1993)

Findlay, Bill (ed.), *A History of Scottish Theatre* (Edinburgh, Polygon, 1998)

Fraser, W. Hamish, and Morris, R. J. (eds.), *People in Society in Scotland: A Social History of Modern Scotland in Three Volumes, Volume II 1830–1914* (Edinburgh, John Donald, 1990)

— and Lee, Clive (eds.), *Aberdeen 1800–2000: A New History* (East Linton, Tuckwell Press, 2000)

Gibb, Andrew, *Glasgow, the Making of a City* (Beckenham, Croon Helm, 1983)

Handley, James E., *The Irish in Scotland* (Glasgow, John S. Burns, 1964)

Harvie, Christopher, *Scotland and Nationalism: Scottish Society and Politics, 1707–1994* (London, Routledge, 1994)

Hay, Marianne H., *Glasgow Theatres and Music Halls*, Mitchell Library Glasgow Room Publications no.15 (Glasgow, Mitchell Library Glasgow, 1980)

Horrall, Andrew, *Popular Culture in London c.1890–1918: The Transformation of Entertainment* (Manchester, Manchester University Press, 2001)

House, Jack, *The Heart of Glasgow* (London, Hutchinson, 1965)

—, 'Hengler's Grand Cirque', in Cliff Hanley (ed.), *Glasgow: A Celebration* (Edinburgh, Mainstream, 1984), pp. 108–112

—, *Music Hall Memories* (Glasgow, Richard Drew, 1986)

Hutchison, David, *The Modern Scottish Theatre* (Glasgow, Molendinar Press, 1977)

Irving, Gordon, *Great Scot* (London, Leslie Frewin, 1968)

— *The Good Auld Days: The Story of Scotland's Entertainers from Music Hall to Television* (London, Jupiter Books, 1977)

Joyce, Patrick, *Visions of the People: Industrial England and the Question of Class 1848–1914* (Cambridge, Cambridge University Press, 1991)

Kenna, R. and Mooney, A., *People's Palaces* (Edinburgh, Paul Harris, 1983)

— and Sutherland, Ian, *The Bevvy: The Story of Glasgow and Drink* (Glasgow, Clutha Books, 2000)

Kift [née Höher], Dagmar, 'The Composition of Music Hall Audiences, 1950–1914', in Peter Bailey (ed.), *Music Hall Q.V. The Victorian Music Hall: Culture, Class and Conflict* (Cambridge, Cambridge University Press, 1996), pp. 73–92

Kinchin, Perilla and Kinchin, Juliet, *Glasgow's Great Exhibitions 1888, 1901, 1911, 1938, 1988* (Wendlebury, White Cockade, 1988)

King, Elspeth, *The Scottish Women's Suffrage Movement* (Glasgow, People's Palace Museum, 1978)

—, *Scotland Sober and Free: The Temperance Movement 1829–1979* (Glasgow, Glasgow Museums and Art Galleries, 1979)

—, 'Popular Culture in Glasgow', in R. A. Cage (ed.), *The Working Class in Glasgow 1750–1914* (London, Croom Helm, 1987), pp. 147–169

Littlejohn, J. L., *Aberdeen Tivoli* (Aberdeen, Rainbow Books, 1986)

—, *The Scottish Music Hall 1860–1990* (Wigtown, G. C. Book Publishers, 1990)

Lynch, Michael, *Scotland: A New History* (London, Pimlico, 1992)

MacDougall, Carl, *Painting the Forth Bridge, A Search for Scottish Identity* (London, Aurum Books, 2001)

Mackenney, Linda, *The Activities of Popular Dramatists and Drama Groups in Scotland, 1900–1952* (Lampeter, Edwin Mellen Press, 2000)

Mackie, Albert D., *The Scotch Comedians* (Edinburgh, Ramsay Head Press, 1973)

Maloney, Paul, '"Curtain Call" on the Britannia Music Hall, Trongate, Glasgow, in *Scottish Field*, April 1994, 44–46

Marchant, Josette Collins, *Journey Through Stageland – The Collins Family of Glasgow* (Wigtown, G. C. Publishers, 1996)

Marshalsay, Karen, *The Waggle o' the Kilt* (Glasgow, Glasgow University Library, 1992)

Maver, Irene, *Glasgow* (Edinburgh, Edinburgh University Press, 2000)

—, 'Leisure and Culture: The Nineteenth Century', in W. Hamish Fraser and Clive H. Lee, *Aberdeen 1800–2000: A New History* (East Linton, Tuckwell Press, 2000), pp. 398–421

McBain, Janet, *Pictures Past: Recollections of Scottish Cinemas and Cinema-going* (Edinburgh, Moorfoot Publishing, 1985)

McCarra, Kevin, and Whyte, Hamish (eds.), *A Glasgow Collection: Essays in Honour of Joe Fisher* (Glasgow, Glasgow City Libraries, 1990)

McGrath, John, *A Good Night Out. Popular Theatre: Audience, Class and Form* (London, Eyre Methuen, 1981)

Medhurst, Andy, 'Music Hall and British Cinema', in Charles Barr (ed.), *All Our Yesterdays: 90 Years of British Cinema* (London, B.F.I., 1986)

Mellor, G. J., *The Northern Music Hall* (Newcastle, Frank Graham, 1970)

Miller, James, *The Magic Curtain: The Story of Theatre in Inverness* (Inverness, Friends of Eden Court Theatre, 1986)

Pearsall, Ronald, *Edwardian Popular Music* (Newton Abbot, David & Charles, 1975)

Peter, Bruce, *100 years of Glasgow's Amazing Cinemas* (Edinburgh, Polygon, 1996)

—, *Scotland's Splendid Theatres* (Edinburgh, Polygon, 1999)

Pittock, Murray G. H., *The Myth of the Jacobite Clans* (Edinburgh, Edinburgh University Press, 1996)

Poole, Robert, *Popular Leisure and the Music Hall in Nineteenth-Century Bolton* (Lancaster, Centre for North-West Regional Studies, University of Lancaster, 1982)

Pratt, Jim, 'Doctor Who? The Amazing Stage Career of Walford Bodie, M. D. (Merry Devil)', in the *Aberdeen Leopard*, 146 (March 1990)

—, *The Music Hall: A Short History* (Aberdeen, City of Aberdeen, 1993)

Rees, Terence, *Theatre Lighting in the Age of Gas* (London, Society for Theatre Research, 1978)

Russell, Dave, *Popular Music in England 1840–1914: A Social History* (Manchester, Manchester University Press, 1987)

—, 'Varieties of Life: The Making of the Edwardian Music Hall', in Michael R.Booth and Joel H. Kaplan (eds.), *The Edwardian Theatre* (Cambridge, Cambridge University Press, 1996), pp. 61–85

Rutherford, Lois, '"Managers in a small way": The Professionalisation of Variety Artistes, 1860–1914', in Peter Bailey (ed.) *Music Hall Q. V. The Victorian Music Hall: Culture, Class and Conflict* (Cambridge, Cambridge University Press, 1996), pp. 93–115

Scullion, Adrienne, 'Geggies, Empires, Cinemas: The Scottish Experience of Early Film', in *Picture House*, 21 (summer 1996), 13–19

Senelick, Laurence, 'Politics as Entertainment: Victorian Music-Hall Songs', *Victorian Studies*, 19:2 (1975), 149–180

—, Cheshire, D. F., and Schneider, U., *British Music Hall 1840–1923: A Bibliography and Guide to Sources* (Connecticut, Archon Books, 1981)

Stedman Jones, Gareth, 'Working-Class Culture and Working-Class Politics in London, 1870–1900: Notes on the Remaking of a Working Class', *Journal of Social History*, 7 (summer 1973–74), 460–508; repr. in Bernard Waites, Tony Bennett and Graham Martin (eds.), *Popular Culture: Past and Present. A Reader* (London, Croom Helm, 1982), pp. 82–151

Stuart, Charles Douglas, and Park, A. J., *The Variety Stage. A History of the Music Halls from the Earliest Period to the Present Day* (London, Fisher Unwin, 1895)

Summerfield, Penny, 'The Effingham Arms and the Empire: Deliberate Selection in the Evolution of Music Hall in London', in E. Yeo and S. Yeo (eds.), *Popular Culture and Class Conflict 1590–1914* (Hassocks, 1981), pp. 209–240

—, 'Patriotism and Empire: Music Hall Entertainment 1870–1914', in John M. Mackenzie (ed.), *Imperialism and Popular Culture* (Manchester, Manchester University Press, 1986), pp. 17–48

Tudor, Florence, 'The Amazing Doctor Bodie', in *The Scots Magazine*, 120:2 (November 1983), 147–157.

Vicinus, Martha, *The Industrial Muse* (London, Croom Helm, 1974)

Walvin, J., *Leisure and Society 1830–1950* (London, Longman, 1978)

Watson, Iain, *Harry Gordon, 'The Laird of Inversnecky'* (Aberdeen, Aberdeen City Council, 1993)

Watters, Eugene, and Murtagh, Matthew, *Infinite Variety: Dan Lowrey's Music Hall 1879–97* (Dublin, Gill and MacMillan, 1975)

## Theses

Brown, Callum Graham, 'Religion and the development of an urban society: Glasgow 1780–1914', unpublished PhD thesis, University of Glasgow, submitted August 1981.

Scullion, Adrienne, 'Media Culture for a Modern Nation? Theatre, Cinema and Radio in Early Twentieth-Century Scotland', unpublished University of Glasgow PhD thesis, 1992.

# Index